Securing Home and Business

Securing Home and Business

A Guide to the Electronic Security Industry

Simon Hakim
Erwin A. Blackstone

Butterworth-Heinemann

Boston • Oxford • Johannesburg • Melbourne • New Delhi • Singapore

Library of Congress Cataloging-in-Publication Data
Hakim, Simon.
  Securing home and business : a guide to the electronic security
industry / Simon Hakim, Erwin A. Blackstone.
    p.   cm.
  Includes bibliographical reference and index.
  ISBN 0-7506-9629-X (alk. paper)
  1. Security systems industry--United States.   I. Blackstone,
Erwin A., 1942–   . II. Title.
HD9999.S453U535   1997
621.389'28'029673--dc20   96-41451
                                                                        CIP

British Library Cataloguing-in-Publication Data
A catalogue record for this book is available from the British Library.

The publisher offers special discounts on bulk orders of this book.
For information, please contact:
Manager of Special Sales
Butterworth-Heinemann
313 Washington Street
Newton, MA 02158-1626
Tel: 617-928-2500
Fax: 617-928-2620

For information on all security publications available, contact our World Wide Web home page at: http://www.bh.com/sec

10 9 8 7 6 5 4 3 2 1

Printed in the United States of America

This book is dedicated to those we hold so dear, who had to incur time without us while this effort was underway.

Liora, Rami, and Doron Hakim
Marijane, Sherri, and Peter Blackstone

Contents

Acknowledgments

This work is based upon research and consulting work in economics, criminal justice, police, and security sciences both by the authors and by others in these fields. We have endeavored to make this book as comprehensive as possible, dealing with burglars' behavior, burglary patterns, effective home and business security, the structure and marketing of electronic security, legal issues, and much more.

This effort could not have been accomplished without the help of many people in police departments and in the security industry, who provided us with information, important insights, direction, and much of their time. We have interviewed people for more than two years and reviewed many of the criminal justice and security journals and magazines. In particular, we used extensively the following magazines: *SDM, Security Dealer, Security Sales,* and *Security News.*

The following people have been of great assistance. Inadvertently we may have omitted some individuals and certainly request their understanding. Thomas Accleston, David Averitt, Andrew Azhir, Norma Beaubian, Robert Bitton, Robert Bonifas, Christopher Cage, Flint Cooper, Thomas Curran, Joseph Daly, Bart Didden, Keith Divine, Michael Drewry, Patrick Egan, Thomas Eccelton, John Fetzer, Anthony Fague, George Flagg, Irv Fisher, Todd Flemming, Steve Flynn, David Folis, John Galante, Jerry Germeau, Maureen Gold, Leo Gudhart, Robert Hall, Colin Harrold, John Hess, Ted Hilton, Andrew Islo, Robert Kerman, Andrew Kilgore, Jason Knott, Peder Kolind, Robert May, Brian McCarthy, Peter Michel, Charles Lacarubba, Keith Ladd, John

Mack, Bruce Moseley, John Murphy, Robert Ohm, Kevin O'Mally, Peter Orvis Jr., Paul Pennypakard, Livanos Pilitsis, Thomas Rankin, Steve Roth, Norman Rubin, Thomas Seaman, Steve Schueren, Michael Shanahan, Margaret Smith, Shawn Smith, Richard (Dick) Soloway, Robert Tilley, Werner Tillmann, Jerry Usher, Lewis Walters, and Jeffrey Whirly.

Thanks are extended to our research assistants, who helped us gather information, research the issues, and provided us with helpful suggestions. They are Chadaporn Chuenjai, Christina Coltro, and Joseph O'Hara. In particular, we would like to acknowledge the immense help from Barbara Blundi Manaka. She made important suggestions and was most instrumental in helping us complete this project.

We are also grateful for the review work of Keith Ladd of The Protection Bureau and Robert McCrie of John Jay College of Criminal Justice, who gave helpful comments and suggestions to the working manuscript.

Clearly, the authors are solely responsible for any errors and omissions.

1

Introduction [1]

BURGLARS: A FRAMEWORK FOR ANALYSIS

Who are the burglars? How do they choose a target? What can be done to best protect homes and businesses? These are issues that law-abiding communities now have to confront. Many ideas exist about both what prompts a burglar to choose a target and what should be done to best protect properties. In the security industry, it is important to understand these issues in order to provide the most effective service and to use the information for effective marketing efforts.

There are, however, differences between what people think and believe and what research and practice show to be the causes and solutions to burglary. An understanding of the considerations of burglars with respect to target choice aids in the development and selection of effective precautionary measures. Two approaches are possible to investigate burglars' motives. The first is to interview and follow burglars in their search process. After all, what is better than hearing and observing the actual behavior of burglars? The other approach to learning is indirect: analyze a large number of individual homes and businesses that have been burglarized, and learn from the data the motives of burglars. Economists put more trust in the second approach, which provides for reliability based on a large number of observations. Further, the second approach shows what the burglars really do rather than merely representing the considerations of burglars, which may not be employed in the actual conduct of their business. Hence, observing their real behavior is more reliable than analyzing intentions. This book will outline the research findings of both these approaches and suggest cost-effective precautionary measures for residential and commercial establishments.

NATIONAL CRIME PATTERNS

We shall now provide an overview of the major trends in burglary and elements characteristic of its occurrence. Interestingly, the rate at which households are victimized by burglary has been declining since 1973. The 1973 rate of 91.7 burglaries per 1,000 households was about 50 percent higher than the 1993 rate of 59.9 burglaries. Figure 1.1 illustrates the 1973 through 1993 trends. The urban and suburban rates have declined by 50 percent while the nonmetropolitan rate has declined by 40 percent. The suburban burglary rate is approximately 25 percent and nonmetropolitan burglary is 30 percent lower than the urban burglary rate. The primary problem with current crime in America is that more people are dying because guns are used more often, crimes are becoming more brutal, and crime prospers among young people. Only among African-Americans do the rates of violent crime and victimization remain disproportionately high, a pattern that has been consistent throughout most of this century. Criminologists agree, however, that despite the diminishing num-

U.S. Burglary Rates Per 1,000 Households

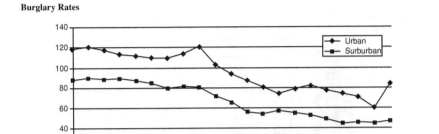

Source: U.S Department of Justice, Bureau of Justice Statistics, 1994. *Criminal Victimization in the United States: 1973-92 Trends,* NCJ-147006, Table 35, p. 110; and U.S Department of Justice, Bureau of Justice Statistics, 1996. *Criminal Victimization in the United States, 1993,* NCJ-151657, Table 53, p. 55.

Figure 1.1

ber of crimes, the fear of crime continues to rise, as the result of the wide coverage of criminal events in the mass media.

The percentage of households affected by all crime dropped from 32 percent in 1975 to 23 percent in 1992. The chance of a U.S. household being burgled over a five-year period is 9.5 percent. It is highest in the South and lowest in the Midwestern part of the country. At the same time, the chance of burglary over 20 years is 80 percent in urban, 70 percent in suburban, and 64 percent in rural localities. Almost 50 percent of the victimized suburban homes will experience two or more burglaries.

Burglary rates are closely related to household income. Figure 1.2 shows that as income rises, burglary victimization drops. For example, households with income below $7,500 a year suffer 90 percent more burglaries than households with income of $75,000 or more.

This is not surprising; burglars prefer to operate within their own community, where they are familiar with access and escape routes. Shifting their operations to an unknown territory requires

Burglary Victimization Rates by Annual Family Income, 1993

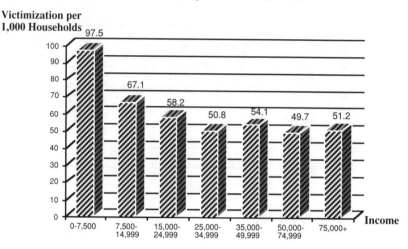

Source: U.S. Department of Justice, Bureau of Justice Statistics, 1995. *Bulletin, Crime Victimization 1993*, NCJ-151658, Table 4, p. 5.

Figure 1.2

significantly more planning. Criminal activity is high in poor communities and in the 1990s has been closely associated with drugs.

At the same time, burglars are attracted to wealthy neighborhoods. The more expensive homes have contents that are usually higher in value than the contents of less expensive homes and thus are most attractive to burglars. Burglary rates are high in affluent communities that are adjacent to major transportation routes, and burglars target those homes that are accessible to routes they often use. Burglars choose the most attractive home or homes on a block. Interestingly, for the same income groups, black households experience a 40 percent higher burglary rate than white households. A burglar examines at least three aspects of a targeted home: its value as determined by the potential contents, the availability of concealed access, and any security measures on the premises.

U.S. Victimization Rates by Time in Residence

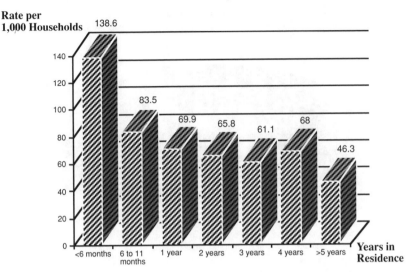

Rate per
1,000 Households

Source: U.S. Department of Justice, Bureau of Justice Statistics, 1996. *Criminal Victimization in the U.S., 1993*, NCJ-151657, Table 51, p. 53.

Figure 1.3

Our previous studies in the Pennsylvania suburbs revealed that most burglaries occur in the first year that home and business owners move to their current address. Figure 1.3 shows that the number of burgled households per 1,000 is the highest in the first six months of occupancy and diminishes thereafter. The same phenomenon is true for commercial establishments (Hakim and Gaffney 1994, pp. 31–32). Newly occupied homes lack the necessary safety precautions. Our studies revealed that alarms, the major precaution against burglary, are usually installed after two years in residence. First, renovations are made to the home, then the alarm is installed after the renovations are completed. The only exceptions are previous alarm owners, who install alarms immediately after moving into a new home and recent victims of burglary. Further, because neighbors are unfamiliar with newcomers, they may believe that an unknown vehicle in the new homeowner's driveway

Victim's Activity at Time of Burglary
(percentage)

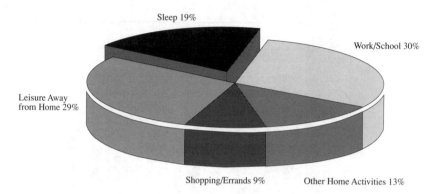

Sleep 19%

Work/School 30%

Leisure Away
from Home 29%

Shopping/Errands 9%   Other Home Activities 13%

Source: U.S. Department of Justice, Bureau of Justice Statistics, 1996. *Criminal Victimization in the U.S., 1993*, NCJ-151657, Table 64, p. 70.

Figure 1.4

belongs to a repair person or someone else who is authorized to enter the home. New commercial establishments usually have new equipment and merchandise with little dead stock and, thus, also attract burglars.

Figure 1.4 provides more evidence of the rational behavior of burglars. Burglars prefer to operate when no one is at home. Sixty-eight percent of burglaries occurred when no one was at home and the whereabouts of the residents were known. In general, homeowner absences follow a routine, which enables planning by the burglar. Thus, most precautions should be of a deterrent nature, lending the impression that someone is in the home, even if this is not the case.

Time of burglary is a finding related to the rational behavior of burglars. The proportion of daytime burglaries has increased over time, largely because of the rise in women's participation in the labor force. In an increasing number of households, no one is at home during the day, and 55.6 percent of burglaries are committed between 6 a.m. and 6 p.m. Interestingly, the share of attempted burglary is significantly higher at night. This probably indicates that burglars attempt to break in at night, assuming that no one is at home. They do not complete the burglary when they realize that someone is home. It may also indicate that, in some cases, an audible alarm has deterred them from actually entering the home.

The National Institute of Justice provides data on the cost of burglary. The average tangible and nontangible costs of burglary in 1993 were $1,100 and $400, respectively. The tangible losses include property and productivity losses and medical bills. The intangible costs include pain, emotional trauma, and risk of death as the result of victimization. Another study estimated the total cost of a burglary to be $1,800 in 1993. Further, almost 6 million households out of 100 million households were victims of burglaries in 1993; however, only 4.8 million burglaries were completed. The total annual cost of burglaries in 1993 dollars is estimated to be $9 billion, $7 billion of which represents tangible costs. Unlike other crimes such as rape, most of the burglary crime costs are tangible. Insurance payments to burglary victims amounted to $3.5 billion in 1993. Almost 50 percent of burglaries go unreported, and the annual take is $7 billion.[2] Finally, Figure 1.5 shows that burglary victimization rates are more than twice as high in the west than in the northeast part of the country. Interestingly, the rate in the southern U.S. is just slightly lower than that of the west.

THE ELECTRONIC SECURITY INDUSTRY[3]

The electronic security industry is an important and growing industry. The total retail revenue of the electronic security industry was estimated at $10.2 to $12.9 billion in 1995, with 2.03 to 4.3 percent annual growth. For comparison purposes, it is one-fourth of the size of the pharmaceutical industry, and less than 10 percent of the automobile industry. About 120,000 workers were

Burglary Victimization Rates by Region
(per 1,000 Households)

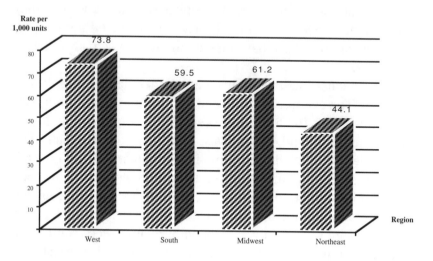

Source: U.S. Department of Justice, Bureau of Justice Statistics, 1996. *Criminal Victimization in the U.S., 1993*, NCJ-151657, Table 58, p. 61.

Figure 1.5

employed by alarm companies in 1995. Overall, 21.4 million electronic security systems have been installed nationwide, with approximately 11 percent residential and 14 percent commercial penetration.

The electronic security industry is composed of four sectors: manufacturing (about $1.5 billion), wholesaling ($1 billion), central monitoring ($6 billion), and dealers/installers ($10.2 billion). All sectors are highly competitive with little market concentration. The growth in the 1990s of mass marketing may lead to some market concentration. In 1995 mass marketers captured about 16 percent of the industry.

Dealers' revenue sources are: 48 percent from original cash installation, 24 percent from monitoring and services, 16 percent from leases, and 12 percent from upgrades. Revenues by type of business are: 57.8 percent from burglar alarms, 17.4 percent from fire alarms, 10.4 percent from closed-circuit television (CCTV), 6.6 percent from access control, 6.5 percent other, and only 1.3 percent from home automation. Contrary to other predictions, our surveys do not suggest much growth of home automation in the economy for the coming years.

Ten million alarm systems in the U.S. are centrally monitored with annual recurring revenues of $6 billion. The 24 largest companies enjoy 20 percent of total revenue; the 1,000 largest, 60 percent. The number of dealers/installers is estimated at 13,000 to 17,000 nationwide. Approximately one-third of the installers lack a permanent address, or remain in the business as part-time workers. An estimated 2 million security systems were installed in 1993.

The three trade associations are the National Burglar and Fire Alarm Association (NBFAA) (dealers/installers), Security Industry Association (SIA) (manufacturers and distributors), and Central Station Alarm Association (CSAA) (central stations). Total membership in all three associations is approximately 4,000, which is no more that one-quarter of all relevant companies. The lowest membership rate is for dealers/installers.

The passage of the 1996 Telecommunications Bill poses dangers as well as challenges to the industry. Ameritech is the first Bell Company to purchase two large alarm companies, making it the second largest company in the industry.

More market entry is expected involving integration between electronic security and other security, home automation, or telecommunications industries. Electronic security is predicted to become part of wider data management packages servicing homes and businesses. This has already occurred in the mid-1990s with closed-circuit TV, access control, and private guard products and services being packaged with traditional burglar and fire alarm systems. Clearly, such a trend offers ample opportunities for all four sectors of the industry to widen their offerings and aggressively penetrate into newly emerging fields.

THE ALARM INDUSTRY AND ITS CHALLENGES

A major element in business and home protection is the burglar alarm. Communities throughout North America have experienced a huge burden on their police resources in responding to false activations. About 10 percent of police manpower in the U.S. is estimated to be committed to responding to activations. Unfortunately, 94 to 98 percent of activations are false, and 70 percent of these are attributed to users' errors. In the case of the 2 to 6 percent bona fide activations, the delay in police response means that the burglars are long gone by the time the police arrive. Thus, many officers who experience the daily frustration of responding to false activations claim that burglar alarms are ineffective and police response should be ceased. Such popular TV programs as *Night Line* and *60 Minutes* have featured uncomplimentary segments on alarms. Contrary to such media reports, burglar alarms are cost-effective.

Overall, it appears that burglar and fire alarms provide net benefits to society. It is fair to say that amateur burglars, who comprise the majority of burglars, avoid breaking into places that are alarm protected. Further, the fire alarm feature of the system prevents the spread of fire by providing for the early detection and dispatching of fire engines to the site, preventing personal injuries and fatalities, and property losses. The benefits of alarms outweigh the costs associated with the unnecessary and costly responses by the police to false alarms.

The sunset of the twentieth century may alter the structure of the industry in a most significant way. Companies that do not adapt to the changing technological and legal environments and consumers' preferences may face difficulties in maintaining their "traditional" business lines and practices. The following are some examples of changes that will affect the security industry:

Upper Merion, Pennsylvania, has 38 patrol officers who respond to alarms. The township has about 2,500 activations a year, many actual burglary attempts, and 25 actual break-ins reported

by alarms. Only one burglary during the year resulted in apprehension of the culprits.

During the same period, a group of four off-duty police officers
from communities near Philadelphia, operating as Fetzer Protection Services, Inc., responded to alarms in commercial establishments in a crime-prone area of North Philadelphia. In 14 years of
operation, Fetzer Protection Services apprehended and turned
over to Philadelphia police officers over 2,000 suspected burglars.
In fact, in a two-week period in 1995, Fetzer Protection Services,
caught 17 burglars who committed burglaries at Fetzer subscribers' premises during that period.

The police are a local public monopoly. The police are much
better funded than private response companies. However, police
are continually struggling with their perceived limited resources,
while the gross profits of many small guard companies tripled between 1994 and 1995, and the quality of service provided was
high. Reliance upon commercial companies to replace government resources is spreading throughout the world. Is it time for
alarm services companies to replace the perceived "free" public
response (which may threaten the very existence of the industry)
with profit-oriented, better-quality private response that will enhance the purchase and use of alarms?

If, in the 1950 to 1975 period, the climate existed for greater
governmental involvement in the marketplace, the arrival of the
twenty-first century shows a significant contrary trend. Deregulation and privatization will touch all state and local services. Just to
list a few, the telecommunications industry will become fully competitive, and telecommunications firms will be among the many
potential (and actual) entrants to the alarm industry. Security services, including patrol, investigations, and management of correctional institutions, are shifting to the private sector.

The false alarm problem will be completely solved only if private
response is provided; indeed, Las Vegas and Toronto are the first cities to exemplify the privatization trend. In Las Vegas the police effectively do not respond to false activations. The police will respond if

an activation is verified by private guards present at the scene. Other large cities are expected to follow with similar ordinances.

Access control and closed-circuit television will be widely installed in commercial establishments and even in affluent segments of the residential market. Integrated systems will become more common, and the market share of stand-alone alarm systems will diminish. Improved two-way audio communications, reliable wireless sensors and transmission, widespread use of cellular, radio, and satellite communications, and the availability of ISDN technology will make communication cheaper, less reliant on wired telephone lines, and not as easily subject to Regional Bell Operating Companies' (RBOCs') possibly unfair competition.

Improvements in computer hardware and software technology introduce significant economies of scale in monitoring. On the other hand, our surveys show that "smart home" features are not being well accepted by homeowners, and the trend is not expected to change in the next five years.

The industry in general is quite fragmented; only modest economies of scale and scope exist, although economies of scale in monitoring have increased. It is relatively easy to enter all segments of the industry, and all products and services are highly price competitive. Manufacturing suffers from stiff competition, and market entry for specific products used in security systems is being competed for by electronics and computer software and hardware companies. Also, sophisticated electronic products developed for national defense are being converted to civilian commercial security products. For example, advanced wireless monitored CCTV designed to identify terrorist penetration for the Israeli Defense Ministry has been modified for commercial surveillance in competition with American products designed specifically for commercial use. Foreign companies compete in North American markets in all components of alarms, but especially in sensors. Monitoring is the only industry segment where economies of scale exist, and further consolidation of central stations is expected. It appears that up to 1 million subscribers can be efficiently monitored at one central station while still allowing for moderate economies of scale. With technological improvements in both computer hardware and software, the capacity of central stations to provide prompt service rises while the costs of production diminish. On the other hand, consolidation increases the risk of interrupted service in the event of a disaster and also raises long-distance telephone costs. An optimal size for centers and the number and location of centers for large companies can be calculated, taking into consideration all the relevant variables.

To better understand the issues and developments in the industry, a large number of interviews were conducted with firms at all levels of the industry, police officials, and others involved in the industry. These interview results are incorporated and reported throughout the book.

ALARM SYSTEMS: MARKETING APPROACHES

The marketing of alarm systems is discussed at length in this book. The following overview provides a brief discussion of the types of issues that this book addresses. For example, at the end of 1995, only 11 percent of households had an alarm. The opportunity for increased market penetration clearly exists. Many methods of marketing have been explored and implemented in the industry, some with more success than others. Methods of marketing vary over time in response to the availability of new products and services, changes in technology, and changes in consumers' preferences. Recommendations will be made on how to improve the marketing effort, in particular, to target the marketing effort to specific segments of alarm buyers. Clearly, better market targeting will save resources and increase the effectiveness of marketing.

Marketing efforts should be developed by both the industry as a whole and individual companies. The first form of marketing involves coordinated public relations efforts by the manufacturers, central stations, and dealers' associations in order to raise the public's awareness of alarms and the benefits their use yields.

Clearly, these efforts should stress the reliability of the alarm institutions by providing information, lists of members, and a prompt response in case of complaints. Our chapter on the costs and benefits of alarms provides valuable information, which can help improve the image of the industry with the general public, state and local legislators, police departments, and insurers.

The second form of marketing involves advertising by the industry and by individual companies, using the mass media, including newspapers and magazines, TV, radio, Yellow Pages, and direct mailings. Advertising messages should stress the feeling of personal safety and the reduction of burglary risk provided by and the affordability of alarm systems.

The third form of marketing includes direct face-to-face contact with potential buyers and cold calls implemented through telemarketing. These efforts are made by individual companies and are quite popular in the industry.

Effective marketing is a matter of combined efforts by both the associations and individual companies. Public relations efforts are required to improve the image of the product and the industry's professional associations along with the usual direct marketing by companies. Mass appeals to the general population are more expensive per acquired system than are targeted efforts of the third form. On the company level, a mix is needed among mass-marketing instruments such as newspapers and magazines, TV, radio, and telemarketing. Interestingly, large mass marketers do not use much telemarketing, but rather rely more upon the use of mass media in order not to aggravate the public. Also, efforts need to be continuous over time for defined geographical areas. A short media blitz in the Christmas season may not yield as good results as a year-long continuous effort made with the same budget.

Most important, the main source of business in the alarm industry is referrals from satisfied customers. Reliable service, prompt response, and follow-up in cases of false activations yield a good reputation and, consequently, referrals. Such warm referrals are superior to cold advertisements or telemarketing. In telemarketing one of 2 to 2 ½ appointments results in a sale. The rate of successful sales is 70 percent for warm referrals, and the time spent in closing the sale is significantly lower. Indeed, mass marketers lose as much as $600 on the actual installation, while at the same time niche companies that install and monitor in high-income neighborhoods or highly valued retail districts are able to enjoy 15 to 25 percent gross profits on their installations. They are successful because of their name recognition, which makes it unnecessary for them to advertise or engage in other forms of cold marketing. Niche marketers that provide superb monitoring and related services usually charge up to 20 percent more for their monitoring services alone. Their name recognition is derived from superb response and service in case of a false activation, which includes sending a technician in the case of a failing system, prompt response to service requests, follow-up in the case of repeat false activations, and frequently educating users about their systems. For highly valued commercial establishments, superb service often includes personal response to alarms by the security dealer.

RELEVANCE OF THIS BOOK

This book outlines the changes that are expected to occur and influence the various segments of the industry. It further recommends directions that can be taken in order to cope with and take advantage of these changes.

This book is of importance to the alarm segment as well as other segments of the security industry. For the alarm segment, the burglary pattern information can help in developing marketing efforts and in enhancing relationships with the community and the police department by explaining how to best protect residences and businesses. It can assist in defusing negative policies and ordinances aimed at the security industry and suggests directions that will improve the industry's overall welfare.

Owners and managers of active security companies are deeply involved in day-to-day operations. Little time is available to learn about the entire industry, where the industry is headed, and what directions firms might choose to take. The industry's associations are involved in "putting out fires" that so often arise, such as responding to an unfavorable national TV program or to an undesirable ordinance in a large city. The associations are further involved in providing services for their members, such as training and insurance programs, and organizing national conventions and other events. The associations have limited resources and are unable to observe the industry objectively from an outside position. Only outside observers can collect information from the various segments of the industry and digest it in a way that provides an understanding of general trends. This book aims to do just that. Again, numerous and extensive interviews were conducted with industry leaders in order to provide a rich and current source of information.

Private guards are the fastest growing segment of the security industry. Privatization of patrol services and correctional institutions is flourishing throughout North America. It is our belief that private response to alarms, which is complementary to patrols, and possibly to stationed guards, is about to gain a huge momentum. It is evident that new alarm ordinances in some large cities reduce the priority of alarm response. Some cities like Las Vegas and Dallas have already resorted to private response; the police do not respond to the site of an alarm unless notified by a private guard service that a possible break-in is occurring. Informal conversations with police executives in large cities reflect their hope that the police will be able to unload the service of responding to alarms. In other countries only private response exists. A major impediment for privatization of alarm response in North America is the liability issue. Companies have been reluctant to offer a package of burglar, fire, medical alert, and a variety of other home response services (which have been successfully offered elsewhere) because of a fear of litigation. However, we shall present a number of examples of firms that are successfully offering private response to alarms. Further, there are a variety of legal and functional solutions to the liability issue, which may help shield large companies from the possibility of litigation that has retarded the development of private alarm response. Private policing is alive and well and is rapidly growing in the other parts of the world. Of the many topics covered in this book, if we are successful only in shedding light on this part of the industry and proving its business merits, then we shall have achieved our goal.

CHAPTER PREVIEWS

Chapter 2 reviews who the burglars are, their motives, and their career path. Empirical findings suggest rational behavior on the part of burglars, with expected costs and benefits determining whether an individual will choose a criminal career and take particular actions. This rational behavior extends to the selection of a burglary target. Chapter 3 outlines and quantifies the cost and benefit variables burglars consider in their target choice. Burglars' considerations are important in the selection and implementation of security precautions by households and businesses. Chapter 4 provides cost-effective precautionary packages, and shows the extent to which burglar alarms enhance security. Alarms provide personal and property protection. However, at the same time they result in a real burden to police departments, which respond to false activations, a subject considered in Chapter 9. Chapter 5 looks at the community as a whole and provides a detailed cost/benefit calculation, which shows that the benefits of alarm systems to the community exceed the costs.

An important issue is the effect that discounts on insurance premiums have on the decision to purchase an alarm. If alarms are effective in deterring burglars (an important consideration in the purchase decision) while reducing insurers' liabilities, then it is in the insurers' interest to promote alarm purchase. Chapter 6 includes a cost and revenue accounting for insurers, which indeed shows that discounts on insurance premiums provide a net return to insurers.

Chapter 7 presents the structure of the four segments of the industry—manufacturers, distributors, dealers/installers, and central stations. Entry/exit to each such segment, economies of scale, technology, and pricing are the major issues discussed. A subject most important to dealers/installers is the marketing of residential and commercial electronic systems. Chapter 8 deals with the characteristics of alarm owners and nonowners, the motives for the purchase, and effective marketing schemes. The chapter makes recommendations to associations and individual companies about cost-effective marketing methods.

Chapter 9 deals with the most prevalent problem of the industry—false alarms. The chapter reviews alarm ordinances and activities in cities across the U.S. Recommendations are made concerning effective ordinances, and the police/city management of response and registration of alarms based upon these experiences and economic theory. Chapter 10 analyzes the legal issues of alarm companies' responsibilities, including those pertaining to private response. The alarm industry has known several entrepreneurs that changed the landscape of the industry and the way in which business is conducted. Chapter 11 includes seven success stories that provide lessons to others in the industry. Chapter 12 discusses the state of the art in the industry and provides predictions of future trends.

REFERENCES

Simon Hakim and Mary Ann Gaffney. 1994. *Commercial Security: Burglary Patterns and Security Measures*. Washington, DC: Security Industry Association.

NOTES

1. Much of the discussion in this section is from S. Hakim, *Securing Suburban Homes*(Bethesda, MD: NBFAA, 1995).
2. These statistics (except for the portion unreported) are drawn from Ted R. Miller, Mark A. Cohen, and Brian Wiersema, *Victim Costs*

and Consequences: A New Look. (Washington, DC: National Institute of Justice, February 1996).

3. The information provided in this section was drawn from SDM releases (Des Plaines, IL), STAT Resources (Boston, MA), J. P. Freeman (Newtown, CT), and the Freedonia Group (Cleveland, OH).

2

*The Burglar's Behavior**

Most of us think of crime as something that cannot touch us. It is something other people have to deal with—people in other neighborhoods, in other socioeconomic strata, in other ethnic groups or races. However, burglary is a crime that can touch any one of us, no matter where we live or what our socioeconomic class. In fact, burglary victims suffered losses of over $3.8 billion in 1993. And although the number of burglaries has dropped by almost 1 million since the peak in 1981 to 1992, police services have not changed significantly during that time period (Bureau of Justice Statistics 1994). Nationally, police outlays rise 3 percent per year, an increase that barely covers price changes and labor costs. This begs the question: Why are burglaries down if not due to increased police protection? One answer may be that more people are looking into

* This chapter was written by Professor Edna Erez, professor of criminal justice at Kent State University, Kent, Ohio, and revised and edited by the authors.

better security for their homes, including purchasing alarms. While police services have remained constant, alarm ownership has risen 6.5 percent per year as the result of the rise in wealth (SDM 1996). As income rises, households demand more and better services to secure their property. The same is true for commercial property owners. However, insurance requirements are the most important reason for alarm purchase for commercial properties.

Those who study criminal behavior emphasize that the likelihood of a particular property being burglarized depends upon the presence of certain conditions that entice those who are already prone or disposed to commit crime to do so. Criminologists view crimes as events that may be explained by the personal characteristics of the perpetrators and by situational and spacial configurations. Theories of crime causation have addressed the characteristics of offenders and identified biological, psychological, and social correlates of criminality (e.g., Adler et al 1995). Yet, with regard to property offenses, in particular burglary, one theory of crime is commonly invoked for explaining the behavior of burglars: Rational Choice Theory. This theory is applicable regardless of the offender's biological make-up, psychological profile, or social characteristics; in fact, the offender, according to this theory, is only one component of the crime event as a whole.

Rational Choice Theory has its origin in the application of economic principles to the explanation of criminal behavior. Gary Becker, who received the Nobel Prize in economics in 1992, applied economic theory to understanding criminal behavior. Becker (1968) in his seminal work claimed that criminals are rational in deciding whether to commit particular crimes. Criminals are utility maximizers in that they maximize the net benefits derived for a given time period, taking into consideration alternative legitimate activities. In their decision to commit a crime, criminals take into account all the expected benefits and costs associated with the act. Their decisions are guided by the same considerations that influence the law-abiding person engaging in legitimate enterprise and business. This theory definitely applies to property criminals, such as burglars, whose motive is to maximize net profits. Becker's approach has been supported by empirical studies and has gained prominence in criminology (e.g., Clarke and Cornish 1985; Cornish and Clarke 1986).

Rational Choice Theory takes each component of the criminal event into account—the offender, the motivation, and the situation. It posits that rational criminals perform a cost and benefit analysis prior to engaging in a crime and that they process information and evaluate alternatives. They can choose between legitimate and illegitimate activities, and among various types of crimes, place, time, and methods of conducting the crime. The theory involves choice, in that criminals make additional decisions throughout the criminal event, all aimed at maximizing their perceived net benefits given the time constraint.

Benefits include the revenues resulting from the crime and, for some offenders, intangible benefits such as personal satisfaction (e.g., excitement, thrill) or social recognition among peers. The costs include out-of-pocket expenses incurred in selecting a target, some "psychic costs" if the criminal act is not enjoyable, reduction in gains from a lawful activity the offender could have pursued in the time period he/she spends on planning and executing the burglary, and the costs of apprehension and, ultimately, punishment. Although some may doubt that offenders conduct such an elaborate calculation prior to committing an offense, the study of a large number of burglaries and of individual burglars reveals that most burglaries do produce a net return, and that burglars conduct such intuitive calculations prior to committing a crime. Rational Choice Theory assumes that the criminal takes both personal factors—such as need, revenge, and thrill—and situational factors—such as how accessible or well-protected a target is—into account when deciding to commit a crime. Before committing a crime, the offender evaluates the risk of getting caught, the seriousness of the expected punishment if caught, the potential value of the loot, and his or her immediate need for criminal gain. Burglars look to receive goods that are highly valued by the fence with a small chance of being apprehended. Within this context, the burglar makes a series of choices, both conscious and unconscious, about committing a particular burglary.

Burglars operate when a need for immediate money arises. Burglars, like many other low-paid workers, have no savings; they do not know how to save for "rainy days." When a need arises, a burglary is planned. This is especially true for drug-related break-ins.

In this context, it is useful to understand offenders' motivations, backgrounds, skills, and target preferences. Because these elements vary among burglars, it is helpful to distinguish among various types of burglars identified by researchers. Studies (e.g., Cromwell et al 1991) suggest that there are three basic categories of burglars: juveniles, professionals, and those who are drug-dependent. Although there is some overlap among the characteristics of these groups (for instance, the overwhelming majority use drugs routinely and commit crime in the face of a perceived pressing need for cash), there are distinguishable patterns that differentiate among them. An understanding of those differences is helpful for guarding against being burglarized.

JUVENILES

These young burglars are just getting their feet wet in the criminal lifestyle. Often, they have begun with shoplifting, and burglary is the next step in the progression of their crimes. Juvenile burglars are often heavily influenced by peers, who promise that burglary will bring them fast cash and the status that money affords. Juveniles also commit burglary for personal thrill, for revenge, and for other psychological benefits that are not as apt to influence older burglars. Studies have shown that the most criminally active burglars tend to be young. In one study (Figgie 1988), half of those convicted under 21 years of age report at least four additional crimes in the year before conviction. Also, the younger these juvenile offenders are at the onset of their criminality, the more likely it is that they will continue in a life of crime. This study found that "early starters" tend to be the most criminally active—about half who began their criminal careers before age 15 committed six or more crimes in the year prior to conviction. These findings also confirm that a substantial number of burglars who begin their criminal involvement as juveniles join the ranks of professional burglars.

PROFESSIONALS

Nearly all professional burglars begin their careers during adolescence, when they are mentored by older, more experienced burglars. These experienced offenders, who are often siblings or relatives, begin to teach novices the skills needed to burglarize, motivating them first by the promise of excitement. In order to survive in this subterranean lifestyle, the novices must learn the various skills and methods needed in order to commit lucrative burglaries. This may include learning how to gain entry into homes and apartments, how to select targets with high potential pay-offs, how to choose items with a high resale value, how to open safes without damaging their contents, and how to use the proper equipment (such as cutting torches, electric saws, explosives, and metal bars). Generally, burglars in the apprentice stage do not travel far to commit their initial crimes (an average of .4 of a mile). As they become more experienced, professional adult offenders tend to travel longer distances than juvenile offenders.

In the next stage of the professional career, the would-be professional burglars begin to make their own connections. They may also form criminal gangs and try to gain access to inside information without the help of mentors. They also gain expertise in searching for lucrative targets, and they carefully plan each move they make. It is at this point that they develop reputations as experienced and reliable criminals.

Once the burglar possesses the advanced skills and organizational understanding that are required, he or she reaches a recognized professional status and adopts the specific patterns that have proven to be successful. One burglar describes it this way:

> [I do burglary] because it's easy and because I know it. It's kind of like getting a specialty or a career. If you're in one line, or one field, and you know it real well, then you don't have any qualms about doing it. But if you try something new, you could really mess up.... I feel like I have a good pattern, clean; go in the house, come back out, under two minutes every time (Wright and Decker 1994, p. 52).

The burglar's peers hold professional burglars in the highest esteem because of their careful deliberation and ability to plan and execute their crimes. One study suggested that almost two-thirds of those who defined themselves as "planners" reported committing six or more additional crimes in the year prior to their last conviction (Figgie 1988). The planning involves the search for information about prospective targets, the property's contents, occupancy patterns, precautions against burglars, and the likelihood of completing the job without being caught. Professionals use various sources of information to select targets. They include social and work networks, newspapers, and community announcements. Professional burglars also take advantage of various local activities (such as "open houses") to find out information about desirable targets. Professional burglars also cultivate buyers for their stolen goods. The characteristics required to acquire the reputation of a professional burglar are, to some extent, related to specific skills burglars possess (e.g., ability to effect an entry); but predominantly, the characteristics needed for a reputation are utilitarian. They are congruent with Rational Choice Theory because they place strong emphasis on planning, processing information, and evaluating alternatives.

It is important to note, however, that what we defined as professional burglars comprise a small minority of the burglars. Our contacts with local police chiefs reveal that only a few of all burglaries are conducted by what we define as professional burglars. For example, the chief detective in Greenwich, Connecticut, where we conducted a major research project, claimed that "in the fifteen years at this police department I came across only two professional burglars."

THE DRUG-DEPENDENT BURGLAR

Drug-dependent burglars initially follow a pattern of apprenticeship similar to that of the professional burglar, followed eventually by break-away. Their descent into a life of crime, however, is more complex. Six basic stages can usually be identified in the progression from a novice to an experienced drug-dependent burglar.

Stage 1

At about age 10 to 13, adolescents in a high-crime area are allowed to join a group of 14- to 17-year-olds who shoplift or burglarize. The apprentice offenders do not believe that they will have to face harsh consequences for their crimes, and the older criminals who teach them help to erode their sense of fear by emphasizing the benefits of their acts.

Stage 2

After 3 to 10 incidents as apprentices, the younger members either become more integral to the older group or start their own group. The burglaries that occur at this stage result in small amounts of stolen property that are not easily fenced.

Stage 3

One to six months after the first stage, the adolescents begin to buy alcohol, pills, and marijuana with some of their proceeds.

Stage 4

The adolescents grow more confident and gain more experience and criminal associates. At this point, they have located an outlet for stolen goods, and they have found themselves on the fringe of a delinquent, drug-using subculture, where drugs are made readily available to them.

Stage 5

Drugs and burglary facilitate each other. More available cash allows for the purchase of more drugs; the more drugs that are consumed, the greater is the need for cash.

Stage 6

Drugs and burglary can no longer be separated; burglary and property crime in general are only the means of obtaining drugs. In this respect, some criminologists have highlighted the spatial link between drug markets and burglaries: drug-dependent burglars often initiate their activities at local drug sales areas (Rengert and Wasilchick 1994). It should be noted, however, that although burglars of all categories use drugs, the offenses of drug-dependents are invariably motivated by the need for drugs.

One study provides a good example of the career path and motivation of burglars, as exemplified by a burglar named Arturo. Arturo began his criminal career while in junior high school, primarily because of his association with a 16-year-old friend, who had already been confined to youth detention centers for various offenses. Eventually, Arturo became a part of a group of five boys, who burglarized and shoplifted in order to get the money to buy alcohol and marijuana. Because Arturo did not enjoy marijuana, he quickly began experimenting with speed, Quaaludes, LSD, and finally, heroin. After becoming addicted to heroin, he increased his burglary activity in order to support his habit. He dropped out of school, and shoplifting and burglary became his occupations (Cromwell et al 1991).

The qualities of drug-dependent burglars have critical relevance to security providers, affecting the way that they protect homes and businesses. One of the primary motivations for an individual to burglarize either homes or businesses is the need for money to buy drugs. In fact, in a study profiling the most criminally active burglars, it was found that most abuse drugs or alcohol; one-third of those reporting at least six crimes in a year indicated that their primary motivation was drugs or alcohol (Figgie 1988). And while not all burglars are drug-dependent, nearly all burglars do use drugs or alcohol before entering a target. Studies have estimated that anywhere from 30 to 90 percent of burglars are drug users. Furthermore, researchers believe that drug use and residential burglary are interdependent, because burglars often use such depressants as alcohol and marijuana before a burglary to reduce anxiety and fear. In this manner, drugs facilitate the criminal event. As one burglar described:

> See, I wanted to do that burglary anyway before I started drinking, but I didn't have no help. So, what I'd do is I'd get me some help. I called it false courage. Because that's the courage that I need and I've never been one to do anything without false courage...(Tunnell 1992, p. 74).

Yet, the addiction does not preclude rationality. Even though a majority of burglars may be addicts, they are still implicitly considering costs and benefits and are rational in the commission of their crime. They must be skilled, dedicated, and careful in order to avoid apprehension and to execute lucrative burglaries to support their drug habits. In fact, burglars who use drugs think of burglary as a job that supports them. As one burglar describes: "I think of this as work just like you think of your job as work" (Cromwell et al 1991, p. 56).

Through the drug-using burglar's eyes, he or she must burglarize—just as the law-abiding person must work—in order to survive.

It is for this reason that drug-using burglars plan drug use in concordance with burglary activities. They use just enough of the drug to get sufficiently high but not feel sick. As one burglar describes:

> Oh, I liked to use [heroin] before I would go and do a burglary, but I wasn't high, high, high, you know. I would have maybe fixed one or

> two papers to take the sick off then go to work [burglary]....When
> I'm sick, I'll stop and think a lot more. When I'm sick, I'll tend to hog
> anything I can whether it be a house, a trailer...I take greater risks
> when I'm sick" (Cromwell et al 1991, p. 112).

Studies have demonstrated that with heroin-addicted burglars, the drug is not an immediate concern with every burglary. These addicts tend to go days or weeks without the drug rather than risk committing an irrational burglary. This is especially true of the burglars who have been addicted to heroin for several years. Therefore, while it can be argued that burglars who use drugs can be less careful in plotting their crimes, the evidence clearly shows that they plan and calculate their actions.

The rationality of drug-addicted burglars, however, may be reduced when they are suffering from withdrawal symptoms. One convicted burglar described how his crime activities were affected by the need for drugs:

> I knew [crime] was wrong, but like I say, man, it was wrong in the
> eyes of the beholder. You know? I mean, I'm needing a shot of
> dope, it's not wrong for me to go get it. I have to get it. I have to get
> it, however I can. To me it wasn't wrong. I had to have it and I had
> to get it from somewhere (Tunnell 1992, p. 66).

Drug-using burglars (as with other drug-dependent offenders who commit instrumental crimes) are likely to consider only the immediate risks and gains, whereas their counterparts, who are not drug-dependent, also examine the long-range consequences of their crimes, such as the expected length of incarceration in the specific crime locale.

THE PAY-OFF

Perceived benefits by burglars include the revenues that will result from their acts (usually the amount expected from the fence) and, for some individuals, the nonpecuniary satisfaction and social recognition that they derive from crime. The costs include the out-of-pocket expenses they incur, the chance of being apprehended, and, if apprehended, the chance of being indicted. If indicted, the cost includes the chance of being convicted and of being incarcerated, the expected time they will spend in prison, and the losses they will incur in their legal income while in prison. In short, whether or not burglaries are conducted depends upon the expected loot on the one hand and on the certainty of punishment, the severity of punishment, and the burglars' lost legal income on the other. Burglars are goal-oriented criminals, with their primary physical motivation being to satisfy an immediate need for cash. Burglars' other motivations are usually secondary to the need for cash, or they work in conjunction with that need.

It is erroneous to assume that burglars never consider legal means of obtaining money. Such thoughts are usually rejected by the burglar, however, because legal alternatives to burglary do not seem to offer either the immediate gain or the amount of profit that burglary provides. The legal alternatives are also not considered viable by the burglars because their legitimate work possibilities are limited, and they are either unable to secure employment or to obtain employment that pays them more than a subsistence wage. The activities of burglars also suggest that legitimate employment cannot provide a fast buck. As one high-rate burglar describes, "[Burglary] doesn't take very long, the profit is quick. If I worked construction I would make a week what I could make in fifteen minutes" (Tunnell 1992, p. 40). Because burglars are often low-skilled and underemployed individuals, crime is actually more attractive for them than legitimate work. They also have less invested in conformity, and they have no status or job that may be jeopardized by criminal activity. Conversely, highly skilled and well-paid individuals have a lot to lose by committing the four street property crimes (burglary, larceny, auto theft, and robbery).

Research also shows that most burglars have considered borrowing money from banks or family members and rejected it as a solution to the need for cash (e.g., Tunnel 1992; Wright and Decker 1994). To burglars, such a solution is perceived as only temporary relief to their financial problems. Burglary offers to the rational criminal an independent and consistent means of obtaining cash that legitimate employment or borrowing money does not offer.

CONCLUSIONS

Criminals appear to be rational in their decision whether or not to commit crime. They assess the expected pecuniary and nonpecuniary costs and benefits of their act, and they will commit the crime if it can be expected to yield net benefits. Benefits include the monetary gains from the sale of the products, and such possible psychological rewards as excitement and thrills. Costs include lost benefits from legitimate activities and the likelihood and consequences of punishment. Motives, skills, and target selection vary with three basic types of burglars: professionals, juveniles, and drug addicts. This order reflects the escalating frequency of burglary cases committed by the three types. Public policies and private measures designed to reduce a particular area's burglary occurrences depend upon the benefits and costs found in the area and the type of criminals who operate there.

REFERENCES

Adler, Freda, Gerhard Mueller, and William S. Laufer. 1995. *Criminology*. New York: McGraw-Hill.

Becker, Gary. 1968. "Crime and Punishment: An Economic Approach." *Journal of Political Economy*. Vol. 78:169-217.

Clarke, Ronald, and Derek Cornish. 1985. "Modeling Offenders' Decisions: A Framework for Research and Policy." In *Crime and Justice: An Annual Review of Research,* ed. M. Tonry and N. Morris. Vol. 6. Chicago: University of Chicago Press.

Cornish, Derek, and Ronald Clarke. 1986. Introduction. In *The Reasoning Criminal: Rational Choice Perspectives on Offending*, ed. D. Cornish and R. Clarke. New York: Springer-Verlag.

Cromwell, P., J. Olson, and D. Avary. 1991. *Breaking and Entering: An Ethnographic Analysis of Burglary.* Newbury Park, CA: Sage.

Figgie International Inc. 1988. *The Figgie Report Part VI: The Business of Crime: The Criminal Perspective.* Richmond, VA.

Rengert, George, and John Wasilchick. 1994. *Space, time and crime: Ethnographic insights into residential burglary.* Final report submitted to U.S. Department of Justice, National Institute of Justice. Grant 88-IG-CX-0013.

"SDM 1996 Industry Forecast Study." *SDM*. January 1996: 51.

Tunnell, K. 1992. *Choosing Crime: The Criminal Calculus of Property Offenders.* Chicago: Nelson/Hall.

U.S. Department of Justice, Bureau of Justice Statistics. 1994. *Criminal Victimization in the United States: 1973-92 Trends.* (July) NICJ-147006.

Wright, Richard T., and Scott H. Decker. 1994. *Burglars on the Job.* Boston: Northeastern University Press.

3

The Choice of a Target*

THE POTENTIAL TAKE

Rational Choice Theory suggests that targets that promise high proceeds will be preferable to those that may yield more modest returns. For all properties, the risk of burglary increases with the market value of the property. Perceived market value and the household's wealth influence the probability of a property's being burglarized. Commercial establishments with higher revenues and larger size have a greater likelihood of being burglarized (Hakim and Gaffney 1994a,b,c). For commercial establishments, however, the risk of burglary is also related to the concentration of businesses in the community. The larger the number of commercial establishments in an area, the more targets a burglar has to choose from. Still, signs of wealth are a stronger attractor for

---

* This chapter was written by Professor Edna Erez, professor of criminal justice at Kent State University, Kent, Ohio, and was revised and extended by the authors.

the commercial burglar than a large number of possible targets. The value of the property is also a factor in residential burglary. Our studies show that the more expensive the homes, the more likely they are to be selected as targets. The reason for this is that wealthy homes suggest expensive contents.

The prospective gain of burglars varies, however, by the kind of target chosen, in particular by whether it is commercial or residential property. For commercial burglars, the risks are high. Yet, the potential pay-off overshadows that risk. Although residential burglary also entails risk and expected benefits, the level of risk that must be balanced against gain increases tenfold when dealing with a commercial property. This is because commercial targets are more likely to have reliable alarm systems, are located in areas that are more visible to passersby, and have heavier police patrols than do quiet residential neighborhoods. The promise of greater and better loot from commercial targets renders the risk-taking worthwhile. However, because of the higher stakes involved, the planning and evaluation of alternatives are of utmost importance to the successful commercial burglar.

The prospects for large proceeds also explain why burglars look for clues to wealth and choose expensive homes as targets. In our study in Greenwich, Connecticut, we found that the burglary rate is high when home values are between $301,000 and $1.2 million. Yet, even though burglary rates increase with the value of homes, expensive homes are less attractive when they have an alarm (in addition to other precautionary measures).

In choosing a residential target, burglars subscribe to two assumptions: Any residence has something worth stealing, and the expected gain from the residence depends on the general affluence of the target's neighborhood. Burglars are attracted by targets that look like they contain "good stuff." If the target meets this specification, the burglar will be less concerned with easy access or how safe the burglary might be. If the burglar thinks that the house contains valuable items, he or she is willing to take the risks associated with the prospective gain. One burglar explains this process of investigation for affluence clues:

Well, some [houses] is kept up more than others. Somebody gone put just a little more umph in theirs than anybody else....I feel [that one's] got more goodies in there. Not for safety, cause it's probably not safe doing either one of them. But [the well-maintained one] might have a little bit more....Now, if you don't give a shit, you let weeds grow....that's people that seldom have company or, if they do, they raunchy people. So you don't want that house. But if you have a upkeeped house and the trash is all put up and the lawn is manicured and the bushes is neatly trimmed and the bird [feeder] got bird seed in it, that's what you want (Wright and Decker 1994, p. 82).

As the burglar describes, the potential gain from the well-maintained house will far outweigh the potential risk. The way in which a burglar determines whether the target contains "good stuff" is through searching for various clues indicating that there are things worth stealing. Such clues include the size of the structure, the condition of the property, the type of car parked in the driveway, and goods that the offender sees being brought to or from the house.

Burglars also want to know about the people who live in the dwelling and what the dwelling contains. One female burglar said that she likes to have inside information about the potential contents of a house before she burglarizes it. She said that she acquires such information by listening to people talk at restaurants and bars. She also spends some mornings waiting at mall entrances or store exits until a woman wearing expensive jewelry comes out. She then follows the individual home, checks out the residence, and returns later to burglarize it. She describes:

So I drive by the front and back, looking for alarms that might go off....When I drive by I pay more attention to the back—I look for a sliding glass door. If it doesn't look like it has an alarm setup of any type I'll come back that afternoon or the next morning (Cromwell et al 1991, p. 112).

LOCATION

Real estate professionals claim that the three major factors that explain home value are—location, location, location. And just as location determines a property's real estate value, it also determines its burglary value. Location is critical in accounting for where burglaries occur, and this manifests itself in two ways. The highest incidence of burglary occurs in the poor neighborhoods of the inner city and in the most expensive neighborhoods. The vulnerability of poor neighborhoods has to do with the familiarity of the area to prospective burglars, who often reside in the area. The high incidence of burglary in expensive neighborhoods is explained by the potential profit they offer to burglars. The rational burglar considers simultaneously several factors in a decision to commit a burglary—the amount of proceeds is only one of these elements. Other considerations are familiarity with the area and ability to blend in with the local population. Even though the expected loot is lowest in poor neighborhoods, burglars are most familiar with these physical environments, and the chance of apprehension in these environments is lowest. Also, the burglars do not stand out as strangers in these areas.

As the distance from a "burglary generating center" rises, the number of burglaries diminishes (Erez and Hakim 1979; Hakim and Gaffney 1994a,b,c). That decline occurs along major arterial routes—meaning that if burglars venture outside their neighborhoods, they will do so along major thoroughfares with which they are familiar. Burglary victimization rates are also high in the immediate vicinity of shopping centers located on or close to city boundaries. Even though these areas may not be in the "burglary generating center" of a poor neighborhood, each of these prime locations offers the burglar both familiarity and the ability to blend in with the people in the area. Burglaries often occur in a corridor of major thoroughfares. Burglars are familiar with the immediate physical environment of major roads that they often use traveling for legal work or for social purposes. Indeed, our studies in both Pennsylvania and Connecticut suburbs show that the chance of burglary is highest within three blocks of major roads or in the proximity of exits from limited access highways (Hakim and Gaffney 1994). As one study found, most offenders burglarize residences with which they are familiar, partly because they know the area and partly because they have "an intuitive understanding of the people who live in the area" (Wright and Decker 1994, p. 88). Burglars can gain this kind of necessary information through knowing the occupants, through receiving a tip, or through observing a potential target. In fact, burglars sometimes attend parties in an unfamiliar neighborhood in order to get information about prospective targets. Burglars also return to a house at which they were a guest and burglarize it. Almost half of burglary victims discover that the burglar is not a stranger.

Burglars also become familiar with their targets by befriending professionals who can give them inside information about potential burglary sites (e.g., insurance agents, plumbers) or by taking those types of jobs themselves, in effect using a "day job" in order to get information that will help them to perpetrate their criminal activity. Two burglars describe this technique: "I like to date maids. They know who has what and how to get it. I get them to talk about their job and the people they work for and I use that information to do burglaries," and

> One time I was working on this roofing job in this real nice area. I got to know the schedules of almost everybody on the block. I knew when they left in the morning and came home at night, and who stayed home during the day. About two weeks after the job was done I came back and did [burglarized] almost every house on that block (Cromwell et al 1991, p. 28).

It is by using these kinds of "legitimate" sources that burglars gain the information they need to commit well-planned, rational burglaries, and it is this kind of information that enables them to be successful at what they do.

Most burglars select a target as a result of spatial search. For both residential and commercial properties, the selection of target is determined in relation to the major roads. The target is selected through a sequence of choices, with the burglar continually narrowing down the choice: the neighborhood, the street in that neighborhood, the property on that street, and finally the point of entry on the property. However, the relative weight each factor has in affecting target choice depends upon whether the burglary is residential or commercial.

Because of the high risk involved in their crimes, commercial burglars often consider and evaluate a target based on just a few key qualities, and accept or reject that target based upon these qualities alone. For example, if a possible target is located in a visible, highly policed area, the burglar will simply reject it, without even evaluating the target's security system and/or the probability of gain from the target. The risk of getting caught is too great to take any chances. This is also the reason that successful commercial burglaries are not spontaneous ventures. Professional commercial burglars hand-pick their targets and put a high premium upon a sense of familiarity. For example, the neighborhood in which to commit the burglary is often chosen because the burglar regularly travels on the major thoroughfares in the area, either for social or work purposes.

Commercial burglars choose the street on which the burglary is to occur based on the following factors: First, they want the business to be located away from major thoroughfares, out of sight, so that they can avoid detection. Our research has shown that commercial burglaries generally occur away from major thoroughfares; a larger proportion of commercial properties located within three blocks of a major thoroughfare were not burglarized compared to those farther away (Hakim and Gaffney 1994a,b). This is true for both alarm-equipped and non-alarm-equipped properties and for thoroughfares with high commercial concentrations. Business concentration offers environmental security. The routes tend to be well lit and have consistent traffic patterns at all times. It is therefore difficult for the burglar to go unnoticed near one of these roads. However, thoroughfares with a smaller concentration of businesses, little pedestrian traffic, and inconsistent automobile traffic attract burglars because there is less risk of being seen. This consideration is critical to burglars because it takes longer to break into commercial establishments than residences, and they offer little access concealment.

Burglars choose the property to target on the street based on other considerations. First, properties on corner lots have a higher risk of burglary because there are four directions in which the burglar can escape. Our studies show that their likelihood of being burglarized is almost double than that of other locations. Suites in office parks are especially vulnerable and have the highest proportion of commercial burglaries, according to type of establishment. Retail establishments have the second highest proportion of burglary. Finally, single office buildings are also vulnerable to burglary, although their probability of victimization is lower than that of other types of establishments (Hakim and Gaffney 1994a,b,c). Alarms, however, reduce the risk for each of these property types. Commercial burglars also show a preference for edge rather than center targets, and surveillability is crucial in determining their choice of target. Commercial burglars generally show a preference for logical, methodical assessment over the use of intuition and emotional reactions. The commercial establishments least frequently burglarized are sole occupant, manufacturing, wholesale, and service buildings, because they promise the least lucrative rewards to burglars.

Commercial burglars also prefer locations that enable them to blend in with the regulars in the area. Sites that allow this kind of camouflage include schools, gathering spots for juveniles (e.g., convenience stores), and treatment centers for drug addicts. These locations are promising because the burglar can blend in with the local population. Also, businesses located within three blocks of woods or parks double their exposure to burglary because the burglar is not likely to be seen, and if seen, not likely to be noticed (Hakim and Gaffney 1994a,b,c).

Residential burglars operate along major arterial roads with which they are familiar. Homes that are located within one-quarter mile of exits from these major roads are most vulnerable to burglary. Our research shows that almost half of all burglarized homes are located within three blocks of one or more major thoroughfares, even though only one-quarter of the houses studied were located in this corridor (Hakim and Buck 1992a,b). The rate of burglary diminishes with the distance from the exits. This is particularly true if the road connects areas of low-income homes or if it has several commercial establishments on it. When choosing a target, burglars like to operate on familiar routes because these offer a means of easy escape. They often select a neighborhood adjacent to a major thoroughfare that they use in their daily travels. Other popular targets include cul-de-sacs surrounded by woods or bordered by an abandoned railroad (Hakim and Buck 1992a,b).

In poor areas, burglaries are more likely to occur near facilities that are known as gathering places for youth and criminal elements, including convenience stores, playgrounds, schools, and wooded areas. Burglaries in the suburbs, however, do not originate from these facilities. In suburban communities, proximity to wooded areas influences the frequency of burglaries (although a greater affluence of such homes may increase their attraction to prospective burglars as well). Homes that are close to a wooded area, particularly if they are adjacent to woods on the back or the sides, provide the burglar with a feeling of security and concealment.

As noted previously, busy residential or commercial streets and corner homes are prime targets for burglary. Townhouses are least frequently targeted for burglary. The reason for this is that a break-in is visible to neighboring units, which is less likely to be the case in a neighborhood of single-family homes on large lots. Homes bordered by a back street that provides concealed access are highly vulnerable. Burglars choose homes that are visible to them in the search phase and at the same time provide for concealed access and easy escape in case of need. A property that is on a commercial street and borders businesses on both sides provides for safe access during times when the businesses are closed, such as at night or on the weekends. Thoroughfares, railroad tracks, or woods on the sides or back of the home provide for safer access than do adjacent homes, which might be inhabited.

TEMPORAL PATTERNS OF BURGLARY

Time is a critical factor in determining the success of a burglary. It manifests itself in several ways: with regard to commercial establishments, the longer a business has been in operation at its current address, the lower is the chance of burglary. Businesses are most susceptible to burglary in their first year of operation. Beyond the first five years of operation the likelihood of burglary drops dramatically. New businesses are attractive for several reasons: the buildings are aesthetically appealing and well cared for to attract customers, they tend to display new, valuable merchandise (rather than sale or clearance items) in their windows, and often they have not as yet installed alarms. Also, businesses that deal with cash or such high-value merchandise and equipment as cameras, jewelry, computers, and office machines are more likely to be burglarized than those that sell less expensive merchandise.

The time of day when burglaries occur also follows a pattern. About two-thirds of commercial burglaries occur at night. At night, burglars can be confident that the business is unoccupied, that the surrounding property will be essentially empty (if in a business district), and that they will be covered by the darkness. For this reason, some argue that precautions other than lighting do little to deter intruders at commercial establishments. Our research has demonstrated, however, that an alarm, not lighting, is the most important security measure for a business. Researchers add that to be effective in a commercial establishment, alarm systems should deter the burglar by signs warning of the system, detect the burglar both with an audible alarm and a connection to a central station, and identify the burglar by the use of hidden cameras to record the burglary. The probability of an establishment with an alarm warning sign being burglarized is about half that of one without a sign. It is also interesting to note that nighttime burglary is more likely for non-alarm-equipped establishments, while the share of daytime burglaries is larger for alarm-equipped establishments.

The reason for this is that if the establishment does not have an alarm and is occupied, the safest time for a burglary is at night. At night there is less chance that the burglar will be noticed. Where alarm-equipped establishments are concerned, the objective of the burglar is to spend minimum time at the premises. The burglar knows that he/she is noticed upon entry, and therefore nighttime adds little in the way of protection (Hakim and Gaffney 1994a,b,c).

Temporal patterns of residential burglary suggest that burglary rates are positively associated with seasons and temperatures. Burglary rates are highest from May through September, peaking in August and September. The reason is obvious: people are more likely to be out of their homes in the spring and summer months. In August and September people take their vacations away from home. This is more likely to occur in wealthy localities, and burglars therefore prefer to operate in wealthy localities during these months (Hakim 1995, pp. 28–29).

Another temporal variable that influences the frequency of burglary is the number of years in residence. Our research has found that burglary incidents diminish as the time residents live at their present residences increases. This finding is supported by national data. The main reason is that when people move to their new home, it takes them time to secure their place. Home renovations take precedence, for most people, over security measures. For example, burglar alarms are usually installed after two years in residence. Also, when people have just moved into a residence, neighbors often do not know the family, so they pay less attention to or may not know who belongs at the property. Since renovations may be taking place when the residents are new, a strange van in the driveway will not arouse suspicion. Residential targets are also more vulnerable within the first five years of residency because the burglar can more easily learn the value of what is in the house, because he or she is likely to have seen people moving things into the house or to have seen new items for the home being delivered.

PLACE OF ENTRY

Both commercial and residential burglars wish to enter quickly, with no special efforts, and without being noticed. Research shows that burglars spend about 60 seconds actually breaking into the house and no more than five minutes within the house (Dingle 1991). Our study of residential properties in three suburbs in the Philadelphia metropolitan area suggests that over three-quarters of entries occur through first-floor openings, and of these, the majority are through the front and back doors (Hakim and Buck 1992a,b). Doors are more likely entry points for non-alarm-equipped homes, while the garage or windows (on the first and second floor) are common entry points for alarm-equipped homes. However, fewer than twenty alarm-equipped homes have been burglarized in all the communities we analyzed. Both indirect data and burglars' interviews suggest that alarmed homes are avoided. This suggests that yard signs and decals that indicate the existence of alarms are desirable. Further, for reasons of cost-effectiveness it is sufficient to protect homes with alarms only on the ground floor.

Studies also show that in about one-fifth of burglaries entry is gained through an unlocked door. Further, in over one-third of alarm-equipped homes that were burglarized, the alarm system for various reasons did not react. In almost two-thirds of these cases the system was not activated, in about a quarter of the cases the system did not cover the point of entry, and in the remaining 11 percent of cases the system was not working properly (Hakim 1995). In very affluent communities, such as Greenwich, Connecticut, where most homes are protected by alarms, in one-third of alarm-equipped homes that are burglarized, the burglar enters through an unprotected garage or the second floor. Thus, in affluent residential areas where most homes are protected by alarms it is necessary to have a whole home security system, which is in a working condition and is used at all times (Hakim 1995). Affluent homes provide strong incentives to burglars, and owners of such houses must have an alarm for deterrence as well as detection.

BURGLAR'S RISK CUES

Burglars consider simultaneously three categories of immediate risk cues in the target selection decision: surveillability (or the extent to which a target is overseen or observable by neighbors or passersby), occupancy, and accessibility.

Target choice is determined, according to our research, by intuitive consideration of these three factors. Consequently, we will suggest how to harden residences and businesses by adopting cost-effective precautionary measures that reduce the chance of being selected as a burglary target.

Surveillability

Burglars determine the surveillability of a target by examining not only the general area but the target's location within that area and the target itself. For commercial properties, surveillability is commonly addressed by the burglar through effective planning of the time at which the burglary will take place. If the burglar is breaking into a property in a business district, all of the businesses are likely to close at a specific time, in which case the area will be for the most part empty. Commercial burglars also try to limit their surveillability through their choice of target, preferring targets with concealed access provided by natural cover, fences, and the like.

Residential burglars use four main cues to determine the surveillability of a target. They include: its location on the street, its visibility from the neighbors' houses, its visibility from the street, and the location and type of windows, both at the target site and at the neighbors' homes. The location and type of windows is especially critical to the burglar, as one study documents: "Notice how that picture window looks out onto the street. The curtains stay open all the time and both the houses across the street can see straight into the living room. I wouldn't do [burglarize] this place" (Cromwell et al 1991, p. 35).

However, surveillability is important on different levels depending on the burglar and his or her level of professionalism in the trade. Whereas an inexperienced burglar may be concerned about being observed at all while committing the crime, the professional burglar is more worried about being noticed and reported. There are also "positive" surveillability cues for burglars, which tell them that they are not likely to be observed in breaking and entering. These include natural covering, such as trees, shrubbery, and other landscaping. Houses with dense shrubbery near doors are especially vulnerable, because they offer the burglar cover from the view of neighbors or passersby. Burglars prefer to break in through a door, which is the easiest way of entry and provides the least attention and noise. In Greenwich, Connecticut, almost 50 percent of entries were through front or back doors. FBI statistics indicate upwards of three-quarters of burglaries are through doors. Dense shrubbery near doors increases a house's vulnerability to burglary.

The privacy fence is also a surveillability cue. This six- to eight-foot-high board or masonry fence enclosing a property's backyard welcomes the burglar; although he may be seen entering the yard, once he is behind the privacy fence he cannot be detected. Burglars generally attribute both positive and negative values to such fences; they are either positive, providing cover, or negative, blocking potential escape routes. Single-family homes that are isolated are preferred to townhouses, twins, or apartments because burglars are less likely to be noticed. In summary, residential burglars choose secluded homes that provide concealed access from neighbors and street traffic, and expensive homes that promise attractive "takes" and lack sufficient security precautions. Burglars view the target as a package of attractive and precautionary features.

Occupancy

Generally, occupancy is of greater concern to residential burglars than to commercial ones. Most businesses keep regular hours that are known to the burglar, and when the business is closed, in most cases, it is a good indication to the burglar that the property is unoccupied.

For the residential burglar, occupancy is a serious concern. For this reason residential burglars are most active between 10 and 11 a.m. and from 1 to 3 p.m. when most people are either at work or running errands. Other prime times for burglaries are when people are on vacation, during Sunday morning church hours, or while the occupants are at a wedding or a funeral (burglars may acquire information about the latter from newspaper announcements).

Research has shown that the rate of residential burglary diminishes with the rise in family size. This is not surprising; burglars prefer to break into homes when no one is there. As family size increases, the probability that somebody is home is greater, and therefore the home becomes less vulnerable to burglary.

Studies of residential burglars' techniques for determining occupancy suggest that burglars have common tricks of the trade. One study revealed the most-often-used probe to be sending the most presentable offender to the door to knock or ring the bell. If someone answered, the prober would then ask for directions or for a nonexistent person without arousing suspicion. One burglar described her use of this technique:

> If the car is gone I go up and knock on the front door. Oh, if someone were to answer the door, you know, I say "Pardon me, is Mr. Brown in?... Mr. Jennings?" Mister anything, anybody
> I know. If they say, "No, you've got the wrong house," I act confused and say, "I'm sorry, thank you" (Cromwell et al 1991, p. 112).

Another burglar practiced a similar strategy, which he called his "acting routine." He described:

> Looking down at my clipboard, I'd go up and knock on the door. I'm looking for a certain house, you know, and in case somebody is looking from across the street, I've opened the screen door with my foot to make it look like I'm talking with somebody. I'll move my arms half-pointing and say, "Okay, I'll go around to the back."

Or after knocking and nobody comes, I'll turn the doorknob. A lot of houses aren't locked. So I'll just walk in. Anybody who's watching thinks I've been asked inside by the owner (Cromwell et al 1991, p. 108).

By using these techniques, the burglar is successful on two counts: First, the burglar is able, in an unsuspecting way, to determine whether or not the target is occupied. Second, burglars can create the illusion of occupancy to passersby in order to divert suspicion that might be directed toward them if it were obvious that no one was home.

Burglars also determine occupancy by first obtaining the name of the resident from the mailbox or sign over the door, looking up that name in the telephone directory, and then calling the house. The burglar then leaves the telephone ringing and returns to the target home. If he or she hears the phone continuing to ring, the burglar can be sure that the house is unoccupied.

Burglars look for other signs of occupancy such as mail accumulated in the mailbox or, in winter time, snowfall around a house. Burglars look for clues such as whether or not walks are shoveled after a few days, whether or not there are automobile tracks in an unshoveled driveway, and whether or not there are tracks to and from the house. The burglar also checks to see if the only tracks to the house are from a neighbor's house, because that shows that the home is not occupied, and a neighbor has been asked to collect mail and to perform other household duties. The tracks from the neighbor's house also provide the burglar with important information about how to approach the house so as not to alert the helpful neighbor. In summary, research has shown that most burglars of residential property employ nothing more than everyday know-how to make checks for occupancy. Wright and Decker (1994) interviewed and accompanied many burglars in establishing their target choice. They claim that burglars use all five senses in determining whether the residence is occupied. Indeed, Figure 1.4 reveals that, nationally, burglars are successful in choosing homes that are unoccupied at the time of burglary. Sixty-two percent of all burglaries are conducted when no one is home.

Accessibility

Another important factor for burglars in the target selection process is accessibility. Burglars look for the placement and types of doors and windows on the premises and the extent of target-hardening at the site (such as locks, alarms, fences, walls, burglar bars, and dogs). Burglars have various means of gaining entry into a target.

The most common ways for residential burglars to gain access into a home are the following: through sliding glass patio doors, by rear door forced entry with a pry tool or by kicking an open garage door and then forcing open the door between the house and the garage, and by using channel lock pliers to twist the door knob off the front door. Indeed, in our Greenwich, Connecticut, survey we found that only 36 percent of all burglaries are not through a door in the residence (Figure 3.1). Because the burglar wants to spend a very short time (often no more than 60 seconds) entering a home, accessibility is extremely important. For this reason, whether a particular property will be burglarized to some extent depends upon the ease with which the burglar can enter it.

RISKS OF GETTING CAUGHT AND OTHER DETERRENTS

Deterrence of burglars can be conceptualized in two ways: on a social level and on an individual level. Socially, economists say that the best way to deter criminal activity is to raise its direct costs (the probability of arrest, conviction, and severity of punishment) and to make legitimate work more attractive. Certainty of punishment is more effective as a deterrent than severity of punishment. In other words, economic studies of crime deterrence

Point of Entry

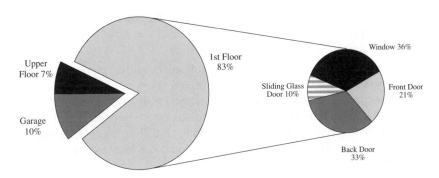

Sample size was 403. Question 40 (Apartments Are Excluded).
Source: Hakim, Simon. *Security Suburban Homes: The Greenwich Case*. Alarm Industry Research and Education Foundation, Bethesda, Md.

Figure 3.1

consistently show that crime prevention activities conducted by police are more cost-effective than administering punishment or applying severe penalties, which are the responsibilities of the courts.

Because burglars make their crime decisions based on the analysis of potential risks and gains, an important deterrent to burglars is a clear message concerning the high risk of getting caught and incarcerated. Making the perceived potential risk outweigh the perceived potential gain requires that victims will report burglary regularly and that criminal justice public policy concerning burglary be modified to increase the costs of perpetrating crime.

Official statistics report an arrest rate for burglary that is very low (14 percent). And because only about half of all burglary victims report the incident to the police, the actual probability of arrest is substantially lower. The fact that burglars do not take the prospect of punishment by the criminal justice system seriously is therefore not surprising. Additionally, many burglars believe that even if they are caught, the relatively light actual penalties make the burglary and the gain it promises worth it. One 48-year-old residential burglar describes his lack of fear of the criminal justice system:

> I always thought [prison] wasn't nothing because I went and did it and come back on here....To you fifteen years would be a lot of time because you don't quite understand it. But, after you get into the system here then they give you so many points for this (good behavior) and so many points for that, and when you get through looking at that you really don't have to stay as long as you might think (Tunnell 1992, p. 93).

Some researchers suggest that the perceived risks of burglary can be increased by reframing the prospects of jail time in terms of a longer period. For example, if one looks at the probability of being sent to jail for one specific burglary, that percentage might be very small. However, if one looks at the probability of a burglar spending any time in jail over the course of a career, that percentage can be as high as 90 percent. Some also argue that by reframing the contingencies of conviction, the rate of burglary could be reduced (Figgie Report 1988). For example, although the probability of conviction may be low, if the burglar knows that all burglars who are convicted must spend time in jail, he or she may be deterred from committing the crime.

Another way to look at deterrence is through individual attempts at target hardening. In fact, most people look at the task of deterring burglars on an individual level, as an issue of protecting what is theirs. Considering that in 95 percent of residential break-ins burglars first case the target, that on average a burglar gets away with $1,281 in cash and loot, that during one in ten burglaries someone is home, and that nine in ten burglaries remain unsolved, the precautions one takes to protect one's home are very important. Research has also shown that the process of actual entry into residential targets seldom required offenders to possess highly specialized knowledge or sophisticated equipment.

CONCLUSIONS

Spatial choice of the site and the type of target emanate from the rational choices of burglars, who maximize net benefits. Commercial targets offer higher returns that more than compensate for the higher risks. More planning and evaluation of alternative targets are required in commercial burglary, which is therefore conducted mainly by professionals, who devote greater effort and expertise to planning their activities.

In choosing residential targets, the more affluent homes in the neighborhood are more attractive because of the greater expected gain in the form of valuable items. This usually outweighs the potentially greater risk involved. Distance from crime-prone neighborhoods has a deterring effect. Burglars prefer to operate in areas where they are familiar with the physical environment and where they cannot be easily identified. Burglaries often occur in the affluent areas adjacent to shopping malls and other areas that burglars often visit. Burglary occurrence is higher within a three-block corridor of major thoroughfares that connect roads that burglars often travel.

Burglars' target choice follows a rational process. In the suburbs, burglars operate along major and familiar arterial routes. For residential targets, as the distance from the route rises, burglary occurrence diminishes. In choosing a street, burglars prefer a quiet street with little expected interference from people passing by. The targeted home is usually the most expensive one on the street. The burglar views the home as a package encompassing opportunities, surroundings, and visible security precautions. Homes that are located further from the street, that provide concealed access because of adjacent woods and shrubs, that do not show signs that somebody is home, and that have no burglar alarm are the most attractive targets.

Burglaries of commercial establishments display a different pattern. Remote and isolated establishments are more susceptible to burglary than are commercial establishments in close proximity to arterial roads. A business location on a major road reduces the chance of burglary. Offices in office parks and in single office buildings are highly susceptible to burglary during nonwork hours.

Burglaries mainly occur within six months of the time residents or businesses move to a new address. Burglary frequency diminishes the longer residents live or businesses operate at the same location. For residences, the initial susceptibility is the result of security precautions not having been installed as yet, and the neighbors being unfamiliar with strange cars or visitors. Businesses, particularly retail establishments, exhibit new and attractive equipment and merchandise. New offices usually have an attractive exterior and new computers and other office equipment. Therefore, burglars are attracted to break into establishments which have recently been occupied.

Two-thirds of commercial burglaries occur at night. Increasingly, residential burglaries occur in the daytime, mainly in two-person working households. Burglaries are particularly high from May to September.

REFERENCES

Adler, Freda, Gerhard Mueller, and William S. Laufer. 1995. *Criminology.* New York: McGraw-Hill.

Becker, Gary. 1968. "Crime and Punishment—An Economic Approach," *Journal of Political Economy.* March/April: 169-217.

Clarke, Ronald, and Derek Cornish. 1985. "Modeling Offenders' Decisions: A Framework for Research and Policy." In *Crime and Justice: An Annual Review of Research*, ed. M. Tonry and N. Morris. Vol. 6, Chicago: University of Chicago Press.

Cornish, Derek, and Ronald Clarke. 1986. Introduction. In *The Reasoning Criminal: Rational Choice Perspectives on Offending*, ed. D. Cornish and R. Clarke. New York: Springer-Verlag.

Cromwell, P., J. Olson, and D. Avary. 1991. *Breaking and Entering: An Ethnographic Analysis of Burglary.* Newbury Park, CA: Sage.

Dingle, Derek. 1991. "Theft-Proof Your Home," *Money Magazine.* August.

Erez, Edna and Simon Hakim. 1979. "A Geo-Economic Approach to the Distribution of Crime in Metropolitan Areas." In *Perspectives on Victimology*, ed. W. Parsonage. Beverly Hills: Sage.

Figgie International Inc. 1988. *The Figgie Report Part VI: The Business of Crime: The Criminal Perspective*. Richmond, VA.

Hakim, Simon, and Andrew J. Buck. 1992a. *Residential Security.* Department of Economics, Philadelphia, PA: Temple University.

———. 1992b. "What Makes a Good Burglary Site," *Security Distributing and Marketing*. April:68-69.

Hakim, Simon, and Mary Ann Gaffney. 1994a. *Commercial Security: Burglary Patterns & Security Measures*. Alexandria, VA: Security Industry Association.

———. 1994b. "The Anatomy of a Suburban Commercial Burglary." *Locksmith Ledger*, March:92-94.

———. 1994c. "Risk Assessment for Commercial Burglary," *Locksmith Ledger*. March:85-90.

Hakim, Simon. 1995. *Securing Suburban Homes: The Greenwich Case*. Bethesda, MD: Alarm Industry Research and Security Foundation.

Rengert, George and John Wasilchick. 1994. *Space, time and crime: Ethnographic insights into residential burglary*. Final report submitted to U.S. Department of Justice, National Institute of Justice. Grant 88-IG-CX-0013.

Tunnell, K. 1992. *Choosing Crime: The Criminal Calculus of Property Offenders*. Chicago: Nelson/Hall.

Wright, Richard T., and Scott H. Decker. 1994. *Burglars on the Job*. Boston: Northeastern University Press.

4

Effective Security Precautions for Residential and Commercial Establishments

INTRODUCTION

To make a home or a business burglary-proof is very costly and practically impossible. The objective should be to spend money on security precautions as long as the benefits of preventing the break-in exceed the cost associated with providing and managing the security precautions. Only cost-effective precautions should be utilized. Further, although it may be possible to reduce the chance of burglary to almost zero, no one would like to live in a fortresslike home. For businesses, overly protected premises may be unattractive to potential buyers and others that visit the property. It is apparent that properties should be protected just enough to lower the chance of burglary in a cost-effective manner.

How can we learn what are desirable types and levels of security precautions? Many books and articles have been written on the topic by security experts. Their suggestions are usually based upon their own perceptions or their own limited experiences. Suggestions for securing homes run the gamut from bars on windows, exterior and/or interior lights, trimming or removing shrubs that hide the front door, to installing dead bolt locks and planting thorny shrubs in front of ground-floor windows. Clearly, there is no guarantee that personal observations about security really reflect what burglars consider important. Experts' considerations do not coincide with those of burglars. Further, as any expert knows, too small a sample does not adequately represent the entire population.

In the early 1990s the National Institute of Justice funded several studies (termed ethnographic analyses) where individual residential burglars were interviewed and followed in order to determine their choices. These studies were very expensive and, again, relied upon a small sample of burglars that does not necessarily reflect the considerations of all burglars.

Our research approach has been to analyze burglaries and a control group of nonburglarized properties over several years in communities that are representative of many others throughout the U.S. We have analyzed a total of 1,153 returned questionnaires in three suburban communities in the Philadelphia metropolitan area, 766 of which are residential and 387 commercial establishments. In a separate study in Greenwich, Connecticut, we sent out 22,000 questionnaires to all residential establishments. Our results are based upon 3,014 returned questionnaires. The Philadelphia study included 490 burglarized establishments and the Greenwich sample included 339 burglarized homes. By observing characteristic patterns in burglaries, we may draw inferences about burglars' behavior. This approach provides a statistically representative sample of the population of residences, and consequently yields reliable results, which have sound policy implications.

In our survey we investigated what security precautions were taken by the burglarized and nonburglarized establishments. Within each group we have analyzed the alarm-equipped and non-alarm-equipped establishments to determine effective security precautions for homes and businesses.

In this chapter we will discuss the effectiveness of various types of security precautions. Special attention will be given to the burglar alarm and its effectiveness in deterring intruders. This chapter will further suggest that the type and level of security precautions indicated depend upon the location and physical attributes of the property. Different types of security precautions are appropriate for residential and commercial establishments.

CLASSIFICATION OF PRECAUTIONS

We can classify residential precautions into the following four groups:

Deterrence—precautions aimed at establishing the impression that somebody is at the residence. These security precautions are designed to encourage the burglar to dismiss the property from consideration when browsing through the neighborhood in search of a target. This category includes a car always parked on the driveway, a yard sign for a burglar alarm, a radio/TV on, and exterior/interior lights set by a timer. An average search by burglars for a residential target lasts twenty minutes. Search time for commercial targets is unknown.

Prevention—mostly mechanical measures aimed at making the actual entry difficult and time-consuming. Usually the intruder is unfamiliar with the extent and quality of the preventive measures until actually conducting the break-in. It is practically impossible to make a residence burglar-proof with preventive measures. These measures simply extend the break-in process long enough to make the burglar abandon the target for fear of being noticed. This category includes bars on windows, a dog, dead bolt locks with solid frames, windows with mechanisms making it difficult to open them from the outside, and pins in sash windows. The actual residential break-in lasts less than 60 seconds. Again, the search time for commercial targets is unknown.

Detection—precautions aimed at detecting the burglar once inside the property. Only a perimeter and interior burglar alarm that covers at least the first floor and is connected to a central station can satisfy the detection criterion. On the average, the burglar spends five minutes in a burglarized home.

Managerial—precautions that indicate the resident's awareness of security, and which require no real products. This category includes a security check by police or other security experts, stopping newspaper and mail delivery when away, maintaining weapons at home, and posting a decal to notify potential intruders of security precautions.

Our research reveals that in order to significantly reduce the chance of burglary all four precautionary categories need to be addressed by the resident. On a regular basis, when residents are away for a significant period of time, measures from the three categories of deterrence, prevention, and detection need to be taken in order to significantly reduce risk exposure.

An effective "generic" precautions package for suburban homes includes a car in the driveway, dead bolt locks with solid frames for all doors on the first floor, and a burglar alarm that is connected to a central station. The dead bolt lock should penetrate the doorframe by at least 1.5 inches. If the lock does not penetrate the frame by at least that much, the burglar only has to break the frame in order to enter the house, and the lock is of no help. A burglar alarm alone or a package of three or more precautionary measures that does not include an alarm is significantly less effective than an alarm and three other precautionary measures. The deterrence, prevention, and detection factors all need to be addressed in order to protect a residence.

A most effective managerial security measure for homes is an active and visible town watch. Burglars do not want to be seen while entering the home. Interviewed burglars have stated that an alarm, a large dog, and an effective town watch deter them. As an example, we would like to present a case from Israel. In an effort to protect the homes in Zahala, an affluent suburban community of Tel Aviv, a town watch of armed residents patrolled the streets every night. The number of nighttime burglaries declined to zero. A neighborhood with a large number of retired people who stay home serves much the same purpose.[1]

We saw in Chapter 3 that in Greenwich, Connecticut, 83 percent, and in the Philadelphia suburbs, 79 percent of burglars' entries were through the first floor. In Greenwich, 64 percent, and in the Philadelphia suburbs, 70 percent of first-floor entries occurred through a door. Burglars avoid breaking windows, which requires time and makes some noise. Burglars prefer not to climb up a building, which makes them visible to residents on upper floors. Thus, protecting the first floor and the doors will significantly reduce risk exposure.

Installing a burglar alarm appears to be the single most effective precaution one can take. Further, our research shows that alarm owners are usually aware of other security precautions and adopt more of them than alarm nonowners. Figure 4.1 exhibits the probability of burglary with and without a burglar alarm, and with fewer than three and more than three other security precautions in place. It shows that the chance of burglary is 10.90 times higher if a home has fewer than three security precautions in place and no alarm than if a home has more than three precautions in place and a burglar alarm. If more than three precautions are taken but without a burglar alarm, the chance of burglary is 2.08 times lower than if fewer than three precautions are taken without an alarm. If fewer than three precautions are taken, then the chance of burglary if an alarm exists is 1.70 times lower than if no alarm exists.

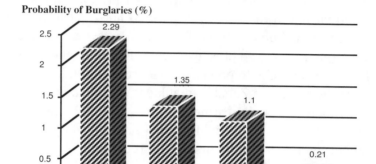

Precautions (3+) Held
Residential

Sample size for alarmed homes was 224 and non-alarmed was 285.
Source: Hakim, Simon, and Andrew Buck, "Proof that Alarms Really Work," *SDM Magazine*, June 1992: 79.

Figure 4.1

Effective protection of homes requires both a burglar alarm and three or more of the other security precautions. The chance of burglary when either an alarm alone or other precautions exist is significantly higher than if an entire security package is maintained.

The question now is: What are the effective security precautions? Both our surveys showed that the following security precautions are cost-effective in reducing risk exposure: 1) deterrence measures: a car in the driveway, exterior lights; 2) preventive measures: dead bolt locks on all doors, a dog; and 3) detection measures: a burglar alarm. Some managerial measures that appear to be effective and serve as deterring factors when no one is home: stop mail and newspaper delivery. To be effective, the package needs to satisfy measures that incorporate all three factors—deterrence, prevention, and detection. Two necessary conditions exist for an effective security package: a burglar alarm, and three or more precautions, covering both deterrence and prevention aspects.

Effective precautions for businesses differ from those of residences. Deterrence measures that are supposed to produce the impression that somebody is home are irrelevant for businesses. Most establishments are vacant outside of business hours (nights, weekends, and holidays). It is easy to determine the name of the business and to verify by phone or by approaching the property that indeed no one is on the premises, and unlawful entry is relatively safe.

Effective prevention measures are difficult to apply for many commercial establishments. Wherever customers visit the premises, businesses want to maintain an attractive entrance and a nonthreatening appearance. Most deterrence and preventive measures are unattractive or may produce the impression that the place is unsafe for the customers. This is particularly an issue for many retail businesses, which need to maintain attractive facades.

Burglar alarms can be used by residents at night and when away from home. Businesses use their alarms only when they are closed. A panic button is the only exception to this rule and is usually used in high-value establishments such as jewelry stores. On the other hand, most commercial establishments need identification measures to control access, prevent employee theft, and identify thefts by customers or other strangers to the establishment. These measures are needed during the regular working hours of the business. Therefore, the use of alarms is of limited value for most businesses except when the business is closed. For identification purposes, most commercial establishments need access-control measures and closed-circuit TV (CCTV) systems integrated with the burglar alarm.

The following are the groups of security precautions required for commercial establishments: prevention, detection, and identification. Prevention measures prolong the forced entry effort while detection and identification measures are effective once the intruder is inside the property. Identification measures are helpful in identifying intruders and in preventing customer and employee theft. In retail establishments, identification measures

Precautions Adopted
Unalarmed Commercial Properties

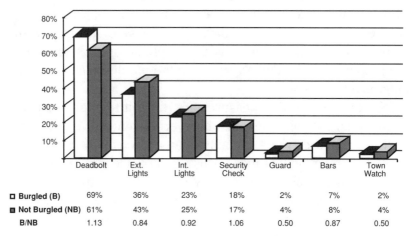

	Deadbolt	Ext. Lights	Int. Lights	Security Check	Guard	Bars	Town Watch
☐ Burgled (B)	69%	36%	23%	18%	2%	7%	2%
▨ Not Burgled (NB)	61%	43%	25%	17%	4%	8%	4%
B/NB	1.13	0.84	0.92	1.06	0.50	0.87	0.50

Source: Hakim, Simon, and M. A. Gaffney, 1994. "Risk Assessment for Commercial Burglary." *Locksmith Ledger*, March: 89.

Figure 4.2

such as CCTV can substitute for deterrence and, partially, for preventive measures. But, the presence of all three types of precautionary measures is required for effective business security. Our commercial establishments' survey in the suburbs of Philadelphia showed that retail and wholesale establishments rarely substitute identification measures for deterrence and preventive measures.

The following discussion centers on the "traditional" factors of deterrence, prevention, and detection in commercial establishments. Figure 4.2 exhibits precautions that commercial establishments adopt in the absence of a burglar alarm. The most utilized measure is dead bolt locks followed to a much lesser extent by exterior lights. Guards, bars, town watch, and exterior lights are shown to exert a possible deterring effect. Town watch and guards are effective because of their personal element, and bars are effective because they are visible and cre-

Effectiveness of Alarms and 3+ Other
Precautions for Commercial Properties

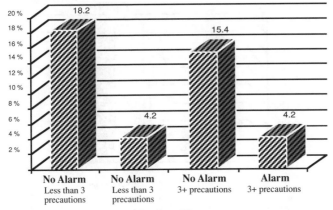

Probability of Burglaries (%)

Sample size for alarmed properties was 181 and non-alarmed was 115
Source: Hakim, Simon, and Andrew Buck, 1993. "Security Systems Cut Burglary Risks," *Security Distributing and Marketing*, April 1992: 80.

Figure 4.3

ate an obvious entry barrier. Exterior lights make concealed entry difficult.

Figure 4.3 shows the effectiveness of alarms in combination with three or more precautions for commercial establishments. It shows that an alarm is effective in deterring intruders. For properties that have fewer than three precautions in place, those not equipped with alarms suffer 4.3 times more burglaries than those that have alarms. For properties that have three or more precautions in place, non-alarm-equipped properties suffer 3.7 times more burglaries than those with alarms. Two inferences can be drawn from these results: a burglar alarm is the most important precaution that can be taken by commercial establishments, and other precautions add marginally to the security of businesses. However, an alarm is an essential precaution and becomes more effective as more precautions are added.

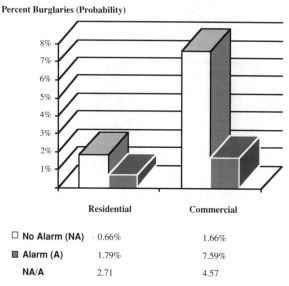

Probability of Burglary

Percent Burglaries (Probability)

	Residential	Commercial
☐ No Alarm (NA)	0.66%	1.66%
■ Alarm (A)	1.79%	7.59%
NA/A	2.71	4.57

Sample size for residential was 766 and commercial was 387.
Source: Hakim, Simon, and Andrew Buck. *Residential Security: The Hakim-Buck Study on Suburban Alarm Effectiveness*, Metrica, Inc., Cheltenham, PA. 1991: 132.

Figure 4.4

THE EFFECTIVENESS OF ALARMS

Our studies analyzed in detail the effectiveness of alarms, and showed that alarms indeed deter intruders. Figure 4.4 shows that in the suburbs of Philadelphia, homes without alarms are in general 2.71 times at greater risk for burglary than homes with alarms. As the value of homes in the suburbs rises, alarms become more effective. In a working-class suburb, non-alarm-equipped homes of less than $100,000 value are 2.65 times at greater risk than alarm-equipped homes. In the high-income neighborhoods, non-alarm-equipped homes are 3.12 times at greater risk.

The probability of burglary for non-alarm-equipped commercial establishments is 4.57 times higher than that of alarm-equipped commercial establishments. As in the case of residential properties, burglars are attracted to businesses and retail stores that are located in affluent areas. Alarms, however, are most effective in deterring intruders where the concentration of businesses is the highest. The greater the concentration of businesses in an area, the more opportunities are offered to burglars, the more burglaries and burglary attempts are made, and the more effective alarms become.

Our survey in Greenwich, Connecticut, one of the 10 wealthiest communities in the U.S., further confirmed our earlier conclusions. Alarm effectiveness is measured as the ratio of the probability of burglary without an alarm to the probability of burglary with an alarm. An alarm appears to be most effective when household income is above $150,000 and home value is above $601,000. The Greenwich survey showed that the probability of burglary for non-alarm-equipped suburban homes rises as the value increases. On the other hand, the probability of burglary for alarm-equipped homes is not only lower by a factor of two but remains constant with the increase in home value. Interestingly, alarm-equipped homes that are burglarized are mainly in the $301,000-600,000 value range. Burglars that break into alarm-equipped homes are looking for expensive homes, which provide greater loot. However, they prefer not to burglarize the most expensive homes, which may have unexpected electronic security measures.

When an alarm is installed it is essential to have a large and visible yard sign. Forty percent of alarm-equipped homes that were burglarized had no sign, while only 33 percent of nonburglarized alarm-equipped homes did not have a sign. An alarm is most effective when an additional three or more deterring and preventive measures are taken from among the following list—a dog, a car in the driveway, exterior and interior lights, and dead bolt locks on all doors. However, to repeat, no other security precaution can substitute for an alarm.

Alarms are also most effective when the home borders a back road, or is located on a quiet residential street. It is most effective when the home is adjacent to woods on both sides or the back. Among all types of housing, alarms are most effective in townhouses, in particular end units, and single family homes; apartments and condominiums gain the least benefit from an alarm system.

As discussed in Chapter 3, an alarm deters myopic burglars. Even professional burglars avoid alarm-equipped properties that are connected to a central station. For example, a professional burglar for three decades who became an international consultant on security (*Security Sales* 1994, pp. 78–86) claims that as far as a residential target is concerned he would avoid an alarm-equipped home or one with a large dog and would switch to another home that lacks both of them.

Different considerations apply to commercial burglary. In many cases he burglarized a target because of his fence's need for a specific product. Burglars often have no choice but to target an alarm-equipped establishment. Here, they claim that not all alarms are the same. In checking the premises before an intrusion attempt the burglar looks for motion detectors, mats, and hard-wired CCTV. The burglar avoids facilities that are equipped with these alarm features. Magnetic contacts on the windows and doors can be either defeated or avoided by entry through the ceiling or the walls. A commercial establishment that appears to have a well-wired, centrally monitored alarm system, with both perimeter and motion detectors, supplemented with CCTV is a difficult target and is not likely to become a burglary target.

But the benefit of alarms to homes is not limited to their deterrent effect. Our studies have shown that burglar alarms improve home security in six additional ways.

Burglar alarms were effective in deterring intruders who chose the home as a target, made an attempt to enter the home, but changed their mind after hearing the siren or noticing the alarm. Of all uncompleted burglaries, 74.3 percent are credited to the existence of an alarm. It is important to note that the audible element is crucial in order to scare away the burglar and prevent entry to the home. On the other hand, a silent alarm probably provides greater social benefit since it is more likely to lead to apprehension of the burglar.

In Greenwich the average value of property stolen is $3,266 for alarm-equipped homes, and $5,343, or 64 percent higher, for non-alarm-equipped homes. The burglar in an alarmed home which is connected to a central station needs to complete his task and get away from the premises in less than 15 minutes. The burglar does not face such a constraint when operating in a nonalarmed home.

The average value of property stolen from alarm-equipped commercial establishments is $1,344, while from non-alarm-equipped establishments it is $1,817, or 35.2 percent higher. Forty-two percent of break-ins of alarm-equipped properties end with no theft compared with 33.9 percent in non-alarm-equipped properties.

Of 319 burglary victims in Greenwich, 9.7 percent confronted the burglar in the house. Nationally, such encounters occur in 13 percent of cases. A third of those confrontations end in assault; more than half the assaults include rape. And no less important is the damage the burglary does to the psyche, which heals slowly. This traumatic experience can be partially alleviated by panic buttons, which are part of many alarm systems.

The best proof that an alarm is effective is the satisfaction alarm owners derive from their systems. Almost all alarm owners who change their residence install an alarm within a short time of moving into their new home. In the Philadelphia suburbs survey, 94 percent of residential respondents who own an alarm are satisfied with their decision to install an alarm. Further, 83 percent said that the alarm makes them/their family feel safer, 12 percent stated that the alarm has prevented break-ins, and another 5 percent claimed that their neighbors/friends have an alarm so they feel it is important for them to own one.

Of the commercial respondents 77 percent are satisfied with their decision to install an alarm, but, only 56 percent of those who are satisfied stated that a feeling of safety was a primary reason for satisfaction. An additional 32 percent stated safety in combination with another reason. Thus, the feeling of safety was important to a total of 88 percent of all satisfied commercial alarm owners.

Commercial alarm owners are primarily concerned about property security, while residential owners care about personal safety. Indeed, a residential burglar alarm is effective when occupants are asleep and when they are away. The panic button adds additional protection when residents are home. For commercial establishments, an alarm is effective only when the business is closed. A panic button adds additional protection in case of robbery. For "traditional" thefts and control over the people at the facility, other forms of electronic security are needed, including CCTV and access-control systems.

People usually think about a burglar alarm while ignoring smoke or fire detectors. Six percent of households and 3 percent of businesses claimed that an alarm prevented a fire. The average loss from fire in the U.S. is $10,199. The damages from fire vary widely. The property and personal cost of a fire can be devastating and can be greater than from burglary. Early detection by an alarm keeps damages minimal.

Overall, as will be discussed in Chapter 5, alarms provide net social benefits to the community. Hence, when all the benefits of alarms and all the costs associated with false activations are considered, our calculations show that alarms are a desirable product for the community.

WEAKNESSES OF ALARMS

Chapter 3 presented the benefits of alarms. However, experience shows that alarms have shortcomings that need to be addressed. The most significant problem is that of false alarms, which is examined in Chapter 9. The other weakness is that of the delay time of alarm systems before the police are dispatched to the scene.

Until the mid-1980s, burglars of commercial establishments spent significant time within the premises searching for cash and other valuables. Electric typewriters and other office equipment, which are attractive items, were often locked away during off work hours, requiring more of the burglars' efforts and time on the premises. Once the use of computers became widespread in most commercial establishments, computers and their accessories such as laser printers, fax machines, and copy machines became readily available. The reception desk itself includes some of these items. Thus, burglars need only spend minimal time within the premises to load those valuables into their vehicle. Three burglars can enter and, within minutes, escape with all their desired equipment. In the case of retail establishments, the burglar can observe from the outside the items of interest and can usually break the window, gain access to the store, select merchandise, and be out within 60 seconds.

Most alarm systems have 30 seconds of delay time before the signal goes to the police department. Then, after the activation is verified and dispatched to the police officers, another 15 to 20 minutes elapse before the patrol car approaches the home/business. The burglar is long gone. Indeed many professional burglars who specialize in commercial targets do not perceive alarms to be a deterring factor.

But these problems can be overcome. To increase alarm effectiveness, the physical order of the preventive and detection measures should be reversed. Usually, preventive measures aimed at delaying entrance into the premises are followed by the alarm, which detects the burglar once he/she is inside the premises. However, if we detect the burglar and then make the actual entry difficult and time-consuming, there is a better chance of apprehension. For example, in the case of window entry, place the alarm contact on the window and the bars inside the window. Further, most businesses have two entrance doors. The alarm contact should be installed on the outside door, and the quality locks and glazing protection should be installed on the inside door. It has been further suggested by Berube (1995) that the delay time should be reduced to zero and the alarm control placed outside the entrance. In doing so, the burglar knows that by breaking through the outside door, the alarm is activated, and now he/she still requires time to overcome mechanical prevention measures such as the dead bolt lock on the inside door. Further, false activations caused by employees unable to deactivate the system upon entering the facility will also decline.

For businesses the main problem caused by a computer's being stolen is the loss of data on the hard disk. Networking the computers and keeping the fileserver well protected in a cage in the center of the facility will significantly reduce loss exposure.

POLICY IMPLICATIONS

The above findings indicate some important developmental directions for residential alarm installers to take. Instead of merely installing alarms, installers might consider expanding their operations to become full-service security companies, offering security packages to clients. In other words, the salesperson that usually presents the alarm could conduct a security check and offer a full security package rather than just an alarm system. An installer should be prepared to install exterior lights and, dead bolt locks, and to remove shrubs, or at least be prepared to have subcontractors available to perform such auxiliary services.

Such a change from being strictly an alarm company to being a security company has valuable long-term advantages. The big fear in the alarm industry is that the regional Bell companies will be allowed to enter the alarm business. Many of the alarm associations' efforts are directed at convincing federal legislators to preserve the judicial restrictions on the Bells' lines of business. However, many in the industry believe that it is just a question of time before the Bells enter this business (Ameritech is already a large player).[2] The Bell companies are interested in entering lines of standardized business that relate to their existing major activity, signal transfer and scanning of telephone lines. They are less interested in entering the installation area and actual operation of central stations.[3] The traditional activities of alarm companies are too labor intensive in the lower echelon of labor skills for the corporate image that the Bell companies have of themselves. So for residential customers, security checks, custom-designed electronic and electrical installation, and dead bolt lock installation are areas presumed to be of no interest to the Bell companies. Thus, by changing the nature of the installer industry to focus on providing more comprehensive and custom-designed service, the alarm installing industry may further reduce the interest of the Bell companies in their business. Further, if the Bell companies enter the market, whether directly or using subcontractors, their business will be of a standardized nature. If the alarm companies enhance their "custom design" service, then their major market of higher-income households will be left intact.

One significant obstacle to such a change in the nature of the alarm companies' operations is the opinion among installers that they would be making a low-tech move, becoming locksmiths, electricians, and landscaping specialists. In addition, a shift to being a security rather than an alarm company is a major structural change, and even small changes can be difficult. It is particularly difficult for small companies in a competitive market, where many need to struggle in order to survive. But such a change in focus will provide important differentiation advantages, whose value will become even greater as competition intensifies.

For commercial establishments, the effectiveness of precautionary measures other than alarms appears marginal. Alarms seem to best address the detection issue. The deterrence factor is irrelevant, and for commercial establishments that are visited by customers, mechanical preventive measures are unattractive. On the other hand, better electronic identification measures are desirable. Companies that provide security for commercial establishments should concentrate on integrated systems that incorporate CCTV and access control with the "traditional" alarm. Such systems will enhance security, since they address the three precautionary factors of prevention, detection, and identification, which are necessary to assure the security of commercial establishments.

Information on effective precautionary measures is important to police departments. Such information can help police in their efforts to enhance awareness of security in their jurisdiction. Sharing information with the police will benefit security companies in their efforts to improve their image in the community and to become an information source for the public.

CONCLUSIONS

The objective in securing properties is not to establish a burglary-proof site. Rather, the objective should be to select security precautions that are cost-effective and will reduce significantly the chance of a site's being targeted by a burglar. Residential precautions can be classified into four categories:

Deterrence: Examples include physical signals that somebody is at home: a car in the driveway and exterior and interior lights.

Prevention: Most important are physical actions that make the actual entry difficult and time-consuming. Effective measures are dead bolt locks and pins in sash windows.

Detection: Once in the property a signal is sent out that makes the stay of the burglar dangerous. Here the only effective measure is a burglar alarm connected to a central station.

Managerial: Examples include precautions that indicate an awareness of security but require no physical measures. Effective measures are police or a security expert's check of the property, stopping newspaper and postal delivery when away, an active and visible town watch program, and posting a sign that weapons are kept in the home.

Improving residential security requires a burglar alarm and three or more additional precautionary measures. Interestingly, preventive measures are of less importance. Once a burglar selects a target, he will vigorously complete his task. Burglars often take drugs prior to an intended burglary in order to suppress fear. The primary objective is to reduce the chance that the burglar chooses the home as a target. A burglar alarm is effective for commercial establishments only during nonwork hours. Precautions other than a burglar alarm are marginally effective for commercial establishments.

REFERENCES

Berube, Henri. 1995. "Putting Alarms in Their Place." *Security Management*. May.

"Former Thief Cites Electronic Security as Deterrent to Crime." *Security Sales*. June 1994.

NOTES

1. See, for example, Lab, Steven (1988). *Crime Prevention: Approaches, Practices and Evaluation*, Cincinnati, OH: Anderson Publishers pp. 43 and 44.
2. We have studied the prospect of the Bells entering the alarm industry. It is our conclusion that it is not in their *interest* to become competitors in installing and monitoring alarms. These parts of the industry are too fragmented and are too small to become profitable for large multinational corporations like the Bells. The services that the Bells can provide are complementary and not competitive to the alarm industry. However, the RBOCs might enter the market, even if it does not appear in their interest to do so. Moreover, the increasing economies of scale in monitoring may change the industry structure somewhat, but the feasibility of long-distance monitoring means that the industry is becoming more national, which reduces monopoly problems.
3. There are a few instances of telephone operating companies entering all phases of the alarm industry. However, in the Pacific Northwest a phone company has met with significant success. The reason why Ameritech has acquired Security Link is unclear, and it is doubtful that similar efforts by RBOCs or cable TV operators will be made. Again, increased economies of scale in the monitoring segment complicate the picture. See footnote 2 above and our discussion in Chapter 7.

5

Costs and Benefits of Alarms to the Community*

This chapter provides a detailed calculation of the annual benefits and costs of burglar and fire alarms to the community. Residents and businesses install alarms in order to supplement police services and to alert the fire department in case of need. At the same time, police departments are burdened by a large number of false activations, which occupy 10 to 30 percent of their manpower resources. If indeed the net benefit of alarms to the community is positive, then the alarm industry has strong ammunition to combat unfavorable ordinances. If, on the other hand, net benefits are negative, then police should raise their fees for false alarm response. Obviously, even if alarms do produce net benefits to

---

* Dr. Yochanan Shachmurove from the economics department at the University of Pennsylvania, Philadelphia, coauthored this chapter.

the locality, it does not preclude current efforts to control and decrease false activations. Revealing the benefits and costs to local communities redirects the attention of local policymakers from the mere cost considerations of false activations to a consideration of the overall costs and benefits.

Tredyffrin Township in Pennsylvania (1990 population 28,028) is a prototypical East Coast affluent suburb. It is plausible to assume that similar results will be obtained for other suburbs, however. The analysis is conducted conservatively; in case of uncertainty, costs are overestimated and benefits are underestimated or even assumed not to exist. The effects on the community are often termed "social" or "real" costs and benefits (National Crime Prevention Institute 1986). These effects can accrue to alarm users and nonusers, installers, police and fire departments, and insurers. We begin with the cost variables, first for the residential units and then for the commercial structures.

COST VARIABLES

Residential Cost Variables

The first cost to be considered is outlays for residential installation. The average cost of a residential system in Tredyffrin Township has been calculated by Hakim and Buck (1991, p. 78) to be $2,244. There were 1,818 residential alarm owners in the township in 1990, the year of our cost and benefit analysis. We estimate the lifespan of a system to be 12 ½ years[1] and the capital recovery rate to be 6 percent. Thus, the annual cost to all residential alarm owners in Tredyffrin Township is:

> Cost of one unit: $2,244
> × Residential units: 1,818
> × Capital recovery rate: 0.11612
> = $473,722

Next, we consider the monthly service charges. Per month cost of monitoring an account ranges from $2.75 for some large nationwide standardized third-party central stations to $15 for upgraded service by companies serving wealthy homes, all in suburban localities. This is the cost of the resources committed to monitoring alarm systems. However, the average price charged to alarm owners is $26. This is the relevant cost, since a community cost-benefit analysis is being considered. However, in a social cost-benefit analysis, which differs from this effort, only the cost of committed resources would be considered.

Eighty percent of all alarm owners in the township are connected to a central station. Thus, the annual cost of the service charges is: monthly charge × months × percent of owners paying the charge × number of alarm owners = $26 × 12 × 0.8 × 1,818 = $453,773

Now we come to the costs accrued to the police department through responding to residential false activations. The police budget for 1990 was $2,849,626. Operating costs included officers' wages, maintenance of facilities and cruisers, fees to the dispatching service, equipment replacement, cost of support personnel, and heat and electricity. The number of officers in the department totaled 47. We concluded that seven officers and the eight civilian employees were allocated to overhead costs, leaving 40 officers available for direct crime prevention. Incidentally, this assumption makes the cost of police response greater than it would be if we assumed all officers were available for crime prevention. In addition, we assumed that the officers actually work at their basic job only 230 working days annually. This calculation allows for days off, vacation and sick time, holidays, and in-service training. Thus, the cost per hour per officer is:

> Yearly police budget: $2,849,626
> Divided by: (40 officers × 230 days × 8 hours)
> = $38.71

Since we have used the total operating budget to calculate the cost per sworn officer per hour, this figure represents the fully loaded cost of one hour of an officer's time. Two officers respond to each activation with two cars, and the average response time is nine-tenths of an hour. This is the average time needed to clear an alarm activation from initial call to response and subsequent follow-up. Since an ordinance was enacted to fine owners for false activations, the number of activations has decreased significantly from previous years. The police in Tredyffrin Township have stated that the officers on regular patrol are diverted from public service and routine patrol to respond to alarm activations. However, in the absence of alarm response, total manpower would not have diminished, but would have been used for other security duties, which yield a similar level of benefit. In order to be conservative about the cost, we assumed that actual cost would have diminished at the rate of average cost. Further, because of the significant share of alarm response in police overall operations, the average rather than the marginal cost is appropriate. Clearly, the real cost of responding to alarm activations in the community is lower than the average cost we calculated. Further, the police enjoy a monopoly, which means that their cost may be greater than would have been the case if a number of firms competed to provide response to alarms. Again, costs are likely to be overstated, making any positive net benefits smaller. In any case, the cost imposed on the police department for each activation for 1990 is calculated as:

$$\$38.71 \text{ per hour} \times 2 \text{ officers} \times 9/10 \text{ hour} = \$69.68$$

There were 1,996 residential false activations in Tredyffrin Township in 1990, which yielded a total cost of response for both manpower and automobiles of $139,081. This figure includes response for both residential burglary and fire. That figure indicates that the alternative benefits that would have accrued to the community from other patrol activities that were denied because the officers responded to false alarms are equal to the real cost.

The total cost to Tredyffrin Township of residential alarms is the sum of residential installation costs, monthly service costs, and the costs of responding to false activations. These figures total $1,066,576 per year.

Commercial Cost Variables

The average cost of an installed alarm in a commercial unit in the township has been calculated by Hakim and Buck (1991, p. 78) to be $3,200. There were 440 commercial alarm owners in the township. As illustrated in our residential analysis we estimate that the lifespan of a system is 12 ½ years, and the capital recovery rate is assumed to be 6 percent. In addition, alarms are considered part of business expenses and are depreciated more quickly for tax purposes. Continuing with our conservative estimate, the tax code states a seven-year lifespan should be calculated for appliances/equipment used in commercial real estate. We also apply the corporate tax rate of 34 percent yearly. The tax benefit means that the firm is really paying only 66 percent (100% – the corporate tax rate) of the cost of installing the alarm. The fact that the tax code allows faster depreciation than the actual lifespan means that the benefits to commercial units are higher than we estimate. Taking all of the above into consideration, it can be estimated that the annual cost to all commercial alarm owners in Tredyffrin Township is:

> Cost of one unit: $3,200 × commercial alarm units: 440
> × Capital recovery rate: 0.179139 × after tax cost: 0.66
> = $166,470

The average monthly service charge has been found to be $100 per month (Hakim and Buck 1991). Only 74 percent of all commercial alarm owners in the township are connected to a central station. This low figure reflects the fact that many retailers are not connected to a central station. All the monthly charges are recognized as business expenses. Thus, the annual cost of the service charges is:

> Monthly charge of $100 × Months: 12
> × Owners paying charges: 0.74
> × Commercial alarm owners: 440
> × After-tax cost: 0.66
> = $257,875

Incidentally, the monthly charge of $100 is high, and probably includes a disproportionate number of high-value commercial enterprises such as banks, jewelry stores, and headquarters of corporations. In addition the figure includes all charges such as opening and closing and testing the system. In general, normal commercial monitoring would be about $40 per month. Again, our calculations are conservative in terms of overstating the costs.

In over 1990 calculation, the cost of police response to false activations was $69.68. There were 528 commercial false activations in Tredyffrin Township, which yields a total response cost for both manpower and automobiles of $36,791. This figure includes response for both burglary and fire.

The total cost of commercial alarms to Tredyffrin Township is the sum of commercial installation costs, monthly service costs, and the costs of responding to false activations. These figures total $461,136 per year. The total residential and commercial cost is thus estimated to be $1,527,712. This is a significant cost to the alarm owners and to other members of the community. The issue now turns to whether or not the benefits of alarms outweigh these costs.

BENEFIT VARIABLES

Residential Benefit Variables

The first, obvious benefit to the alarm owners is avoided burglaries. Avoided nonmonetary costs of burglary include personal injuries and emotional discomforts to the victimized persons. On the national level, in 13 percent of all break-ins, burglars encountered someone in the home; in almost one-third of these cases, the confrontation ended in assault, 10 percent of which were rape (Dingle 1991, pp. 96-97; National Crime Prevention Institute 1986; Rand 1991). Cohen has calculated the cost of crime to victims using national statistics and jury awards in personal injury incidents (Cohen 1988a, pp. 343-353; Cohen 1988b).

Using the findings of our survey in the township, we calculated avoided violent crime as the difference between the probability of burglary with and without an alarm multiplied by the actual number of homes with alarms in the township. Then, this figure was multiplied by the average cost of crime as estimated by Cohen (1988a: Table 1) and updated for 1990 using the change in the Consumer Price Index (CPI) from 1988 to 1990, when the CPI increased by 10.5 percent. To calculate the annual cost of assaults, we multiplied:

> (Probability of burglary without an alarm: 0.0306 minus the Probability of burglary with an alarm: 0.0104)
> × Alarm owners: 1,818 × the average cost of assault of $12,028
> × Proportion of homes where somebody was present at the time of the break-in: 0.13
> × Proportion of occupied homes that ended in assault: 0.333
> = $19,122

> (Probability of burglary without an alarm: 0.0306 minus the Probability of burglary with an alarm: 0.0104)
> × Alarm owners: 1,818 × the average cost of rape is: $51,058
> × Proportion of houses occupied: 0.13
> × Proportion of occupied homes that ended in assault: 0.333
> × Proportion of assaults that ended in rape: 0.10
> = $8,117

The direct monetary losses of burglary to a victimized home-owner (which include the costs of repairs and lost wages from time off from work), excluding the value of the goods stolen, were estimated at $1,038; pain and suffering, $350; risk of death, $128, yielding an average cost per burglary of $1,516. Therefore, the calculation of the annual nonmonetary costs of burglary is:

> (Probability of burglary without an alarm: 0.0306 minus the Probability of burglary with an alarm: 0.0104)
> × Alarm owners: 1,818 × nonmonetary costs of burglary: $1,516
> = $55,673

To summarize, because of alarms the avoided annual monetary costs of burglary, including pain, suffering, and risk of death, in residential units add up to $55,673. The avoided annual cost of the same three categories for assaults is $19,122, and of avoided rapes is $8,117. Thus, the benefits to Tredyffrin Township in avoided violent crime is $82,912.

Next, we consider the direct costs of residential property stolen that are avoided by alarm owners. Our computations are illustrated in Table 5.1. The first column assumes that there are no residential alarms in the community. Applying the historical burglary rate to all housing units without alarms yields an expected 317^2 burglaries that would have occurred in the Township in 1990 if no alarms existed. On average, non-alarm-equipped residences lose $1,674 per incident, yielding a total loss of $530,524. If there are alarms in the community, 1,818 homes suffer a successful attack rate of 0.0104, giving us an expected number of burglarized, alarm-equipped properties of 19. To these add those burglaries expected to occur in the remainder of the population, 262 incidents. Now, applying the average loss to each yields expected losses of $24,106 in alarm-

Table 5.1 Direct Costs and Benefits of Residential Alarms in the Community

	No Alarms	**Equipped**	**Unequipped**
Housing units	10,425	1,818	8,607
× Burglary Rate	.0304	.0104	.0304
Expected Number of Burglaries	317	19	262
× Loss per Burglary	$1,674	$1,275	$1,674
Total Expected Loss	**$530,524**	**$24,106**	**$438,007**

Source: Survey conducted by authors. Funded by the Alarm Industry Research & Education Foundation (AIREF).

equipped and $438,007 in non-alarm-equipped residences. The difference between these two states, alarms versus no alarms $[(2) + (3) - (1)] = 24,106 + 438,007 - 530,524]$, is a reduction in losses of $68,411 because of the existence of burglar alarms in Tredyffrin Township.

Not all burglary attempts in Tredyffrin Township were successful. We also must consider the cases of incomplete burglary. Two percent of alarm-equipped properties experience unsuccessful burglary attempts. Burglars are presumed to have been scared off by the alarm's activation. This means that .02 × 1,818 = 36 properties that suffered no loss. Each would have lost $1,674 had they not had an alarm. Thus, the total loss avoided is $60,264.

A further well-recognized impact of successful burglaries is demoralization cost incurred to the victims. These are emotional costs associated with the trauma of the invasion of privacy, the feeling of vulnerability, and the loss of items with little marketable value but with significant sentimental value.

In affluent communities like Tredyffrin, it is assumed that all residences are insured against the monetary loss of assets. Alarm installation protects against the demoralization costs of future burglaries. The survey in the township showed that 90 percent of the burglarized population in the township installed alarms after a burglary. Therefore, paying for alarms today saves the homeowners from the costs of both buying an alarm in the future and from being burglarized in the future. Accordingly, the annualized cost of alarm installation and the monthly charges may be conservative estimates compared to the demoralization costs, which are not recovered from insurers.

The annualized demoralization costs associated with burglaries avoided by alarm owners are:

> Installation costs:
> Homes installing alarms after burglary: 0.9
> × Unit cost: $2,244
> × Capital recovery rate: 0.11612

× Number of alarmed homes expected not to be burglarized:
1,799

= $421,894

Monthly charges:
Homes installing alarms after burglary: 0.9
Monthly charges: $26
× Months: 12
× Capital recovery rate: 0.11612
× Alarm-equipped homes expected not to be burglarized: 1,799
= $58,659

Thus, total demoralization costs are ($421,894 + $58,659=)
$480,553.

Most systems protect against both fire and burglaries. Therefore, one other benefit to the township is the avoidance of fire. Indeed, fire protection alarms do not get the attention they deserve. About 2.5 percent of the homes in the sample claimed that their alarm systems detected fires over a period of one year (Hakim and Buck 1991, p. 106). Using our survey responses, we find that 19 percent of expected fires are detected earlier because of the use of alarms. The fires at alarm-equipped residential properties had minimal damages because of early detection. Thus, we conservatively assume that alarms help reduce fire damage in 2.5 percent of all households. We may assume that this includes the upper 50th percentile in the seriousness of fires. If those residential units had no alarm system, an additional 118 homes in Tredyffrin Township would have had a serious fire. Using national figures, average U.S. residential loss because of fire is $7,286. (National Fire Protection Association, 1989). This is a very conservative measure for a high-income suburb like Tredyffrin Township. Using these figures, avoided residential losses resulting from fire total $859,748 annually.

Demoralization costs also accrue from fire loss. Again, as in the case of burglary, these costs pertain to devastation associated with destruction of a home and loss of personal items with senti-mental value. Estimating these losses is very difficult, so we chose to maintain our conservative estimate of benefits and pro-vide no monetary value for these benefits.

The total benefits of alarm ownership to Tredyffrin Township sum to $1,551,888. These are conservative estimates of avoided losses because of the existence of alarms in the township.

Commercial Benefit Variables

Maintaining conservative estimates, we assume that the probabil-ity of rape in commercial structures resulting from burglary is zero. The benefits of prevented burglaries consist only of avoid-ance of assault and the indirect nonmonetary benefits. The proba-bility of burglary without an alarm is 0.15480 and with an alarm is 0.04776.

Following the residential calculation, the annual cost of assaults is estimated as:

> (Probability of burglary in commercial units without alarms: 0.15480 minus the
> Probability of burglary in commercial units with alarms: 0.04776)
> × Commercial alarm owners: 440
> × The average cost of assault: $13,490
> × Proportion of commercial units where somebody was present at the   time of the break-in: 0.13
> × Proportion of occupied structures ending in assault: 0.333
> = $27,504

The total cost of rape in commercial establishments is assumed to be null. The direct nonmonetary losses of burglary to a business owner (which include the costs of repairs and lost wages from time off from work), excluding the value of the goods stolen, were estimated at $1,038, pain and suffering, $350, and risk of death, $128. The average cost of burglary is $1,516. Therefore, the calcu-lation of the nonmonetary costs of burglary is:

(Probability of burglary without an alarm: 0.15480 minus the
Probability of burglary with an alarm: 0.04776)
× Commercial alarm owners: 440
× Nonmonetary costs of burglary: $1,516
= $71,400

To summarize, the avoided costs for pain, suffering, and risk of
death for alarm-equipped commercial units is $98,904.

Next, we consider the direct costs of property stolen that are
avoided by the owners of alarm-equipped commercial establishments. Our computations are illustrated in Table 5.2. The first column assumes that there are no commercial alarms in the
community. Applying the historical burglary rate to all commercial
units without alarms yields an expected 120 burglaries, which would
have resulted in the township in 1990 if no alarms existed. On average, non-alarm-equipped commercial units lose $2,008 per incident,
producing a total loss of $241,185. If there are commercial alarms in
the community, 440 units suffer a successful break-in rate of 0.04776,

Table 5.2 Direct Costs and Benefits of Commercial Alarms in the
Community

	No. Commercial Alarms in the Community	Equipped	Unequipped
Commercial units	776	440	336
× Burglary Rate	.15480	0.04776	0.15480
Expected Number of Burglaries	120.12	21.01	52.01
× Loss per Burglary*	$2,008	$1,529	$2,008
Total Expected Loss	**$241,185**	**$32,132**	**$104,425**

Source: Survey conducted by authors. Funded by the Alarm Industry Research & Education Foundation (AIREF).

* The loss figures have been adjusted for inflation similar to what was done for the residential figures to make them comparable to the cost and other data.

giving us an expected number of burglarized, alarm-equipped properties of 21.01. Adding the expected number of break-ins to the remainder of the population yields 52 incidents. Now, applying the average loss per incident yields expected losses of $32,132 in alarm-equipped, and $104,425 in non-alarm-equipped businesses. The difference between these two states, alarms versus no alarms [(2) + (3) − (1) = 32,132 + 104,425 − 241,185], is the amount of prevented losses attributable to commercial alarms, which is: $104,628.

As noted previously, about 2 percent of alarmed properties experience unsuccessful attempts, where intruders have been scared off by the alarm's activation, but they did break in and cause damages. This means that .02 × 440 = 8.8 properties suffered no loss. Each would have lost $2,008 had they not had an alarm. Thus, losses avoided because of unsuccessful burglary attempts on commercial establishments are $17,669.

The demoralization costs reflect emotional costs associated with the trauma of the invasion of privacy, the feeling of vulnerability, and the loss of items of sentimental value. About 62 percent of the owners of burglarized commercial units reacted to burglary by installing alarms. Installing alarms provides valuable protection against future burglaries. Therefore, paying for alarms today prevents the owners from having to buy an alarm in the future and reduces the chance of being burglarized in the future. Accordingly, the annualized cost of alarm installation and the monthly charges may represent a conservative estimate of the nonmonetary costs, which are not recovered by insurers. The annualized demoralization costs associated with burglary that are avoided by alarm owners are reflected in both the installation cost and the monthly payments. The installation cost component consists of:

Burglarized businesses that install alarms: 0.62
× Unit cost: $3,200
× Capital recovery rate: 0.11612
× Number of alarmed firms expected not to be burglarized: 437.9
× After tax cost: 0.66
= $66,584

The second component in the calculation of the demoralization costs is the monthly charges which can be estimated as follows:

> Burglarized firms that install alarms: 0.62
>
> × Monthly charges: $29 (12.5 percent higher than residential) (*Security Sales* 1994, p. 14)
>
> × Months: 12
>
> × Capital recovery rate: 0.11612
>
> × Number of alarmed businesses expected not to be burglarized: 437.9 (U.S. Bureau of the Census 1994, p. 329)
>
> × After tax cost: 0.66
>
> = $7,241

Thus, the total commercial demoralization costs are equal to $73,825. Most alarms provide protection against burglaries and fire. About 0.0238 of the commercial units in the sample claimed that their alarm systems detected fires. Fires at alarmed properties incur minimal damages due to early detection. If those businesses had no alarm system, an additional 18.47 commercial units would have had a fire. Using national figures, average commercial damage in the U.S. caused by fire is $10,199. This is a very conservative measure for the commercial establishments in this affluent community (median family income in 1989 of $75,571). Thus, avoided fire losses attributed to commercial alarms totals annually $188,376.

Other costs also accrue from fire loss. Again, just as in the case of burglary, these costs pertain to devastation associated with the destruction of the business and loss of business records that have no resale value. Estimation of such losses is difficult, and maintaining our conservative approach we chose not to give them any monetary value.

The total benefits of commercial alarm ownership to Tredyffrin Township sum to $483,402. These are conservative estimates of losses avoided because of the existence of alarms in the township. The total residential and commercial benefits to the township are estimated conservatively to be:

$1,551,888 + $483,402 = $2,035,290.

THE BALANCE OF COSTS AND BENEFITS

In this section the balance of costs and benefits is presented, first for the residential units and then for the commercial units. Table 5.3 provides the summary estimate of the costs and benefits that resulted from residential alarm systems. It shows that the net benefits from the 1,818 systems are $485,312. Thus, overall, residential and commercial alarms are beneficial to the community.

Table 5.3 Total Annual Costs and Benefits of Residential Alarms to the Community

A. The cost variables are:	
1. To owners	
Installation outlays	$473,722
Monthly charges	453,773
2. To the Police Department	
Response to false activations	139,081
Total Costs	**1,066,576**
B. The benefit variables are:	
1. Avoidance of burglaries	
Cost of violent crimes (assault and rape)	82,912
Cost of property stolen	
Cost to homeowners	68,711
Incomplete burglary	60,264
Demoralization costs	480,553
2. Avoidance of fires	
Cost to homeowners and insurers	859,748
Demoralization costs	N/A
3. Discounts on insurance premiums	
Total Benefits	**1,551,888**
Net Benefits	**485,312**

Source: Survey conducted by authors. Funded by the Alarm Industry Research & Education Foundation (AIREF).

The community includes alarm owners, the police department, and non-alarm owners. It is likely that one group bears the costs and another group enjoys the benefits. For example, the police department bears the costs of responding to alarms but alarm owners enjoy the additional security. Application of real costs may increase the efficient use of alarms. For example, the fee charged for false activations should be the average cost to the police department of answering these calls. Response to alarms requires the use of real resources, which have alternative uses of similar value to the community. Thus, one can not argue that if an officer responds to false activation the community bears no cost. As long as officers do not sit idle in the station, their commitment to false activations adversely affects security elsewhere with no gain at the site of the false activation.

The amount collected by the township for false activations usually enters the township's general fund. Thus, rising costs of alarm response and subsequent increased collection of fees are not channeled to the police department, which bears the actual costs. The extensive burden to the police of responding to false activations with no additional resources is indeed the false alarm problem. These charges should be transferred to a special fund for the police department to be used solely to cover the police costs of responding to false activations. For further discussion see Chapter 9.

It is important to note that the one element in Table 5.3 that gets the most attention is the cost to the police department of responding to residential false activations ($139,081). However, the overall picture is more important to township officials, who must reconsider local ordinances restricting alarm response.

Table 5.4 provides the summary estimates of the costs and benefits resulting from commercial alarm systems alone. The results show that the net benefits of the 440 systems are $22,266. Thus, overall, commercial alarms are beneficial to the community. The overall net benefits to the community from residential and commercial burglary and fire alarms are summarized in Table 5.5. The net total benefits are $507,578.

Table 5.4   Total Costs and Benefits of Commercial Alarms to the
Community

A. The cost variables are:	
1. To business owners	
Installation outlays	$166,470
Monthly charges	257,875
2. To the Police Department	
Response to false activations	36,791
Total Costs	**461,136**
B. The benefit variables are:	
1. Avoidance of burglaries	
Cost of violent crimes (assault and rape)	98,904
Cost of property stolen	
Cost to business owners	104,628
Incomplete burglary	17,669
Demoralization costs	73,825
2. Avoidance of fires	
Cost to business	188,376
Demoralization costs	N/A
Total Benefits	**483,402**
Net Benefits	**$22,266**

Source: Survey conducted by authors. Funded by the Alarm Industry Research & Education Foundation (AIREF).

CONCLUSIONS

In this chapter we calculated whether the benefits from burglar alarms for both residential and commercial establishments outweigh the costs. On the benefit side is the prevention of break-ins, and on the cost side is the cost of responding to false activations. It shows that the total benefits accruing to the community in the form of enhanced security outweigh the costs of installing residential and commercial alarms and of the police responding to false activations. Homeowners and businesses install alarms

Table 5.5 Total Annual Costs and Benefits of Alarms to the Community

A. Total Costs to the Community	
Total Residential Costs	$1,066,576
Total Commercial Costs	461,136
Total Costs to the Community	1,527,712
B. Total Benefits to the Community:	
Total Residential Benefits	1,551,888
Total Commercial Benefits	483,402
Total Benefits to the Community	2,035,290
C. Net Benefits	
Net Residential Benefits	485,312
Net Commercial Benefits	22,266
Net Benefits to the Community	**$507,578**

Source: Source: Survey conducted by authors. Funded by the Alarm Industry Research & Education Foundation (AIREF).

because they believe that their private benefits are greater than the associated private costs. The benefit is the perceived greater security and the cost is the fines to be paid for false activations. Individuals can be trusted to make correct decisions provided they bear all associated costs and benefits. What is good for individuals is not necessarily good for the community as a whole. An overall community assessment requires the consideration of the cost of police response to alarms and the benefit of arresting burglars and preventing them from stealing.

Costs and benefits were conservatively calculated. Costs were biased upwards, and benefits downwards. Still, alarms appear to be beneficial to the community. Benefits outweigh the costs by $507,578. Ninety-six percent of net benefits are attributed to residential alarms and about 4 percent to commercial alarms.

This work provides policy direction for municipal officials. They should consider redistributing fees collected from alarm owners to the police, who bear the costs associated with the alarms. For example, the total amount of users' fees collected in 1990 was only $14,796. The amount collected did not cover the real costs to the police department. Further, the money was credited to the general fund of the township. Thus, the township is still underpaid for its real costs. By 1992, the system of collection became more efficient, and fines better reflected the real response cost. However, collection for false activations, annual permits, and installers' licenses added up to $56,200. Thus, the township is still underpaid over its real costs by $18,400.

An efficient use of alarm-related collections can be achieved if the following two conditions are fulfilled: First, the fines should represent the real costs to the department. The amount should represent the long-term average cost associated with false alarms. Hence, each and all false activations would be charged a flat fee of $70 per false activation. Second, the police department should enjoy all receipts associated with alarms and should use this amount to provide alarm-related services. If this were the case, much less friction would exist between the police and alarm owners. The police would benefit, or at least break even, and the public would benefit from alarm installation. An alternative solution is simply to mandate private response to alarms, a subject discussed in Chapter 9.

The analysis shows that alarms provide positive net benefits even when the costs and benefits were estimated so as to make any positive net benefits as small as possible. The community should recognize alarms as being complementary to police services and not place impediments on the purchase and use of alarm systems. However, this does not mean that users should not pay for false alarms. Further, reducing false alarms would presumably increase the net benefits from alarms.

In this effort, the local community was used to calculate costs and benefits. This type of calculation is of assistance to alarm associations and dealers in their interactions with local jurisdictions. A social cost-benefit analysis includes the overall effects and is less practical. If a social analysis were conducted, then the actual cost of monitoring would be considered, while in our community calculation the higher retail monitoring prices are included (e.g., monitoring cost for residential users is in the range of $2.75 to $15 per month, while the retail price is in the range of $20 to $26). Benefits will also be lower in a social analysis than in a community analysis.

Monetary losses from burglaries in a social analysis may be considered as redistribution from one person (the victim) to another (the burglar) and are not technically a cost. In a community analysis the value of property stolen is considered in full. In any case, a social cost-benefit analysis of burglar and fire alarms will yield greater net benefits.

Finally, if more alarms are installed, it is not clear that they would provide the same benefits. Marginal net social benefits may decline. Displacement of crime may result as more establishments are equipped with alarms. Displacement can be to other burglary targets, to other forms of crime, or to other times when alarms are not armed. For example, if many or all homes and businesses were equipped with alarms, burglars might be displaced to committing armed robberies, or they might be forced to select an alarmed establishment, or to victimize the same business but at a time when the alarm is not armed. Displacement will be of greater magnitude when a social rather than a community analysis is conducted, since the new target is likely to be in another jurisdiction. However, recent research shows that areas that exhibit a high degree of security precautions provide a security umbrella for the immediate area. For example, if a majority of homes on a street display yard alarm signs, the remaining homes experience a lower than expected probability of burglary (Clarke and Weisburd 1994).

Many express concern about the benefits of alarms when displacement considerations are taken. There are, however, important arguments against such a concern. Alarm ownership is at the range of 11 to 15 percent of all homes and businesses. Thus, the displacement to other types or times of committing crime will not occur before alarm ownership reaches a much greater number of establishments. Further, our own and other research efforts found little to support the existence of displacement (Hakim and Rengert 1981; Reppetto 1976, pp. 166-172).

CONCLUSIONS

Tredyffrin Township, Pennsylvania, was selected as a case study for the calculation of the costs and benefits of residential and commercial alarms to the community. Costs include installation and monthly charges, and police response to false activations. Benefits include the avoidance of burglaries and fires and avoidance of their associated adverse effects. Net benefits to the community amounted to almost $500,000 a year. This chapter can assist alarm associations in their public relations efforts with police and city officials. It shows public officials that alarms are indeed beneficial to the community and efforts should be made to encourage alarm installation while vigorously promoting efforts to reduce false activations without adversely affecting alarm ownership.

REFERENCES

Clarke, Ronald V., and David Weisburd. 1994. "Diffusion of Crime Control Benefits: Observations on the Reverse of Displacement." In Ronald V. Clarke, ed. *Crime Prevention Studies*, vol. 2. Monsey, NY: Criminal Justice Press, pp. 165-183.

Cohen, Mark. 1988a. "Pain, Suffering, and Jury Awards: A Study of the Cost of Crime to Victims." *Law and Society Review.* Vol. 22(3).

———. 1988b. "Some New Evidence on the Seriousness of Crime." *Criminology.* Vol. 26(2):343-353.

Dingle, Derek. 1991. "Theft Proof Your Home." *Money Magazine.* August.

Hakim, Simon, and Andrew J. Buck. 1991. *Residential Security: The Hakim-Buck Study on Suburban Alarm Effectiveness*, Philadelphia, PA: Temple University, (April).

Hakim, Simon, and Mary Ann Gaffney. 1994. *Commercial Security: Burglary Patterns and Security Measures.* Alexandria, VA: Security Industry Association.

Hakim, S. and G. Rengert. 1981. *Crime Spillover.* Newbury Park, CA: Sage Publications.

National Crime Prevention Institute. 1986. *Understanding Crime Prevention.* Boston: Butterworth-Heinemann.

National Fire Protection Association. 1989. "Fire Experience Survey, Fire Loss in the United States During 1988." In *NFPA Journal*, vol. 85, no. 5, table 2.

Rand, Michael. 1991. "Crime and the Nation's Households, 1990." *Bureau of Justice Statistics Bulletin.* Washington, DC.

Reppetto, T.A. 1976. "Crime Prevention and the Displacement Phenomenon," *Crime and Delinquency.* Vol. 22.

Security Sales. 1994. Vol. 15 No. 13.

U.S. Bureau of the Census. 1994. *Statistical Abstract of the United States: 1994*, 114th edition. Washington, DC, Table 350.

NOTES

1. The annual survey of 3,000 dealers, which is conducted by *Security Sales Magazine*, revealed that in 1995 the average length of a subscriber contract was 12.5 years.

   Understanding Crime Prevention (Butterworth Publishers, 1986); Michael Rand, "Crime and the Nation's Households, 1990" (U.S. Department of Justice, *Bureau of Justice Statistics Bulletin*, Washington, DC, 1991).

2. The computational number of housing units without alarms that would have been burglarized is 316.92. This number is maintained in the computations that follow.

6

The Effectiveness of Alarms for the Insurance Industry*

INTRODUCTION

This chapter shows that alarms are monetarily beneficial to insurance companies. Encouraging installation of alarms increases the economic gain of insurance companies by reducing the insurance companies' exposure to losses. The benefits from alarm installation increase with the value of the house. The higher the value of the house, the greater the exposure to burglary is and the more effective the alarm is in avoiding burglaries or reducing the average burglary's loss. Based on United States national statistics as

---

* Dr. Yochanan Shachmurove from the economics department at the University of Pennsylvania, Philadelphia, coauthored this chapter.

well as data from the affluent Greenwich Township in Connecticut and the more modest Tredyffrin Township in Pennsylvania, it is shown in this chapter that the installation of more alarms is beneficial to the insurance companies. Substantially greater benefits accrue to the insurance companies for alarm installations in the more affluent township.

The insurance industry, in part through insurance premium discounts, could be a powerful vehicle for increasing alarm sales. Alarms reduce the losses resulting from fire and burglary, while insurance discounts effectively lower the cost of alarms. However, a lack of communication exists between the alarm and insurance industries. As a result, insurance discount policies vary from one company to the next, and there is little promotion of the installation of alarms. One would expect that users of systems that incorporate features that are proven effective in deterring and detecting intruders would be rewarded with larger discounts. However, the current premium discount structure is erratic and ineffective.

The rest of the chapter is organized as follows. The next section, "Net Benefits to Insurance Companies—The Greenwich Study," analyzes the net benefits to insurance companies based on a detailed study of the affluent Greenwich Township in Connecticut. The section entitled "Net Benefits to Insurance Companies—The Tredyffrin Study" derives the benefits net of based on data from Tredyffrin Township in Pennsylvania. The section following discusses the criteria that must be satisfied for the discounts to be effective from the insurers' viewpoint. Policy implications that will increase sales and reduce the risk of burglary are then provided for the alarm industry and insurers.

NET BENEFITS TO INSURANCE COMPANIES—THE GREENWICH STUDY

The total dwelling units in Greenwich, Connecticut, based on 1992 data number 23,649. Alarm-equipped homes comprise 43.73 percent of the dwellings. Thus, the number of residential units with alarms is 10,342 and without alarms is 13,307 units. The probabilities of burglaries are 6.68 percent for an alarm-equipped home and 14.8 percent a non-alarm-equipped unit. Non-alarm-equipped properties face 2.22 times the risk of burglary as alarm-equipped properties. The average loss from burglary for the alarm-equipped houses is $3,266, and the corresponding loss for non-alarm-equipped units is $5,343 (Hakim 1995). Assuming a 10 percent deductible on insurance claims, insurance companies must pay on average to burglarized homeowners $2,934.40 for alarm-equipped units and $4,808.70 for non-alarm-equipped units.

Given the above data for Greenwich Township, Table 6.1 summarizes how much the insurance companies save from avoided burglaries due to alarm installations. Based on Table 6.1, the net benefit to insurance companies from avoided payments on claims

Table 6.1 Total Insurance Claims for Alarmed versus Nonalarmed Homes, Greenwich Township

	Homes with Alarms	Homes without Alarms	Total Residential
Number of Homes	10,342	13,307	23,649
× Probability of Burglary	× 0.0668	× 0.1480	× 0.1480
Average Number of Victimized Homes	690.85	1,969.44	3,500
Average Claim Net of Deductible	× $2,939.40	× $4,808.70	× $4,808.70
Total Claim	**$2,030,684.4**	**$9,470,446 .1**	**$16,830,450**

Note: The probabilities of burglary for homes without an alarm and for total residential units are the same because in the last case the assumption is that no home has an alarm. If no home has an alarm, then the burglary rate and the resulting average claim will be at least as high as that for an unequipped home in the current environment. In general, the existence of alarms systems in a neighborhood reduces the overall burglary rate.

in Greenwich Township amounts to ($16,830,450 – $9,470,446.1 – $2,030,684.4) $5,329,319.5.[1]

Alarms serve not only to avoid burglaries but also to detect, prevent, and reduce fires. Insurance also covers fires, and claims based on fire damages need to be considered as well. In the U.S., there is one structural fire every 50 seconds. About 2.5 percent of homeowners in the Greenwich sample stated that their alarms had detected fires. Based on national data (1990 United States Census), the total number of residential units was 102,263,678, and the number of residential fires was 2,437,000, and, thus, 2.38 percent of residential units experience a fire in any year. It can be assumed conservatively that alarms prevent 1 percent of all household fires. If those homes were without security systems, the insurance companies would have had to pay claims to an additional 103.42 homeowners in Greenwich. The average loss due to fire is $6,786, net of the deductible. It follows that as a result of their clients' having alarms, insurance companies saved an additional $701,808.

The total benefit in avoiding insurance claims from installing alarm systems is the sum of avoided burglaries and avoided fires ($5,329,319.50 + $701,808) which is equal to $6,031,127.50. This is a conservative figure since we are not including physical and psychological injuries. Medical insurance companies and homeowners (to the extent such injuries are covered) derive some additional savings from alarm systems.

On the other hand, the monetary costs to the insurance companies from offering discounts to owners of alarms can be estimated as follows. Discount policies vary among insurance companies, both in the specification of what is required and the level of the discounts. Table 6.2 details these insurance discounts. The average discount level is approximately 10 percent. The protection requirements differ among companies. Discounts range from 2 to 25 percent, depending on the company and the level of protection. The higher rate requires complete protection of all openings, including ceilings, floors, and walls enclosing the premises. If there is at least one regular employee on duty at all times, a 5 percent discount is awarded for a hold-up alarm connected to a

Table 6-2 Discounts for Homeowners Insurance.[1]

Company	Max Discount (in percent)	Protection Requirements
Aetna[2]	25	Large co. CS burglary or fire 10% each Small co. 5% to 7% each. Audible burglar—none. SD, 2%; DB, 2%. SD + DB + FE = 5%
Allstate	15	10% for CS burglary. 10% for fire alarm connection to CS or fire dept. 5% for audible burglary. SD + FE + DB = 5%.
Prudential	20	10% for CS burglary. An additional 10% for CS fire. 5% audible burglary. 2% for SD.
State Farm	15	10% or 7% for both CS burglary and fire. Audible burglary, 2%, SD 5%.
Travelers	10	CS burglary or fire 5% each, 3% audible burglary, 2% for SD. SC + DB + FE = 5%.
Maryland Casualty	10	CS burglary or fire 5% each. Audible burglary 2%, 2% for SD.
Penn Mutual	15	CS burglary or fire 5% each, 2% for SD, 3% for DB.
Ohio Casualty	10	CS burglary or fire 5% each, 2% for SD, 2% for audible burglary, and 3% for DB.
USF&G	15	CS burglary and fire 10%. 2% for SD. SD + FE + DB = 5%.
Nationwide	20	CS burglary or fire 10% each. Audible burglary—none. 1% for SD. 1% for DB.

[1]Legend: CS—A residence that is connected to a central monitoring station or directly to
            the fire department.
        DB—Dead bolt lock.
        FE—Fire extinguisher.
        SD—Smoke detector.
[2]Aetna Homeowners was sold to Travelers Insurance in the fall of 1995.

Source: Telephone survey conducted by authors.

central station or police station. Usually, Underwriters Laboratories' listed systems and alarm systems monitored by a central station enjoy higher discounts.

The average annual premium in Greenwich Township is $700. Therefore, the total cost of the discount premiums is the number of alarm-equipped homes multiplied by the average discount of 10 percent. This calculation leads to the following cost to the insurance companies: 10,342 alarm-equipped units × $70 = $723,940. The net benefit to the insurance companies is the total benefit, which was calculated to be equal to $6,031,127.5, minus the total cost of the premium deduction of $723,940. Thus, the net benefit is equal to: $5,307,188.

NET BENEFITS TO INSURANCE COMPANIES—THE TREDYFFRIN STUDY

The benefits and costs to insurers were calculated for all properties in Tredyffrin Township (Buck et al 1993, pp. 107-111). The probability of the burglary of a home with no alarm system in any given year, based on the Tredyffrin area study, is 1.79 percent. The property loss in a home without an alarm system is $1,674. For alarm-equipped homes, the burglary rate is 0.66 percent with an average loss of $1,275. There are 21,128 homes with no alarm and 4,923 homes that are alarm-equipped. The average deductible is $500. Table 6.3 shows the calculations for the gain to the insurance companies from installing alarms.

In addition, fires are another cause for filing an insurance claim. About 2.5 percent of the households in Tredyffrin stated that their alarm systems had detected fires. Conservatively, one can assume that alarms prevented 1 percent of all household fires. Furthermore, one can assume that this includes the upper 50th percentile by seriousness of fires. If those houses were without security systems, insurers would have had to pay claims to an additional 49.23 homeowners in Tredyffrin. The average loss due to fire, net of the deductible, is $6,786. Thus, insurance companies saved $334,075.[2]

Table 6–3 Total Insurance Claims for Alarmed versus Nonalarmed Homes, Tredyffrin Township

	Homes with Alarms	Homes without Alarms	Total Residential
Number of Homes	4,923	21,128	26,051
× Probability of Burglary	× 0.0066	× 0.0179	× 0.0179
Average Number of Victimized Homes	32.49	378.19	466.31
Average Claim Net of Deductible	× $775	× $1,174	× $1,174
Total Claim	**$25,180**	**$443,995**	**$547,448**

Note: The probabilities of burglary for homes without alarms and for total residential units are the same because in the latter case the assumption is that no home has an alarm. If no home has an alarm, then the burglary rate and the resulting average claim will be at least as high as that for an unequipped home in the current environment. In general, the existence of alarm systems in a neighborhood reduces the overall burglary rate.

Source: Andrew J. Buck, Simon Hakim, and Mary Ann Gaffney, "Burglar/Fire Alarm Discounts: Cost Effective for Insurers?" *CPCU Journal,* June 1993, p. 109. Reprinted by permission of the *CPCU Journal,* published by the CPCU Society, Malvern, PA.

The total benefit in avoided claims to the insurance companies resulting from the installation of alarms is the amount of the avoided burglary and fire claims. This sum is equal to $412,348.

The monetary costs to the insurance companies from offering discounts to owners of alarm systems can be estimated as follows: The average discount level is approximately 10 percent, and the average annual premium in Tredyffrin Township is $420. Thus, the total cost of the discounts is: the number of alarm-equipped homes multiplied by the average discount, which amounts to 4,923 homes × $42 = $206,766.

This calculation shows that the discounts are cost-effective for the insurance companies. The net saving to the insurance companies in Tredyffrin Township is equal to $412,348 − $206,766 = $205,582.

DISCUSSION

This study shows that discounts are cost-effective to insurers; the amount sacrificed on discounts is less than the savings on claims from burglaries prevented by, and fires that were controlled as the result of, alarms.[3] Therefore, properly offered discounts on alarms are in the insurers' own self-interest.

In order for insurers to decide whether premium discounts are worthwhile, the following questions need to be addressed:

1. Are alarms effective in deterring intruders or preventing break-ins and the spread of fires?
2. Are alarm owners aware of discounts and do they take them into account when purchasing their system?
3. Are nonalarm owners aware of these discounts?
4. Do alarms provide a net return to insurers? Or, in other words, is the total amount sacrificed on discounts less than the avoided payments on burglaries and fires to victims?

If the answer to any of these questions is negative, then it is not worthwhile for insurers to offer discounts. The rationale is that net return is the insurers' primary objective when offering discounts.

In response to the first question, Greenwich Township data show that the risk of burglary is 2.22 times higher for non-alarm-equipped homes compared to alarm-equipped units. In addition, alarms have been proven to deter burglars and prevent the spread of fire. In Tredyffrin Township, non-alarm-equipped homes are an average of 2.71 times more likely to be burglarized than similar alarm-equipped homes. The more expensive the home is, the more cost-effective and valuable the alarm becomes. In Tredyffrin Township, non-alarm-equipped houses valued at $60,000 have a risk of burglary of 1.37 times greater than alarm-equipped homes of the same value. Non-alarm-equipped homes valued at $100,000 are more than three times more likely to be burglarized than alarm-equipped homes (Hakim and Buck 1991). These facts clearly show the effectiveness of alarms.

The second and third questions deal with the effect of discounts on the purchase of alarms. It was found that 25 percent of businesses installed alarms because of requirements from insurers; only 9 percent of businesses took the discount into account when they had free choice in the purchase decision. Of residential owners with no alarms, only 2 percent in Tredyffin and 4.6 percent in Greenwich knew that their insurer offered a discount for alarm ownership; 69 percent of residential and 64 percent of commercial respondents did not know whether a discount was applicable to their establishments. Homeowners did not even consider insurance discounts in their decision to buy alarms while nonowners of alarms were not even familiar with the discount policies of their insurer. Only 8 percent of current residential alarm owners in Tredyffrin and 18 percent in Greenwich considered the discounts when purchasing their alarm system, and only 3.2 percent of them in Tredyffrin and 10 percent in Greenwich sought some form of advice from their insurers before the purchase of the alarm system (Hakim and Buck 1991, pp. 61-65; Hakim 1995, pp. 72-74; Hakim and Gaffney 1994, pp. 50-54).

Discount policies could be good instruments for increasing alarm purchases; however, the lack of public knowledge of discounts is a major deterrent to growth in their use in the community. Notably, the higher the levels of income and education, the more aware the homeowners were about their insurance policies.

To answer question 4, this study has shown that the loss in premiums due to discounts is less than the potential loss from claims resulting from burglary and fire, and thus insurers gain by providing discounts. The benefits are the reduction in burglaries and the consequent claims on the insurance companies. In addition, alarms shorten the time a burglar has in which to commit his crime and thus reduce the average loss from an alarm-equipped unit. The affiliated cost is the discount offered by the insurance company for homeowners and commercial establishments that install alarm systems. The insurance discounts are effective from the insurance companies' point of view if and only if the total cost of the discounts is less than the savings from fewer and smaller

claims for burglaries and fires. This study shows that such benefits are in the millions of dollars for the affluent Greenwich Township in Connecticut and in the hundreds of thousands of dollars
for the more modest township of Tredyffrin in Pennsylvania.

POLICY IMPLICATIONS

This chapter shows that alarms do deter intruders and detect fires
and provide net benefits to insurance companies. Discounts have
been proven to yield a net monetary benefit to insurers. What can
be learned from these findings? Premium discounts offered by
insurance companies promote alarm ownership, which will reduce
their claims and losses. However, discounts are not considered in
alarm purchase decisions. Alarms are seen as luxury items for
high-income families, which cause many possible owners to
believe that alarms are out of their price range. In fact, alarm systems are often not expensive. Further, they are even cheaper when
insurance discounts are taken into account. With these discounts,
alarms are affordable for many families other than just the rich. For
example, in Tredyffrin, the $42 annual discount reduces the $26
monthly monitoring charge by $3.50 or about 18 percent. Further,
even after providing such a discount, insurance companies derive
substantial net benefits, suggesting the possibility of an increase in
discounts.

What are the policy implications of these findings? The alarm
industry should work with the insurance industry to encourage the
purchase of alarms. Insurers should restructure their discounts in
order to enhance alarm installation. We suggest redesigning the
discounts in a way that raises their effectiveness while not changing the total amount allocated for discounts. The greater the concentration of establishments in an area and the more affluent it is,
the more effective the alarm is in avoiding burglaries and minimiz-
ing their effect. Thus, insurers should raise the discounts for properties where their loss exposure is higher, and lower them in areas
where property values are low. Insurers already differentiate auto
insurance premiums based upon the neighborhood. The same

practice of price differentiation in discounts for alarms should be applied, but in a reverse way. Houses that are more likely to be burglarized without an alarm should be encouraged to install alarms by offering them larger discounts. Owners of more valuable houses with a high average expected loss should be offered higher discounts in order to encourage them to install alarms. The focus of discounts should be the high- and middle-income segments of the population, namely, the affluent neighborhoods. Further, the possibility that discounts even in less affluent areas may be profitable is suggested by the positive net benefits in Tredyffrin Township.

In addition, increasing the awareness of discounts is a key to the changes mentioned above. More cooperation between the alarm and insurance industries is required in order to increase homeowners' awareness of the mutual benefits from alarm installations. Joint seminars and brochures should be developed by the two industries. Methods of promoting alarm sales, establishing hardware standards that warrant premium discounts, and listings of installers who provide accepted hardware and adequate service are some of the issues that should be addressed by the industry.

CONCLUSIONS

The insurance industry is a natural ally to the alarm industry in its efforts to promote the sale of alarms. Insurers have an interest in reducing the risk exposure of their subscribers in order to avoid payments for personal injuries and stolen property. The purpose of offering discounts on alarm ownership is to encourage businesses and residents to install a system. Three conditions need to be satisfied in order to justify the discounts from the insurers' viewpoint.

1. Alarms are effective in deterring intruders. Indeed, the chances of burglaries are approximately three times higher for non-alarm-equipped than alarm-equipped homes, and over four times higher for non-alarm-equipped versus alarm-equipped commercial establishments. Thus, this condition is satisfied.

2. The public is familiar with the discounts, and it is a consideration in purchasing a system. This condition is not satisfied. Of nonalarm owners, only 4 percent of residential and 2 percent of commercial occupants knew about the discount offered by their insurers. Of alarm owners, only 8 percent of residential and 9 percent of commercial establishments took the discount into consideration when buying a system. Thus, from the insurers' viewpoint, the discounts are a waste. Insurers would have almost the same number of alarms installed even if they did not offer the discounts on premiums. If indeed alarms are effective for insurers—yielding net returns—then they should more actively promote alarm purchase by their policyholders.

3. Alarms provide a net return to insurers. We calculated the cost of sacrificed income resulting from the discounts and the benefits to insurers of avoided payments for property claims. The net savings for insurers in Tredyffrin Township was over $200,000 per year.

These results suggest that insurers need to participate in promoting alarm sales to their subscribers. Efficiency of the discounts can be increased by offering higher discounts on properties where potential avoided losses from burglaries are higher. For example, discounts on expensive single-family homes, where an alarm is most effective in deterring burglars and where expected claims are high, should increase, while they should decrease on moderate-priced housing, assuming that insurers maintain the same total budget for discounts.

REFERENCES

Buck, Andrew, Simon Hakim, and Mary Ann Gaffney. 1993. "Burglar/Fire Alarm Discounts: Cost Effective for Insurers?" *CPCU Journal.* Vol. 46 (2) June: 107-111.

Cohen, M. 1988a. "Pain, Suffering and Jury Awards: A Study of the Cost of Crime to Victims." *Law and Society Review.* 2(3):231-249.

————. 1988b. "Some New Evidence on the Seriousness of Crime." *Criminology.* 26(2):343-353.

Hakim, Simon. 1995. "Securing Suburban Homes: The Greenwich Case." Philadelphia: Department of Economics, Temple University.

————, and Andrew Buck. 1991. "Residential Security: The Hakim-Buck Study on Suburban Alarm Effectiveness." Philadelphia: Department of Economics, Temple University.

————, and Mary Ann Gaffney. 1994. *Commercial Security: Burglary Patterns and Security Measures.* Alexandria, VA.: Security Industry Association, 50-54.

————, and Yochanan Shachmurove. 1996. "Social Cost Benefit Analysis of Commercial and Residential Burglar and Fire Alarms." *Journal of Policy Modeling.* 18(1) February: 49-67.

NOTES

1. In addition to the direct monetary costs discussed above, there are other nonmonetary costs of burglary. These costs include personal injuries such as confrontation with a burglar, assaults, rape, and the risk of death, in addition to the emotional discomfort suffered by the victimized residents. In 13 percent of all break-ins, burglars encounter someone at home; in one-third of these cases, the confrontation ends in an assault, 10 percent of which are rapes. Based on national statistics and jury awards in personal injury accident cases, Cohen (1988a and 1988b) estimates the direct monetary loses to the victimized homeowners at $939, pain and suffering, $317, risk of death, $116, yielding an average cost per burglary of $1,372. (These figures are for 1988.)

2. In Tredyffrin Township, the installation of alarms resulted in avoided costs for pain, suffering, and risk of death adding up to $55,673. The avoided costs of assaults and rape were $19,122 and $8,117, respectively. Thus, the total avoided costs of violent crime are equal to $82,912. Although these costs cannot be recovered by the insurance companies, avoiding these costs represents a benefit to the consumers of alarms.

   These benefits are excluded from our estimation since we would like to concentrate here on property insurance companies and the owners of alarms.

3. See also Buck et al. (1993), and Hakim and Shachmurove (1996).

7

Structure of the Electronic Security Industry

INTRODUCTION

The structure of any industry, including the electronic security industry, provides the environment in which firms operate. Among various consequences, industry structure is important because it determines the power a firm possesses in setting prices. Future structure is important in order to evaluate present investment strategies and such issues as whether diversification of product is desirable. Major elements of structure include the number and size distribution of sellers and buyers and the magnitude of entry barriers. The size distribution can range from a monopoly to an industry with thousands of firms. The greater the number of suppliers and the smaller each firm's market share, the more competitive the industry is likely to be. Competition means that firms have very little discretion over price. The easier entry into an industry is, the closer price will be to cost. Indeed, if the industry is competitive, price in the long term will be at marginal and average cost, which is the lowest price that is sustainable. Firms will be earning a normal return on their investment, which in 1995 would probably have been around 10 percent. Other elements of structure include product differentiation (whether consumers regard the products of each firm as interchangeable), vertical integration (operating at more than one stage of the production process, such as producing alarm equipment and wholesaling the alarms; or installing, monitoring, and responding to alarms), economies of scale (the cost advantage enjoyed by larger producers), and economies of scope (lower cost per unit from producing more than one product such as alarms and locks). These elements affect both entry into and the character of competition within the industry.

The electronic security industry is composed of manufacturers, distributors, and installers of alarms and other intrusion detection systems, and firms that monitor the alarms and request response to intrusions or other problems. Each segment is highly competitive.

MANUFACTURING

Manufacturing of alarms (SIC 36691) encompasses a large number of firms, insignificant economies of scale, easy entry, and also satisfies the other conditions for a highly competitive industry. In 1992 there were 127 manufacturers of alarm systems, about the same number as in 1987, when there were 132. The average firm had $11.1 million in alarm system sales in 1992, reflecting its small scale. Similarly, the average manufacturing establishment had only 72 production workers in 1987 compared to 125 in telephone and telegraph equipment manufacturing companies. Concentration, the share held by the largest firms (which may be suggestive of monopoly-type problems), is moderate. The largest manufacturer for alarm equipment has between 10 and 15 percent of the market, and the top eight have no more than 80 percent.

The Herfindahl Index for the industry would be no more than about 1,000, which is considered to be at the high end for unconcentrated industries.[1] If one looks at, for example, particular types of electronic alarm equipment such as sensors, concentration is still low. The top four firms were estimated to have 38 percent of the glass breakage sensor market in 1991, and the top three had 42 percent of the ultrasonic motion detector market (Frost and Sullivan 1994, p. 204). The modest concentration in the industry will keep prices competitive. In any case, the large firms are constrained by the large number (119) of smaller industry participants. Concentration, in fact, declined between 1982 and 1990, which is indicative of the absence of economies of scale or other advantages of large size. In addition, new entrants to the industry will assure the high degree of competition. For example, AT&T now manufactures detection equipment, marketed through licensed installers/dealers, and Michigan Bell designed a control panel to monitor its remote switching stations and has licensed its manufacture.[2]

Easy entry and the large number of potential entrants ensure that prices will remain competitive. As mentioned, economies of scale in manufacturing alarm systems are not significant. Modest economies arise in purchasing materials and components in large quantities. There are also modest economies of scale to be gained from running a production line continuously. Training of workers and developing skills in, for example, production of sensors provides some advantages for larger firms. Economies of scale arise in manufacturing from the advantages of specialization and training. The firm has to be large enough to avoid having to shut down the production line and shift to another product. Switching imposes a substantial cost penalty, and its avoidance results in economies of scale. Further, other entry barriers, such as patents, access to raw materials, or other key inputs (including capital) or advantages provided by product differentiation, do not seem significant. The absence of substantial product differentiation means that new entrants can easily convince knowledgeable buyers such as wholesalers and installers that their products are of a quality commensurate with existing manufacturers' products. Consumers have not exhibited much brand loyalty in such electronics purchases as televisions. Alarm equipment would be unlikely to command any greater brand loyalty. Advertising costs, not surprisingly, have been very low, and these would not make entry difficult. Advertising is primarily directed at dealers, not final consumers. It usually occurs through industry magazines and via conventions. Patents do not play an important role in the alarm industry since the technology is generally well known. Capital costs do not pose much of a barrier, as evidenced by the widespread presence of small, non-publicly-traded firms that raise sufficient capital without resorting to public offerings. Product development is also well within the capability of many firms. A new product typically takes nine months to develop and requires an investment of only $150,000. Further, economies of scope from producing more than one product are largely absent (existing possibly only in marketing). New entrants would thus ensure that prices do not exceed cost for any substantial period.

The number of potential entrants is large and includes telephone and electronics firms. For example, in 1992, 148 firms manufactured telephone sets, answering machines, or fax machines. Moreover, firms producing related security products could easily enter the alarm industry. For example, firms producing only fire alarm control systems could easily enter the burglar alarm segment of the market.[3] In addition, foreign firms could enter electronic security manufacturing and export their products to the U.S. Indeed, in another related segment of the industry, one firm imports closed-circuit televisions used for surveillance and security. Moreover, vertically integrated firms that sell directly to consumers (and install their own systems) could sell to the nonintegrated wholesalers should wholesale prices exceed cost.

The presence of large and knowledgeable buyers, including wholesalers, also helps ensure that prices remain competitive. These wholesalers sometimes have great purchasing power, which can be employed against manufacturers. In fact, almost 40 percent of alarm equipment passes through wholesalers. These wholesalers have a strong incentive to obtain low prices from manufacturers because they sell to installers, who typically buy from four wholesalers. In addition, companies such as Sears also purchase alarms. Such companies presumably obtain competitive prices.

Indicative of the presence of active competition in the manufacturing segment is the fact that in 1987 price to wholesalers was only 60 percent in excess of variable cost, which implies, given profit maximization, a price elasticity of demand of 2.7. That value is reflective of competitive behavior, because a high price elasticity normally means that good substitutes are available. Moreover, prices for systems have fallen substantially, which is symptomatic of a high level of competition. Basic systems have fallen from almost $3,000 in the 1970s to $100 in 1995 (and in some cases they are installed at no charge). In part, prices for systems have fallen because of price reductions at the manufacturing level. For example, in 1987 control panels were sold to dealers for $150; in 1995 they were sold for $75. Over time, panels come to include more features; dealers are sometimes able to switch to such panels at marginally higher or even lower prices.

Firms also compete in developing better products. One firm employs 70 engineers that work on such projects as better control panels and improved glass breakage detection. The security industry usually adopts developments from other industries. Product development is based upon adopting technology from the related fields of computers and electronics. Already more adoptable innovations have come from the telecommunications industry, mainly from its wireless segment, and this will definitely be the case in the future. New firms are often established, producing a particular product that is based upon new technology. These new firms rely upon large distributors such as ADI for their marketing efforts. The rate of technological innovation that is relevant to the alarm industry is expected to increase in future years. The restructuring of and alliances among the cable TV, telephone, and electronics industries will generate innovations that will affect the alarm industry. Thus, the frequent emergence of firms producing a single or a few new alarm components will continue, and the concentration in manufacturing will further decline. The manufacturers also compete in terms of service to dealers.

In manufacturing, the absence of substantial economies of scale means that a large number of firms can compete with larger, multiproduct firms. Firms that specialize in one or a limited number of products also can compete. An industry structure with a large number of firms and modest entry barriers means prices should remain at the competitive level.

WHOLESALERS

Distribution of alarms by wholesalers is a highly competitive segment of the industry. These firms purchase alarm equipment from manufacturers and sell the equipment to installers. This distribution function, getting the alarm equipment from manufacturers to installers, must be performed by manufacturers or by wholesalers. Even some of the largest installation firms employ wholesalers to perform the distribution function. The national sales of wholesalers totaled approximately $1 billion in 1995. ADI, which operated 80 branches, was the leader, with an estimated national market share of about 30 percent. For example, ADI has eight branches just in Florida. The firm even has branches in New Mexico and Rhode Island. The 10 largest wholesalers, including ADI, compete in a given local area with local firms. The nature of selling in the industry, typically through catalogues, means that perhaps 70 percent of products are shipped to the installer, and, consequently, the market area can be large. Salespeople travel to installers to sell their products. Still, about 30 percent of the products are purchased at the wholesaler. The relevant local and national markets are highly competitive, containing a large number of small firms and some national firms. Entry into the business is not difficult. The buyer-installers are knowledgeable and, because of strong pressure to keep their costs down, they are highly sensitive to prices. The demand faced by wholesalers is, accordingly, elastic. The industry's highly competitive nature is also indicated by its gross profit margin, which is typically in the range of about 18 to 23 percent. The entire wholesale distribution function has to be performed for less than 23 percent of the industry's sales revenue, a figure comparable to that for the highly competitive retail food distribution industry.

The major function of wholesalers is to get the products from manufacturers to the installers at the lowest possible cost. Along these lines ADI has been quite successful with its innovative supermarket concept. Computerized ordering and delivering are also extensively employed. Buying power and knowledgeable sales representatives are important for firms to remain competitive. To perform the distribution function, wholesalers use advertising in security magazines, offering specials, trade shows, visits to customers, and, most important of all, catalogues. Indicative of the focus of activities performed by wholesalers is that in 1995 out of one firm's total employment of 30, 18 were engaged in selling. Interestingly, there are advantages to having local sales offices and a centralized shipping facility. One firm has 12 sales offices but ships from only one location. Wholesalers sometimes try to achieve product differentiation, similarly to the use of store brands in supermarkets. For example, one wholesaler markets such a brand-named wireless system, and its retail dealers employ telemarketing to sell the system.

One problem with the wholesale segment is the difficulty the end users have in getting complaints transmitted to the manufacturers. Communications from manufacturers to wholesalers and then to installers and end users work better than the reverse communication channel. Aside from this problem the segment performs its function well.

INSTALLATION

The installation of alarms is a highly competitive segment of the industry. At least 12,000 firms installed alarms in the U.S. in 1994 (Blackstone et al 1994; Hakim and Buck 1991; Hakim and Gaffney

1994, pp. 44-56). If we include firms and individuals that install alarms on a part-time basis, the figure rises to 17,000. Most of the firms are small. Fifty-six percent of installers have annual gross sales of less than $249,000. Only 4 percent have annual revenues of $2.5 million or more. Ninety-eight percent employ fewer than 10 workers. The top 25 firms account for an estimated 40 to 50 percent of the industry's sales. There are also large vertically integrated firms like ADT, Brinks Home Security, and Westinghouse Security Systems. These large firms in general have competed for the mass market by offering low prices for standardized systems.

On the local level, which is the relevant market in relation to competition in installation, a large number of firms compete, including small ones and large vertically integrated firms. For example, 88 firms were advertising installation of burglar alarms in Lower Bucks County, Pennsylvania, in 1988.[4] Tredyffrin and Upper Merion townships in Pennsylvania in 1989 had 120 and 82 firms installing alarms, respectively. The respective populations for the two suburbs of Philadelphia were 23,019 and 26,138, indicating again that even in an area of small population a large number of firms compete. The top 14 firms installed 65.2 percent of the alarms in Tredyffrin and the top 13 installed 60.14 percent in Upper Merion, with the remaining 35 to 40 percent handled by 69 to 106 firms. The industry obviously has a large number of different-size firms. In Tredyffrin, for example, the large and small firms on the average installed 43 and 3 alarm systems, respectively. These firms operate in other communities as well. A large number of firms compete in the large cities. For example, in Portland, Oregon, in 1994 the top eight installed 78 percent of the systems but 167 firms competed.

Since labor costs represent such a large part of installation costs, a larger firm does not gain significantly lower costs. Actually, many of the large companies contract out installation to small independent installation outfits. Table 7.1 shows that installation time varies from 5 hours to 4 days. High-end customized installation can take 4 days. Few conclusions can be drawn about installation time

Table 7-1 Installation Statistics

Number	No. Install/Yr.	Installers	Installation Time	Clientele	Wages	Cost Components	Cost Tele-marketing	Selling Expenses[1]	Direct Cost[2]	Price
1	150	3	1 day, 1 installer (22 openings)	90% residential higher-end	$200 ($25/hr)	$395	No	None		$1500-$2000
2	180-240	11		90% residential	$110	$165	No	None	$400	$560
3	240	6	4 days, 1 installer	residential high-end	$9-$12/hr		No			$2200-$2500
4	250	2 + 5 sub-contractors	1 day, 2 installers	95% commercial	$385	$735	0	$525	$1645	$1500-$2000 for a retail store $800 for wireless
5	360-408	8	1 installer, 3 days	95% residential high-end	$480($12-$13/hr)	$860	No	$900	$1800	$2700
6	300-500	20			$490	$330	No		$820	$1500
7	428			70% residential	$35/hr		No	$350	$1765	Residential: $1600 Commercial: $2100
8	900-1200		1 installer, 1 day		$150	$150	Yes, $83 per installation	$75 commission	$458	0
9	excess of 1200		5 hours, 1 installer		$100-$110	$240	No	N.A.	$350 not including selling	less than $100
10	excess of 1200		1 day, 1 installer		$120 ($12-$17/hr)	$230	No	$296	$800 (fully loaded)	less than $200

Table 7-1 Continued

Number	Price Monthly Monitoring	Profit (Gross)	Vertical Integration[3]	Location	Business	Comments
1	$4.25 - $7.25	20% to 30%	No	PA Metro	Referrals	
2	Residential: $4-$5 Commercial: $10-$15	40%	No	PA Suburbs	Referrals	4 managers/administrators; when general and administrative expense included, no profits earned on installation.
3			I,M,S,P	VA	Referrals	4 service personnel, 1 on call at all times. If service required, priced at $55 per hour.
4	$65 retail	6%	None		Referrals— especially existing clients & police	Telemarketing to special commercial lists of new and re-located businesses.
5	$25-$30 retail	0%	I,M	PA Suburbs	Referral— signs, real estate agents	Out of 400 sales leads, 50% comes from referrals, 40% signs, 10% other, including real estate agents.
6	$15-$20 retail	10%-12% (Net)	I,M			
7	Burglary $24, fire $32 retail	14%	I,M	WI		Marketing expense is 20% of gross sales.
8	$24.95 for 3-year contract period		I,M	NJ Suburbs	Mass tele-marketing	Telemarketing: .66 appointments per hour; one installation for 2 appointments. Average installation includes $400 of extras. Firm provides both mass marketing and custom installations. Information in table is only for mass marketing.

Table 7-1 Continued

Number	Price Monthly Monitoring	Profit (Gross)	Vertical Integration[3]	Location	Business	Comments
9	$19.95-$24.95 retail		I,M	National	Mass media	Mass marketer
10	$21.95		I,M	National	Mass media, mainly TV	Average installation price is $400, 70% of appointments yield a sale. Firm uses same manufacturer for each component.

1. Selling expenses include salesmanship, advertising, and miscellaneous direct marketing.

2. Direct cost may include some additional items.

3. I = Vertical Integration

M = Monitoring

S = Service

P = Private Response to Alarms

N.A. = Not Available

Some numbers have been reported so as not to identify a particular company.

Source: Survey conducted by authors.

for commercial establishments because the size and requirements of each job vary too much. In general, about 4 to 5 hours are usually required to install a standard wired system no matter how many systems are installed. Accordingly, economies of scale are not significant in the installation segment of the industry. Since the per installation cost is essentially the same for large or small firms, the industry supports firms of far different sizes. The absence of economies of scale means that many firms can compete.

Not only is concentration modest and do a large number of firms compete, but entry is also quite easy. Negligible entry barriers mean that price cannot exceed average cost without attracting new firms, a process that will return price to the competitive level. The large number of firms itself means that price is likely to be competitive. In any case, entry barriers are negligible. In particular, very little capital is required to enter the industry, and the required skills and training can easily be obtained. The industry even has a training institute and also conducts training seminars at many regional, state, and national association meetings. Moreover, since alarm installation involves only low-voltage electrical work, there are few governmental regulations or restrictions on entry. A permit is sometimes required to install alarms, but it is usually under $100, and no test is required. Product differentiation also does not appear important. The only possible entry cost is some modest advertising, such as in the Yellow Pages, and such a requirement is unlikely to be much of a deterrent to entry. In fact, many new installation firms are composed of former employees of established alarm installation firms.

Part-time installation by electricians and locksmiths, among others, occurs. If prices temporarily rise above the competitive level, part-time firms can easily expand to return prices to the competitive level. And, in the opposite case, their exit could help raise price to the competitive level, where a return equal to opportunity cost is earned. Further, self-installation is feasible in some cases (about which more will be said later in this chapter).

Indicative of the ease of entry is the fact that 68 firms entered the alarm installation business in Lower Merion Township, Pennsylvania, between 1988 and 1989. Easy entry and exit (few nonrecoverable costs besides opportunity cost should a firm leave the industry) means that 12 percent of the installation firms have been in the business fewer than two years and 32 percent have been in the field fewer than five years.

Competition in the installation segment of the industry has been strong. An indication of low profitability in installation comes from the following statement:

> A lot of dealers believe that they have to make a substantial cash investment in a system, so they constantly lose money up front on new business with the intention of making it up down the road on the monthly service fee (Spooner 1990, p. 67).

Companies, especially the large vertically integrated ones that install and monitor their systems, offer standardized systems below cost. For example, in 1995 a simple system with sensors on two or three doors, one motion detector, and a control panel, including wiring and labor, cost about $220 to install. A technician normally takes from 4 to 6 hours to install the system at the premises.[5] At least three firms, ADT, Scott Alarm of Jacksonville, Florida, and Guardian Security of Detroit, will install such systems at either no charge or at a minimal charge such as $99 provided a monitoring agreement exists. Such agreements generally run from 3 to 5 years. One oil delivery firm on Long Island, New York, will even provide an alarm at no charge if a customer obtains oil delivery for five years. On the other hand, some companies try to earn modest profits on installation. Such firms typically provide custom installations for expensive homes. Other companies try to just break even on installations.

Installation costs include both direct and overhead elements. Marketing and overhead add $400 to $800 per account, according to interviews. Table 7.1 provides detailed results from our extensive interviews. Installers also provide warranties ranging from 90 days to 1 year, and service calls are common. The cost of a service call can easily exceed $100. A phone connection is usually not included in the installation price and adds another $80 that the residence owner must pay.

Interestingly, interviews report that the marketing of alarms has become quite expensive, since television and radio are now extensively employed. Companies such as Security Link, Brinks Home Security, and ADT can afford advertising through realization of economies of scale whereas smaller firms may not be able to.[6] Increased concentration in installation may well occur.

Losses on installation are covered by monitoring profits. The average cost of installation has been estimated to be $600, which includes both direct and indirect costs. Accordingly, the loss on some installations can be as much as $600. Since the average monthly monitoring price is $20, and the direct operating cost is estimated to be $4, about 38 months are required to recover the loss on installation for a vertically integrated firm, without including interest to account for the time value of the money. Including opportunity cost represented by the loss of interest, the recovery period becomes even longer.

Specifically, the firm must determine how long it will take to recover its loss on installation. The firm has incurred a $600 loss, and it must calculate how many months it will take (using an appropriate discount rate) to provide net revenues equal to the initial loss. Each month provides $16 of profit ($20 less the monitoring cost). The following equation represents the situation:

$$\$600 = \$16/(1+i) + \$16/(1+i)^2 + \ldots + \$16/(1+i)^n$$

where i=interest rate, and n=years.

Using a 10 percent discount rate for the above figures, about 53 months are required. The firm must essentially discount future profits until it obtains enough discounted profits to equal the losses on installation. In the above example, earnings in the fifth year add only $109 in present value, illustrating the significance of the discount rate. High interest rates obviously mean a longer recovery period, whereas higher monitoring fees yield a shorter recovery period.

The importance of monitoring revenues is clear. The industry refers to this notion as "recurring revenues." Normally, a dealer's subscribers turn over every five to six years. This turnover makes it difficult but not impossible to recover initial losses. Incidentally, the above figures suggest that a three-year contract just covers the loss on installations, when the loss is under $450. In any case, the strategy of low installation prices adopted by some large firms means that earnings from systems occur over time instead of immediately, when the system is installed.

Firms on occasion don't consider their total cost. One firm sells its accounts for $600 to $700, but the firm may not be fully considering its overhead, which may mean that its total cost is $800 per installation. Firms may be losing even more than they realize on installations if they do not account for the time value of money. If the loss on installation is, conservatively, $400, the opportunity cost for the $400 is substantial, adding months to the time required to cover the losses on installation.

The length of the monitoring contract, as previously mentioned, is important in determining profitability. Often four to five years are required to recover the losses on installation. After that recovery period, the profits on monitoring are high. One firm reported that the margin after the four- to five-year period was 70 to 80 percent. The key to profitability in the installation and monitoring segments of the industry is maintaining long-term service.

Firms that can afford the delay in recovery, a group that presumably includes the large integrated firms that both install and monitor systems, may be at an advantage with such a pricing system. Some large firms can afford to lose $40,000 per month to obtain installations, whereas small firms may not be able to lose such an amount. An inexpensive funding source is required to follow a low-installation-price strategy, which suggests an advantage for large firms that can obtain cheap credit. However, small firms may be able, in effect, to sell their accounts to a finance company or obtain credit based on their monitoring contracts. We expect further development of the financing market. Smaller firms that do not offer monitoring services can also sell their installations to monitoring firms and earn revenues from their share of monitoring revenues, or they can pay third-party monitoring companies to monitor their accounts. More will be said about such issues later in this chapter.

In any case, installation is a competitive segment of the industry: concentration is moderate and entry is very easy. Indeed, installation prices are often less than cost. Given such easy entry, it is hard to imagine this segment to be anything but highly competitive. This means that installers can expect to earn only normal profits in the long run.

MONITORING

The other retail segment of the industry is the monitoring of alarms. These activities include verification of an alarm, cancellation of alarms known to be false, dispatching of the remaining activations to police or private response companies, and notification to subscribers or other designees.[7] Monitoring establishments include those operated by vertically integrated firms and third-party firms that monitor the accounts of independent installers. Self-installed systems may also be monitored by third-party firms. The quality of service may differ among monitoring facilities. Some, for example, may verify an alarm before dispatching police. Others may simply dispatch the authorities whenever a signal is received. Like other segments, monitoring is competitive. In the U.S. as a whole in 1992, there were 2,724 monitoring establishments. For example, in Bucks County, Pennsylvania, in 1992, there were six monitoring establishments. Montgomery County, Pennsylvania, had 17, and Philadelphia County had 10. Pennsylvania had 119.

These establishments were generally small. The average annual revenue of Bucks County establishments in 1992 was $195,833. The comparable figures for Montgomery and Philadelphia Counties were $1,747,529 and $2,508,900, respectively. For the entire state of Pennsylvania, average annual revenues were $1,170,361, again reflecting the small scale of operation. The figure for Bucks County suggests the very small size of some establishments. In terms of employees, the average monitoring company in Bucks County had only 2.3 paid employees in 1992. In Montgomery and Philadelphia Counties they had 18 and 34, respectively, and in Pennsylvania, about 16.[8]

A large portion of the expenses of monitoring establishments arises from labor. For Bucks, Montgomery, and Philadelphia Counties in 1992, labor expenses represented 29, 36, and 37 percent of total revenue, respectively. Labor costs were 35 percent for monitoring establishments for Pennsylvania as a whole. Interestingly, Bucks County establishments, by far the smallest, had the lowest portion of revenues attributable for labor expense, suggesting the possible absence of substantial economies of scale.

Concentration figures on a national basis suggest that the industry is unconcentrated. The top four firms in 1987 earned 39.5 percent of the industry's revenues, the top eight 49.8 percent, and the top 50 65.6 percent. However, those figures do not reflect local market concentration, the real locus of competition for this industry. However, long-distance monitoring has become commonplace because of reduced telecommunications charges, so that the market has become more national. An interesting question is whether consumers would be willing to pay higher prices to obtain local monitoring. In any case, these figures do suggest the existence of a large number of firms. The national figures show that the leading firms operate a large number of monitoring establishments. The top four on the average in 1987 operated 65 central stations, the next four largest, 41 central stations, the next 12, about 6, and the next 30, about 2 each. The government figures in Table 7.2 show the wide range of sizes of monitoring establishments.

The figures suggest a modest increase in the second largest and largest-size classes (500-999 and 1,000 or more employees). At the same time, the smallest-size class has also grown. Since there has been a large increase in the number of monitoring establishments (26.9 percent over the 1989-1992 period), it appears that entry occurs mainly into the small-size classes and

Table 7-2 Monitoring Establishments

Total Number of Establishments			Employment - Size Class								
			1-4	5-9	10-19	20-49	50-99	100-249	250-499	500-999	1000 or more
1989	2146	Number	708	385	441	389	154	55	13	1	–
		%	33	18	20.5	18.1	7.2	2.6	0.6	0.05	–
1992	2724	Number	1024	509	490	454	163	66	14	3	1
		%	38	19	18	16.7	6	2.4	0.5	0.1	0.04

Source: U.S. Dept. of Commerce, Country Business Patterns, 1989 and 1992, Table 1b.

then the successful companies grow to the larger-size categories. Although only a few years of government data are available, the data suggest that modest economies of scale exist. Again, these data come from a period of substantial growth, so a longer period is necessary to discern any more subtle trends. We have also conducted a large number of interviews to try to gain a more detailed understanding of the monitoring sector, which appears to be the segment where economies of scale and changes in technology are most likely to occur. These findings are discussed below and are reported in detail in Table 7.3 at the end of the chapter.

Economies of scale are a significant factor in the monitoring sector. They primarily arise from the efficient use of labor. A central station does not begin to be efficient until it has a least 3,000 to 3,500 subscribers. For example, it is generally less expensive for a firm to have 2,000 accounts monitored by another firm (a third-party) than to have its own central station. In addition, 53,000 residential accounts can be monitored with eight operators per shift, whereas 3,000 residential accounts require at least one and probably two operators per shift. Increasing the size of the operation by almost 18-fold increases labor cost by eight to 12 times. Doubling the size of the central station often requires only a 20 percent increase in the number of operators. In smaller central stations, operators are busy 40 minutes per hour; in larger central stations, operators are busy 50 minutes per hour.

A step function exists for costs, where costs are constant for some ranges of subscribers. For example, 4,000 or 5,000 accounts can be monitored with the same personnel. In other words, there is no extra cost to monitor the additional 1,000 accounts.[9] However, when approximately 5,000 residential accounts are added, an additional operator per shift is required. Then again, the same personnel can handle up to an additional 5,000 accounts. By fully using labor, which, incidentally, represents about 70 percent of expenses, per subscriber cost can be reduced by 10 to 15 percent.

To summarize, substantial economies of scale exist for establishments monitoring up to 60,000 subscribers. Establishments with fewer than 3,000 subscribers have substantially higher costs.

Beyond 60,000 accounts there are some modest additional effi-ciencies available in terms of labor. Finally, average costs of mon-itoring establishments as large as 200,000 accounts are only slightly lower than those of smaller facilities. Officials of large national monitoring companies in excess of 200,000 accounts claim economies of scale exist for maintaining one large center. One company states that monthly monitoring costs would decline to $3.50 per subscriber for a 500,000 subscriber facility, a figure considerably below its 1995 monthly cost for monitoring in excess of 100,000 subscribers. The best proof that economies of scale are significant is the continuing decline in the number of central stations maintained by large national companies. ADT had 118 central stations in 1988, while in 1995 the number shrank to 14 and will probably decline further. The main reason why some companies operate more than one central station is the need for compliance with local fire codes, which require local monitoring. Clearly, such a requirement stems from historical reasons and is likely to change in many local jurisdictions over time. Westing-house monitors 236,000 accounts at one facility, and National Guardian also operates, for all practical purposes, one center. Economies stemming from operations larger than 200,000 accounts result from more efficient software, better use of space, and better prices from long-distance carriers. Further, large mon-itoring companies can move their facilities to remote locations where semiskilled labor is less expensive, and real estate costs are lower. Figure 7.1 illustrates our empirical findings on econo-mies of scale in monitoring. Again, it illustrates that economies of scale are significant up to 200,000 accounts; from that point on, economies of scale are modest.

Let's discuss other costs of central stations: computers, soft-ware, telephone lines and receivers, rent, and electricity. One central station designed to monitor 4,000 to 5,000 accounts had capital requirements of $50,000 in 1995. Underwriters Laborato-ries (UL) certification added $25,000 to $30,000 in costs. Among other requirements for UL certification, the building must be fire-proof and have sprinklers and a dual-generator system to handle

Average Cost of Monitoring Establishments
(computed)

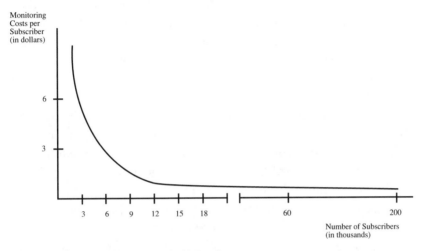

Source: Hakim, Simon, and E. Blackstone. 1995."Outside Attraction:
    Economies of Scale, Scope and Cost...," *Security Dealer,* (April): 106.

Figure 7.1 Average Cost of Monitoring Establishments

such services as air conditioning, as well as having a battery backup system. Increasing the number of accounts monitored by the central station requires, after some point, additional space, keypads, and monitors. About 2,000 square feet of space is required for every 20,000 to 30,000 accounts. Such space is generally not expensive; additional computers and other equipment are also inexpensive. Larger central stations require more sophisticated software, which can add $50,000 to capital costs. Such software is required to maintain a short response time for the operators.

The average, or fully loaded, cost of monitoring establishments, excluding marketing costs, was reported to be around $3 per subscriber for large establishments (around 50,000 subscribers) in 1995. Small monitoring facilities (those with 3,000 subscribers) had higher average costs (about $6 per subscriber), and the largest had costs somewhat below $3 per subscriber. Confirming that costs were in the range given above is the fact that the typical per subscriber charge by central stations that monitor the accounts of other installers was $6 in 1995. A large installer with thousands of accounts might be able to monitor for as low as $3.75 per account. These are typical charges and vary depending upon the number of zones in each monitored account, which essentially means the sophistication of the alarm system in terms of areas of the facility protected.

The increasing significance of economies of scale is again reflected in the fact that firms have consolidated their operations. ADT, for example, consolidated 118 monitoring centers into 14. A firm in Florida consolidated five central stations into one. Westinghouse monitors its many accounts nationwide from one central station. Even for monitoring establishments of over 200,000 accounts, economies of scale were still realized. A factor that is a disadvantage for larger nationwide central stations is their telephone charges, which are higher than those realized when regional centers are maintained. Further, larger central stations require more technical personnel with greater skills to troubleshoot for hardware and software.

In any case the consolidation into larger-size establishments is likely to continue. However, economies of scale do not mean that the industry is going to be dominated by a few firms. Even the largest facility has only a small share of the industry, and the cost advantage beyond 50,000 or 60,000 subscribers is very slight. In addition, since some consumers prefer local monitoring, some local facilities are likely to remain. Concentration, accordingly, will remain moderate. Further, the ability to monitor from a distance means that local facilities face competition from distant ones. Long-distance monitoring means that even if the number of local monitoring facilities declined consumers might have more, or at least the same number of, choices since they can use facilities located throughout the U.S. instead of only local establishments.

Discussions with manufacturers revealed that any problems that may have occurred with wireless systems have been overcome. Wireless systems are expected to become more "immune" to false activations. Some hard-wired system producers intend to enter the "install it yourself" alarm market and supply the systems to large chain hardware stores. Clearly, that may open the door for inexpensive third-party monitoring, which will bypass the installers. Homeowners and businesses will contract directly with a monitoring company and, in the absence of the middleman, probably do so at lower prices. This fact will add to the lower concentration in the monitoring segment of the industry.

Installers' marketing costs to obtain accounts were substantial, approximating or exceeding the direct costs of monitoring. Installers often lost $400 to $600 per installation. Accordingly, if such costs (for owned accounts) are added to other costs, monthly per subscriber costs could easily exceed $10 (assuming a five-year monitoring contract). Firms that monitor other installers' accounts do not have to cover losses incurred on installation and can charge only for monitoring. Radio and television advertising is expensive and is usually employed by only the largest firms for marketing of alarms. Telemarketing is also expensive and is used by many firms.

Another important element in explaining industry performance is entry barriers. Entry barriers into the monitoring segment in the past were low. All costs could be covered with only 1,000 subscribers. As mentioned above, the average annual 1992 revenues for Bucks County, Pennsylvania, monitoring establishments were about $196,000, somewhat below but close to the $240,000 minimum size necessary to cover all costs ($20 per month × 12 months × 1,000 subscribers). Entry by firms outside an area is possible and, as mentioned above, monitoring from a distance occurs using current telephone and computer technology. Firms can and do monitor from low-labor-cost areas. Given the increased significance of economies of scale, we expect entry to be somewhat more difficult but still fairly easy in the future.

Most important is the possible entry of major competitors like the Regional Bell Operating Companies (RBOCs). In fact, in December 1994 Ameritech, the RBOC in the Chicago area, acquired the assets of Security Link, a monitoring firm with revenues in excess of $37 million. In 1995 Ameritech acquired National Guardian, the fourth largest alarm company, for an amount in excess of $200 million. Ameritech then ranked among the top four alarm companies. Incidentally, Ameritech has petitioned the court to allow it to monitor at a distance. Under current judicial rules, RBOCs cannot generally provide long-distance service. Accordingly, Ameritech requested a judicial waiver to monitor what amounts to 30 percent of Security Link's customers (*The Bellringer* 1995, p. 15). (These issues will be discussed further later.) Moreover, the RBOCs already have systems to monitor their unmanned remote switching stations for intrusion, fire, and other environmental changes. The telephone companies also provide reporting services such as 911 and derived channel services, which report any break in a line, such as may result from burglars cutting the telephone line to prevent notification of a break-in.

Potential market entry is likely by other types of companies as well. For example, New Jersey's Public Service Electric and Gas Company is developing a system in conjunction with AT&T that will read meters and provide appliance control, home security, and medical alert services (*Business Week* 1995, p. 94). A similar network is being tested in Chenal Valley, Arkansas. Further, companies like Circuit City that sell security systems could enter on a large scale. Circuit City "opened a central station in their corporate office. They had been doing their own security installations in their own stores, so it made sense to monitor their own alarms" (Stepanek 1995, p. 74). Circuit City was monitoring only in Richmond, Virginia, in 1995, but it could easily expand.

Monitoring, like the other segments of the industry, is highly competitive both in terms of the number of existing establishments and in terms of potential entry. However, recent changes in the industry suggest the development of greater economies of scale in monitoring than previously existed, about which more will be said later in this chapter.

ISSUES IN THE STRUCTURE OF THE MARKET

Vertical Integration

Large, vertically integrated firms compete in all segments of the market, while specialized firms operate in just one segment. Moreover, the vertically integrated firms can expand in any segment that provides opportunities for profit, thereby helping to keep all segments competitive. If prices rise in any segment of the industry so that profits in excess of opportunity cost are earned, vertically integrated firms like ADT can provide other firms with components, installation, and monitoring, and increase their own supply as well. Such behavior serves to keep prices competitive.

One issue concerns whether advantages exist for vertically integrated firms. Since both vertically integrated firms and specialist firms have coexisted for some time, the advantages, if any, are not likely to be great. If they were, the more efficient type of firm would have supplanted the inefficient. Nevertheless, vertically integrated firms enjoy some advantages. For example, an installer that also maintains a monitoring facility can market the concept that the firm does not sell or "dump" the accounts to another firm that performs monitoring, but the one firm does both. Moreover, the firm can point out that it will provide all services, including repairs and system improvements. In addition, a vertically integrated firm does not have to negotiate monitoring prices and/or sell accounts. The costs of negotiation and sales, referred to as transaction costs, can be substantial. Further, most of the profit comes from the monitoring segment, which covers any losses on installation. Vertically integrated firms may be better able to retain customer accounts than third-party monitoring firms and thus be more willing to incur losses on installation. The single-firm approach may provide the basis for greater stability in customer accounts. In any case, the continued existence of both vertically integrated and specialist firms suggests that any advantages of vertical integration are not consequential.

Further, companies can and do use dealers who regularly sell their installed accounts to a firm that does monitoring in order to reduce transaction costs. Such in effect vertical integration can help ensure that the acquired accounts were installed by competent workers using high-quality materials.

Telephone Company Entry into the Alarm Industry.

The Telecommunications Reform Act of 1996 has now made it possible for the RBOCs to enter information services industries, including the provision of alarm services—but, in the case of alarms, after a five-year period. In the case of Ameritech, which is already in the industry, restrictions have been placed on its ability to make acquisitions. An interesting question is why would the RBOCs or other telephone companies want to enter the industry. Since the alarm industry is competitive, the prospects for high profit appear remote. However, as mentioned, Ameritech has already entered the industry, raising some issues, including the possibility of cross-subsidization. The RBOCs enjoy monopoly power in local telephone services (although that power is being challenged). Alarm companies have expressed concerns about the telephone companies' using profits from protected businesses to reduce competition in the alarm industry, and then recouping their investment once competition has been reduced. We have elsewhere[10] argued that the absence of substantial entry barriers makes such a strategy unlikely to be successful. Moreover, the telephone companies are now regulated to a far greater extent on an incentive basis, where rates are established for some period and the telephone companies have the incentive to cut costs and retain the profits. Under the previous method of regulation, the telephone companies would lose little and possibly even gain by entering an industry such as alarms and incurring losses.

The previous method of regulation established rates through a type of cost-plus approach. As long as the costs of the alarm operation could be included in the company's overall costs (capital and operating), the firm could not lose, since rates could be raised on the protected monopoly's customers to cover any losses on alarm operations. Now, the regulated operations are supposed to be kept distinct and separate from the unregulated activities. However, the use of cost-separation procedures to prevent discrimination has not been very successful, as noted by the judge overseeing the AT&T breakup (Blackstone et al 1994). Especially important is the use of incentive regulation where the gains are increased from cost-cutting as opposed to expanding the rate base, the source of gains under the former method of regulation.

The local telephone market is likely to become more competitive, so the RBOCs and other telephone companies may not be able to raise telephone prices as easily in the future to cover losses on alarms. For example, MCI announced plans to offer local telephone service to business customers in New York and nine other large cities by the end of 1995 (Andrews 1995, p. D1). Under the plan, MCI will offer ordinary local telephone service, data transmission on private lines, and the ability to bypass the local telephone company to reach long-distance carriers. Two smaller companies already provide competitive local telephone service similar to what MCI is planning. The cable television operator Cablevision Systems Corporation was planning to offer residential and business telephone service on its cable network and entered into an interconnection agreement with Nynex, the RBOC in its area. Time Warner was planning to offer local telephone service on its cable systems, most notably in New York. Rochester Telephone Corporation as of January 1, 1995, allowed any other telephone provider to connect to its network and its customers. It also agreed to reduce rates 11 percent and freeze them at that level for seven years. In exchange for allowing unlimited local competition and cutting and freezing rates, it was no longer to be subject to New York Public Service Commission's 11 percent rate of return rule and it also could offer any services that it wants, including video, alarm, and long distance (*Business Week* 1995, p. 94). A number of states, including New York, Illinois,

Michigan, and Maryland, have aggressively encouraged new competitors to enter the local telephone industry (Andrews 1995, p. D2). Incidentally, RBOCs that face local competition would be able to offer long-distance service, a product they strongly desire. In any case, the RBOCs will face more competition in the future in the local telephone market, reducing their ability to subsidize operations in competitive markets, such as the alarm industry.

The alarm industry, not surprisingly, does not look favorably upon the prospect of additional RBOC entry. The Executive Director of the National Burglar and Fire Alarm Association in referring to the Ameritech acquisition of Security Link noted:

> These tactics have strengthened the alarm industry's resolve to prevent domination of our communication link with alarm customers. This domination could afford access to the alarm industry customer lists and potential exploitation of these customers through direct and multiple-service marketing strategies. Especially egregious is that all of these activities, including the acquisitions themselves, are financed through funds generated as a protected monopoly to the detriment of small entrepreneurial companies forced to compete on an unlevel playing field (*The Bellringer* 1995, p. 15).

Alarm companies are concerned that the name recognition provided by Ameritech will yield an unfair advantage to its subsidiaries (Litsikas 1995, p. 31). They believe both that customers will associate the name with the alarm subsidiary and that the subsidiary will be able to borrow at lower interest rates than they can. They are also fearful that the alarm subsidiary will learn quickly about requests for new telephone service, information that other alarm companies do not have. Further, there may be concern that alarm services could be used to sell home automation, information, and entertainment services. The danger might be loss-leader pricing of alarm services, including monitoring. However, a top Ameritech official stated that the company would not be a leader in cutting monitoring prices. Whether other telephone companies would follow a similar policy is unclear (*Security Sales* 1995, p. 54).

An Ameritech representative argued:

> I think the advantage that we have is the name Ameritech and
> deep pockets. But, I don't think that's a significant advantage over
> Motorola or GE Capital or anybody else. And frankly, Westing-
> house and some of the others that have had the privilege of having
> that much of an advantage have not done exceptionally well (*Secu-*
> *rity News* 1995, p. 26).

Society, on the other hand, might benefit by having new technologically sophisticated firms such as the RBOCs enter the
alarm industry. Although the benefits from their entry are not
apparent, there may well be some, and they could be quite important. That is the nature of dynamic competition. Further, keeping
the RBOCs out would entail considerable resources. Finally, it is
not clear how successful the RBOCs will be when they have to
compete. Firms that have been regulated do not necessarily do
well in a competitive environment or, at least, formerly regulated
firms have to learn how to compete.

Entry by an RBOC entails some regulatory issues. An RBOC
cannot currently provide long-distance service outside its local
access transport area (LATA). Accordingly, Ameritech cannot
monitor any accounts from its central stations if long-distance
telephone service is involved. Security Link's five central stations
are located in Cleveland, Philadelphia, Indianapolis, Oakbrook,
and Peoria; the latter two are in Illinois. Ameritech is confined to
monitoring accounts from each of its central stations only within a
given LATA. Such restrictions are likely to be eliminated as part
of the increased reliance upon competition in the telecommunications industry.[11]

Accordingly, concentration in the industry would be expected
to increase if everything else were held constant. However,
demand for alarms is growing substantially, so concentration
may not increase, since the market can accommodate more
firms. Further, monitoring of alarms can be done from a distance, so the market is widening, reducing effective concentration in the industry. Capital requirements, even for sophisticated

systems, remain low, and other entry barriers are quite low. Accordingly, entry remains a threat should prices temporarily rise above the competitive level. Entry would soon return them to the competitive level.

Pricing and Vertically Integrated Firms

Currently, a substantial number of outlets exist for an installer to sell accounts, if the installer lacks a central station. If concentration increases in monitoring, there will be fewer buyers for accounts and perhaps higher wholesale prices for monitoring accounts of installers without their own central stations. In either event there will be a reduced incentive for installers to lose money on installations. Vertically integrated firms, which both install and monitor alarms, would not be affected in the same way. Indeed, some vertically integrated firms would have an increased incentive to offer low-price installation.

Vertically integrated monitoring firms would be affected adversely if the RBOCs were to enter into just the central station or monitoring part of the industry. Monitoring prices would be reduced and the vertically integrated firms would have a reduced incentive to lose on installations. Like the situation where the installers were paid less for their accounts or had to pay more to have them monitored, now vertically integrated firms would also have a reduced incentive to lose on installations. Interestingly, entry into just monitoring would tend to increase installation prices. Further, increased competition in monitoring may occur once demand ceases to grow as rapidly as it has.

Small, non-vertically-integrated firms may encounter competitive problems. One dealer states: "What happens when competition or technology starts to lower the pricing for monitoring services?" (Schueren 1995, p. 3). He noted that the low-installation-price companies cannot lower their monitoring prices because of their need to recover installation costs. That is partially correct. However, the very large companies enjoy lower costs because of economies of scale, saving perhaps as much as $3 per subscriber per month over small companies. The large vertically integrated companies may thus be able to drive prices to levels that hinder the competitive ability of small companies. On the other hand, the additional marketing and advertising costs of large companies weakens their cost advantage. In fact, the advertising and marketing costs for the large companies may approximate $7 per month per installation over a five-year period. Accordingly, the advantage of economies of scale enjoyed by the large firms may be far less significant ($3 lower monitoring cost versus $7 extra in their marketing and advertising). The independent installers and small firms may be able to offer monitoring at rates that threaten the competitive position of the large integrated firms. In any case, the competitive environment is likely to become more intense once demand ceases to grow as rapidly. Interestingly, entering additional large mass marketers, including telephone companies, may find their advertising stimulates sales for other firms as well, maintaining demand growth.

CONCLUSIONS AND IMPLICATIONS

Economies of scale and cost conditions in the alarm industry explain why installation is and will remain competitive. Manufacturing enjoys some economies of scale by limiting the high cost of shifting from one line of production to another. Some vertical economies may exist for manufacturers who own major national and international distribution channels. Manufacturers of alarms develop new products, which are usually adopted from the research output of the computer and electronics industries. Currently very little basic or applied research, essentially only development work, is done within the industry. Technology is moving toward the integration of cable TV, telephone, access-control, and security systems. The regulatory environment is changing to allow invasion by companies in these industries of each other's territory. Indeed, business practices show acquisitions and alliances among

Table 7-3 Central Station Operation

ID Number	Number of Subscribers	Type of Central Station	Total Employees	Operators	Operators Distribution	Space Sq. Ft.
1	1,500	Specialized UL; C=100%	40	10	2: 12am-8am; 3: 8am-4pm; 5: 4pm-12am	1,500
2	1,500	Non-UL	40	6		900
3	2,200	Regional R=50%; C=50%	40	8	1: 11pm-7am; 2: all other times	
4	2,600	Regional	15			1,000
5	3,000	Regional UL & FM; R=40%,C=60%		10	2: 24 hr./day; 2 12-hr. shifts	5,000
6	3,800	Regional UL		7		
7	4,000-5,000	Regional Non-UL; R=95%		8	2: 8am-4pm; 2: 4pm-12am, 1: 12am-8am	
8	9,200	UL				
9	13,000	Regional UL; R=50%		11-12 operators 1 manager	3 all day	
10	13,000	Regional; R=60%		12	4: 8am-4pm; 3: 4pm-12am, 2: 12am-8am	3,000
11	25,000	Regional UL & FM; R=70%	180	24 operators 4 managers 4 supervisors	8 at all times (including supervisor and manager)	1,500 enough for 100,000 accounts
12	20,000	Regional UL; C=100%	100	21	5 operators all the time	1,500 enough for 100,000 accounts
13	28,000	National 3rd party UL; R=70%		16	Day: 3-4, 1 supervisor; Night: 4	7,500

Table 7-3 Continued

ID Number	Number of Subscribers	Type of Central Station	Total Employees	Operators	Operators Distribution	Space Sq. Ft.
14	40,000	National 3rd party UL; R=55%		17	5 operators,1 supervisor: 8am-8pm; 3 operators, 1 supervisor: 8pm-12am; 2 operators: 12am-8am	5,000 (needs only 3,000 sq.ft)
15	53,000	National UL for 300 accounts		24	4: 12am-4am, add 1 oper./hr. until 8am; 8: 9am-9pm; 3-4: 9pm-12am	5,000
16	81,000	National 3rd party UL; R=90%	60	21	6:11pm-6am; 3:6am-11pm 1 supervisor at all times	
17	100,000 or more*	National UL; R=62%	117	75	12-15: 8am -5pm; 15: 5pm-8am	
18	100,000 or more*	National UL; R=90%	2,000	50	15: 6:30am-7:30 am 6-8: 7:30am- 6:30am 1 supervisor at all times	3,500 monitored 3rd party accounts
19	100,000 or more*	National UL; C=80%	352	251		
20	100,000 or more*	National UL; R=96%		37	20: 6am-12am; 5: 12am-6am	15,000 including customer service

*Subscribers exceed 100,000 but are grouped together for confidentiality reasons.

Table 7-3 Continued

ID Number	Equipment	Subscribers/ Operator	Fully Loaded Cost/ Subscriber/Month	Labor Cost/Hr.	Economies of Scale	Price of Service/ Month
1		750				$222 including armed response
2			$4		6 operators/10,000 accounts	$15 - $20
3	Ademco Radio Receivers	2,200	$15.15		1 operator/4,000 accounts 2 operators/9-10,000 accounts	$20 residential $40 commercial
4			$19		None	$30 residential $65 commercial
5			$12 - $15	$15	Multiply subs by 10 requires adding 1 supervisor and 2 ⅓ operators	Avg. = $25 Range: $20-$200
6	3 Terminals		$8	$6.75 - $8.75	Can add 5,000 accounts without an increase in resources	$21-$24 residential $24-$30 commercial
7		4,000	$4.17	$12	Can add 1,000 at no additional cost	$23 residential
8			$9			$25 - $30
9		4,333	$8.91		Adding 4,000 accounts would involve an extra cost per account of $4 and average cost would become $7.82	$22 average

Table 7-3 Continued

ID Number	Equipment	Subscribers/ Operator	Fully Loaded Cost/ Subscriber/Month	Labor Cost/Hr.	Economies of Scale	Price of Service/ Month
10		4,333	$3.99		Increases from 9,000 to 13,000 subscribers required 2 additional operators. Average cost at 9,000 was $5.50; marginal cost for extra 4,000 was $.58 per subs.	
11	$1-2 million	2,250	$5	$5	Can increase 4-5,000 accounts with 1 operator around the clock	$18-$22 residential $20-$25 commercial (prices vary by geographic area)
12	Total start-up cost is $2 million; computer and software share is $1 million	4,000			Can add 5,000 accounts with no additional cost. At 25,000, to add 3,000 would require 5 operators	Burglary $20
13		7,000			Doubling in size would require 16 additional operators	

Table 7-3 Continued

ID Number	Equipment	Subscribers/ Operator	Fully Loaded Cost/ Subscriber/Month	Labor Cost/Hr.	Economies of Scale	Price of Service/ Month
14	Upgrade computer system every 2-4 years	13,000	$2	$2	Can add 10,000 accounts with no additional cost. From 50,000 to 65,000 accounts must add 1 operator around the clock. To reach 65,000 accounts requires a total of 5 additional operators.	
15		8,150			At 60,000 full capacity of operators; cost per account is reduced by 15% from that at 53,000. After 60,000 subscribers, costs rises.	
16	Start-up: $1 million; replace 2 mainframe computers: $480,000	6,750	$2.55	operators w/ benefits $10.50; without $7.50	Expand by 10% by adding 1 operator per shift or 5 per week	$5.25 (3rd party) opening/closing unsupervised $12 additional supervised $22 additional
17		7,570	$2-$3 without marketing	operators $7-$10, fully loaded technicians $20,000-$60,000 per year	Economies of scale extend beyond 225,000 accounts. Lowest average total cost possible is $2	

Table 7-3 Continued

ID Number	Equipment	Subscribers/ Operator	Fully Loaded Cost/ Subscriber/Month	Labor Cost/Hr.	Economies of Scale	Price of Service/ Month
18		23,600	$2.25 or less	operators $8.50-$9 unloaded $10.60-$11.25 w/ benefits	If double size from 100,000 to 200,000 accounts, must increase operators by 20%	
19		4,380	$2.25-$2.50 (excluding top executives)		For every 4-5,000 accounts need 1 operator around the clock	
20	sufficient capacity for 500,000 accounts	20,477		$8-$10	Can increase subscribers by 10% with no additional resources. At 1 million accounts must have another central station	

Table 7-3 Continued

ID Number	Vertical Integration	Price for 3rd Party	Total Revenue/ Subscriber/month	Comments
1	I,M,P	None	$278	Operator- annual wage $30,000; manager day,$50,000; manager night, $45,000; overall supervisor, $60,000; technicians:4
2	I,M			
3	I,M,Pc			No verification
4	I,M,Pc			800 Audio; 1800 digital
5	I,M		$600	Approval for UL adds $10,000/year; Total central station investment = $100,000; Insurance: 6.5% of total revenue; False alarm rate 0.53 police dispatches per alarm per year; verifies and screens out 93% of all calls.
6	I,M,P			50 activations per day and 8 dispatches per day
7	I,M	$6 not including opening and closing		UL approval would cost $2,500 per year. Break even at 2,000 subscribers; profit begins at 3,000 subscribers. Expense for 800 numbers is $.20 per minute; central investment is $200,000
8	I,M,Pt			Savings from having 800 lines exceed other savings
9	I,M			UL adds 30% to labor cost; gross profit is 60% of revenue. Doubling size would enable use of superior software.
10	I,M			
11	I,M		$43	
12	I,M,P			
13	M	$4		UL adds 10-50% to the cost of a system
14	M	Residential: $3 Commercial: $3.75	$50	Commission to dealers is 22% of price; can turn off false activation from central station

Table 7-3 Continued

ID Number	Vertical Integration	Price for 3rd Party	Total Revenue/ Subscriber/month	Comments
15	M	$6		Long-term profit is 1.5% of total revenue
16	M	See price for service		Back-up system for every function. Telephone expense per account is $.58.
17	M	Avg=$6; range is $3.75–$9 depending on volume and zones in premises		Maximum subscribers per operator is 10,000. Software crucial in determining length of service time. As central station size increases, skills of technical personnel must improve.
18	I,M			Operators busy 50 minutes per hour; smaller central station operators busy only 40 minutes per hour. All residential activations are verified: 20 seconds to verify and an additional 15 seconds to take action. Average dispatch: 22 seconds
19	I,M		$34.17	For an additional 4-10,000 accounts need more sophisticated software, which is priced at $50,000
20	I,M			Back-up station exists

Notes: Some numbers have been placed in categories so as not to identify particular companies.

I = Installation
M = Monitoring
P = Private Response
Pc = Private Contract Response
Pt = Private Technician Response
C = Commercial
R = Residential
UL = Underwriters Laboratories
FM = Factory Mutual

Source: Survey conducted by authors.

all these industries. As a consequence, we should expect to see in the near future manufacturing of integrated systems allowing for some economies of scope and scale. The current pricing policy of losses on installation and profits on monitoring is likely to continue, but it may be threatened somewhat by companies entering into just the monitoring segment. Monitoring is experiencing increasing economies of scale and, accordingly, is likely to become somewhat more concentrated. Entry into all segments, including monitoring, will remain fairly easy, and competitive returns are likely to be earned.

REFERENCES

Andrews, Edmund L. 1995. "MCI Will Compete in Local Phone Services." *New York Times.* March 6, 1995: D1.

———. "U.S. Plans More Phone Competition." *New York Times.* March 1, 1995: D2.

"Ameritech: Questions and Answers." *Security News.* May 1995.

The Bellringer. March 1995. "Baby Bell Seeks Court Waiver: Clean-up for Alarm Company Acquisition."

Blackstone, Erwin, Andrew J. Buck, and Simon Hakim. 1994. "An analysis of telephone company entry into unregulated markets: The electronic security case," *Antitrust Bulletin.* Fall.

Business Week. "Phone Frenzy," February 20, 1995.

Frost and Sullivan. 1994. *The US Market for Commercial and Industrial Security Equipment and Services.* Mountain View, CA.

Hakim, Simon, and Erwin A. Blackstone. 1995. "Outside Attraction: Economies of Scale, Scope, Cost in the Electronic Security Industry," *Security Dealer.* July.

———, and Andrew J. Buck. 1991. *Residential Security: The Hakim-Buck Study on Suburban Alarm Effectiveness.* Philadelphia: Department of Economics, Temple University.

———, and Mary Ann Gaffney. 1994. "The Structure of the Installers Market," *Locksmith Ledger.* May.

Litsikas, Mary. 1995. "Ameritech Enters the Alarm Industry." *Security Distributing and Marketing* January 1995.

Schueren, Steve. 1995. "Washington Blitz Who Cares?" *The Bellringer.* May.

Security Sales. "Ameritech Says Telecom Act Restrictions Are Unfair." August 1995.

Spooner, Lisa. 1990. "Pricing for Profit Now, Not Later." *Security Distributing and Marketing.* July.

Stepanek, Laura E. 1995. "ADT Links with Radio Shack Amidst Retailing Alliances." *SDM.* September.

NOTES

1. The Herfindahl Index is the sum of the individual market shares (in percent) squared. Herfindahl numbers 1,000 and under are considered unconcentrated by the U.S. government. Between 1,000 and 1,800, the industry is considered moderately concentrated, and above 1,800 it is considered highly concentrated.
2. This discussion comes from Erwin Blackstone, Andrew J. Buck, and Simon Hakim, "An analysis of telephone company entry into unregulated markets: The electronic security case," *Antitrust Bulletin* (Fall 1994). Some of the discussion about economies of scale and scope comes from Simon Hakim and Erwin A. Blackstone, "Outside Attraction: Economies of Scale, Scope, Cost in the Electronic Security Industry," *Security Dealer* (July 1995), pp. 102-108.
3. For example, the Pittway Corp has begun to concentrate on security system manufacturing opportunities. See Kevin Hillstrom, ed., *Encyclopedia of American Industries*, Vol. 4. (New York: Gale Research Inc., 1994).
4. The population of Lower Bucks, which borders Philadelphia, in 1984 was 310,000.
5. These figures were derived from extensive interviews conducted during the summer of 1995 with more than 20 firms that install residential alarms. Highly specialized firms that operate in high-income areas (whether residential or commercial) appear to spend significantly more time on installation. Expensive installations require unseen wiring run through the walls, involving more time and more highly skilled workers. Rewiring of structures also requires on average only 4 to 6 hours. See Table 7.1 for a compilation of interview results.
6. Ameritech, the Midwestern Regional Bell Operating Company, acquired Security Link in 1994 and National Guardian in 1995.

Clearly, Ameritech has the resources to engage in substantial advertising. See below for additional discussion.

7. Private response became more common in 1995 as some small companies provided or contracted for that service. Because of its small current size, we are not covering that segment in the structure chapter. We do, however, report some interviews with private response firms in chapter 9. Further, this segment is likely to become more important in the future. Again, see chapter 9.

8. Data came from the U.S. Department of Commerce, *County Business Patterns, 1992*, Table 1b. A minimum of four operators and a supervisor/administrator are required. However, there are part-time monitoring companies that contract out their subscribers for part of the time. Further, some of the monitoring workers may be the owners or contract employees, and are thus not considered paid employees. Thus, the figure of 2.3 employees does seem well below the minimum threshold but is reliable and indicates the small scale of many monitoring establishments. Table 7.3 provides more detail on the monitoring segment.

9. The following statement illustrates the low marginal cost: "with the big players in the game, the incremental cost to monitor another account is pennies per month..." See David J. Massarelli, "Niche Marketing Is Most Profitable," *Canadian Security* (October 1995): 35.

10. See note 2.

11. Indeed, in 1995 Ameritech gained the right to offer long-distance telephone service in the Chicago and Grand Rapids, Michigan, markets. See Patrick O'Toole, "Ameritech Goes National...Guardian," *SDM* (Sept. 1995): p. 25.

8

Marketing Alarms

In this chapter we will discuss the motives for alarm purchase, the characteristics of the buyers, how an installer is chosen, whether alarm owners are satisfied with their systems, and what features they like or dislike in their systems. Marketing strategies and methods will be recommended for installers and for the alarm associations. The material in this chapter is based upon our detailed surveys in two suburbs of Philadelphia and in Greenwich, Connecticut. Further evidence from other sources will be incorporated in the discussion.

NATURE OF THE PRODUCT AND THE PURCHASER

In discussing marketing strategies and methods with installers, we found that their efforts run the entire gamut of options. Installers advertise in the Yellow Pages, on bulletin boards, in local papers, on radio and TV; they use direct mailings and employ cold calls to potential prospects. Further, they provide incentives to encourage existing customers to refer new customers.

Since the mid-1990s we have witnessed a rise in telemarketing efforts. Even installers who target the high-end residential markets use telemarketing under other trade names. Advertising is important in developing customer confidence, because the quality of the product or service cannot be known until after purchase. The companies must convince the buyer to purchase the product. Also in the case of alarms, there is promotion of the powerful emotional motive of security, which can be compelling, especially for residential buyers.

Alarms are also purchased by businesses, which are more concerned about the cost-effectiveness of alarms than other issues. Business buyers are less likely to be swayed by emotional claims. Further, the moderate concentration in the industry makes it likely that nonprice rivalry will be intense. Firms generally find in these kinds of markets that nonprice rivalry is profitable. Monitoring prices exceed cost so that firms have a strong incentive to increase sales. Promotion including advertising is the method usually employed.

The large vertically integrated companies such as ADT, Guardian Security, and Westinghouse run selected regional advertising campaigns over radio and TV. Alarm companies spend much on mass media advertisement, perhaps as much as $100 to $400 per installation. However, promotion involves many activities besides advertising and in total is slightly below what large companies in other similar industries spend. We estimate that promotion of all types equals at least 10 percent of industry revenues.[1]

Marketing efforts, in general, and advertising, in particular, are productive if the amount spent yields more than the cost associated with these efforts. Our frequent contacts with installers show some interesting, innovative, and promising marketing approaches, but many turn out, surprisingly, to be cost-ineffective. For example, some installers targeted costly marketing efforts toward minority groups in moderate-income neighbor-hoods. Indeed, these people suffer most from burglaries and can afford a basic system. Yet the salespeople quickly learned that their efforts were unsuccessful. There was little interest in alarm systems in these neighborhoods. Those that were interested had poor or insufficient credit records, which disqualified the sale of their account to a financing company. Other installers believed that the elderly should be targeted since they are and feel vulner-able to burglary. However, here, too, installers found that their efforts were not cost-effective.

The question indeed is: What are the most cost-effective mea-sures to follow? It is recommended that frequent market surveys similar to ours be conducted, where buyers' and nonbuyers' motives and impediments to buying are investigated. Frequent surveys are important in order to detect changes in consumers' preferences in and motives for alarm purchase. Indeed, our sur-veys have consistently shown that alarms are perceived as a lux-ury product, and efforts need to concentrate on the middle- and high-income segments of the population, using promotional efforts that appeal to them.

There is no absolute formula for the effective marketing of alarms. Marketing efforts need to vary depending upon the target (residential or commercial, type of commercial establishment, and the socioeconomic profile of residents). For example, differ-ent types of marketing are necessary to address high-income sub-urban communities, middle-income urban households, and owners of commercial establishments.

WHO BUYS ALARMS?

Income is the single most important factor in targeting alarm buy-ers. We found that as income rises or the value of a house increases so does the likelihood of alarm purchase. Even when dealing with a relatively high-income population like that in Greenwich, Connecticut, the proportion of alarm owners relative to nonowners rises starting at an income of $150,000, or when homes are valued at $601,000 and more. In our Philadelphia sub-urbs survey we found that the income and home value of alarm owners are, respectively, more than 10 percent and 14 percent higher than that of nonowners.

Alarm systems are perceived as a luxury product. In spite of the low initial price for alarms, alarm ownership is more prevalent in higher-income areas. In 1995, several alarm companies offered installation of standardized systems free or at nominal prices. ADT offers coupons to its subscribers to be given to friends and relatives. The coupon offers free installation. An oil supply com-pany in Long Island, New York, offers free alarm installation in exchange for a five-year contract for oil supply. Other similar offers are made by numerous alarm dealers across the country. In its TV advertising ADT offers one keypad, a control panel, two door contacts, and a motion sensor for $99. Still, alarm ownership had reached only 11 percent of households and 14 percent of businesses by 1995, in an industry that has been in existence for over 100 years.[2] For comparison purposes, in 1995, over one-third of households owned one or more personal computers in an industry that has been in existence for barely one decade, and for a product that is not a necessity. Twenty-eight percent of house-holds own camcorders, and over 90 percent own VCRs, again industries that have been in existence for just over one decade.

The main reason for the low market penetration is the percep-tion of the product. Personal computers are perceived as neces-sary goods. Thus, PC acquisition is weakly related to income level. Alarms are perceived as luxury goods, and therefore their acquisition is strongly related to income. As income rises, the demand for alarm installation increases. Households with annual income above $300,000 spend over two times more on alarm pur-chases than those with income below $50,000.

Mass marketers have changed the landscape of alarm sales, and may significantly increase alarm ownership rates. They have introduced aggressive telemarketing campaigns and/or have increased significantly the amount per system sold spent on mass media advertising. The promotional style is similar to long-distance carriers' marketing efforts but on a smaller scale. These efforts have accelerated since 1994 and are expected to continue to grow. Executives of some large mass marketing companies believe that by the year 2000 fifty percent of households will be equipped with an alarm. Clearly, such efforts are limited in their effect unless resources are expended on continuing public relations efforts to increase public exposure to the benefits of alarms and change their entrenched luxury image. Without such concentrated efforts by the three major alarm associations in conjunction with the large mass media companies and property insurers, it is unlikely that the 50 percent penetration will be attained.

Economists like to discuss the price elasticity of demand for products and services. Our findings show that indeed demand for burglar alarms is very sensitive to change in price. A price reduction will increase sales by a larger percentage than the percent cut in price. Consequently mass marketers are likely to be successful in increasing penetration as a result of their price cuts. As income rises, price considerations lessen. Hence, demand for alarms becomes more price inelastic as income rises. However, the low installation prices have attracted customers who more often fail to pay their monthly fees. Low prices appeal to lower-income households. Further, high installation prices cause consumers to protect their initial investment. Companies need to consider all the consequences of low-pricing policies.

Another interesting finding is the relationship between alarm ownership and family size. Alarm purchase rises with family size. Alarm ownership rises as the size of household increases from two to five members with two or more children under the age of 18. Alarm purchase is significantly higher for families with children than for childless couples. After the five-member family size, the rate of alarm purchase remains constant. After all, income per capita declines as family size increases, if everything else is kept constant.

In our Pennsylvania survey we included open-ended questions on the characteristics of alarm buyers. The same answer kept appearing: "I am absent often from home, and I wanted my family to be protected." Women responded in similar terms, stating that they felt insecure when their husbands were not home. Alarm purchase is clearly a family-oriented decision, and the woman appears to be the main force in making the purchase decision. Family size and the presence of young children are related to personal rather than property protection concerns. Suburban home-owners are usually insured, so burglary losses are covered. However, no compensation is provided for the personal trauma associated with the invasion of privacy and possible confrontation with the burglar. Therefore, it is not surprising that households purchase alarms merely for personal protection.

Single-family homes, followed by townhouses, are the types of housing most popular for alarm installation. Renters and twin-home residents tend not to install alarms. This finding in our Greenwich survey suggests two conclusions: homeowners who intend to live for long periods in their residence are the major customers for an alarm. This observation further enhances the strong association of alarm purchase to income. Residents of twin homes often own the property; however, they buy alarms less often than owners of single-family homes and townhouses, whose incomes are usually higher.

WHY BUY (OR NOT BUY) AN ALARM?

Now that the characteristics of alarm owners are known, let's turn to why residents buy alarms. We saw that personal protection is the single most important factor. This sense of security is heightened when a family member or a neighbor has experienced a burglary. Personal protection is strongly tied to the protection of the family; an alarm is commonly purchased for households where the head is frequently away on business trips. Again, demand for an alarm is usually motivated by the woman in the household.

Price plays an important role in the decision to purchase a residential system. Here, the income effect is crucial. When the price of an alarm goes down, the effective income of households rises, and more alarm systems are purchased. The purchase is remotely related to the substitution effect; residents do not perceive other security measures as substitutes for an alarm. Indeed, as we reported in Chapter 4, a burglar alarm fulfills the detection requirement for security precautions and has no other substitute. All other precautions satisfy either the deterrence or prevention requirements. Further, we showed that an alarm, more than any other security precaution, provides residents with enhanced security.

It is important to understand why some people buy alarms. However, it is as important to understand why other households with similar socioeconomic attributes do not buy one. Knowledge of the reasons why an alarm is not purchased is important to better target-marketing efforts. In general, alarm owners have higher income, live in more expensive homes, and their families have three or more members. Non-alarm owners state that they chose not to purchase an alarm because of the price, because they never thought about it, and because of the false alarm problem. Interestingly, false alarms were a minor reason in the Pennsylvania survey, which was conducted in 1991. In a second survey three years later, it increased from 11 percent of all reasons to over 35 percent. Both surveys were of suburban residents of major metropolitan areas and could be assumed to be similarly informed. In particular, the residents of Tredyffrin Township in the first survey and the residents of Greenwich Township in the second survey are of similar socioeconomic and educational levels. However, the false alarm reason for nonpurchase significantly increased in this three-year period.

Much has been said in the media about false activations, and many more alarm owners have experienced the problem themselves. In general, ordinances were tightened and more stringently enforced during this three-year period. Police departments began to crack down on frequent alarm activators. The problem of false alarms changed from only an industry and police concern to one that affected the general public and began to adversely affect sales.

Alarm owners are satisfied with their decision to purchase an alarm. Ninety-four percent of alarm owners in the Pennsylvania survey expressed satisfaction with their decision to purchase an alarm, and 83 percent of this group said that it made them feel safer. In the Greenwich survey, 93 percent were satisfied with their security company. Seventy-seven percent of the commercial alarm owners were satisfied with their system.

Satisfied customers are the best proof that the product and the service are effective. Such a theme should be considered in the marketing efforts of both the industry and the individual security companies. Having consumers express their satisfaction with the product and the service can be most convincing in encouraging nonowners to purchase. This is particularly true if they know the individuals making the endorsement. People cannot know about the usefulness of an alarm until they acquire it. Therefore, endorsements of the product/service by people they trust are very important to potential buyers.

Attributes and motives of commercial alarm owners differ significantly from those of residential owners. The three most important motives for commercial system acquisition, in declining importance, are insurance requirements, affordability, and having experienced a burglary. Retail establishments gave only affordability and the experience of burglary as reasons for alarm purchase. Incidentally, it appears to be easier to sell alarms to commercial operators than to residential owners. Commercial customers require only one reason to purchase a system, while residential buyers need 1.43 reasons. Forty-four percent of businesses that responded to the question of why they installed a system stated that they had done so for one reason, while 17 percent needed two or more reasons.

In response to an open-ended question, most commercial respondents gave property protection rather than personal protection as the motivation for alarm purchase. This fact makes good sense; residential alarms are also used at nighttime for personal protection while the residents are asleep. Commercial alarms are used only when no one is on the premises; thus they provide less personal protection. CCTV and access control are the major complementary security devices for commercial alarms; these security measures serve to deter employee and customer theft. These complementary measures serve to identify unlawful entry at all times. Integrated systems that include all three elements are sometimes used for commercial protection. Factors that play a role in alarm purchase include insurance, head office requirements, and possessing merchandise that is highly valued on the street. A burglary disrupts regular business operation, creating a lack of merchandise and equipment. Prolonged dealings with insurers and, often, delayed compensation are major factors in motivating alarm purchase and could be stressed in marketing efforts.

Commercial establishments that do not own alarms were questioned as to why they did not purchase a system. Thirty percent of respondents felt that they had adequate security, even without having had a professional security check for their property; 22 percent of respondents stated that an alarm is too expensive, 16 percent never thought seriously about it, and another 16 percent felt that false alarms were a nuisance.

Ignorance about the features of alarms seems to prevent purchase. Many retailers stated that audible alarms often activate, particularly in shopping malls, and no one pays attention to them, a situation similar to that encountered with car alarms. Surprisingly, they are unaware of the connection to the central station and the possible notification to the mall's security guards, who can rush to the location of the alarm. Participants in the alarm industry have difficulty comprehending that such a fundamental attribute of alarm systems is unknown to the general public. Indeed, the attributes of security systems should be emphasized in the industry's public relations efforts.

When a burglary occurs, an urgent demand arises to obtain an alarm. Indeed, 79 percent of businesses without an alarm are unfamiliar with a burglary victim. Further, 38 percent of residential alarm owners bought an alarm because a neighbor was victimized, 21 percent because they have experienced a burglary, and

32 percent because they are familiar with a victim. Twenty-four percent of commercial establishments mentioned their having been a burglary victim as a motive for alarm acquisition. Thus, approaching businesses in the vicinity of burglarized properties provides a reasonably high probability of an alarm sale.

Because of the experiential nature of alarms, a strong referral basis exists in the industry, where buyers search for a reliable dealer by questioning other alarm owners. Accordingly, it appears not to be cost-effective to rely on cold calls to burglary victims or their neighbors but rather better to approach them with a reference to a satisfied customer.

In the residential market the decision to install an alarm is made within the household, and most often by the woman. Emotional motives pertaining to security can be stressed. In the commercial market two separate cases need to be addressed. In independently owned establishments the owners and managers can be directly targeted since they are the decision makers. Identification of the initiating force is more complex when chain stores, corporate subsidiaries, bank branches, and government agencies are concerned. The latter are often required by their respective home offices to install an alarm. Most often, the specification of the system and the installer is made by the home office.

Now that many banks are consolidating on a national scale, and many retail stores are part of national chains, the nature of business initiation is likely to change. Advertisements should be placed in national business newspapers and journals, and should reflect particular attributes of systems.

The targeted audience in commercial and institutional organizations is sophisticated and well informed. Contacts should be made with the security directors, and should indicate the entire spectrum of problems that can be addressed with the proposed electronic security systems. Alarm systems yield limited benefits and need to be integrated with other security systems such as CCTV and access-control systems. Often in commercial cases nontraditional technical solutions are needed. For example, in a multistructure organization, access could be limited to certain hours and only to specific individuals. Thus, in order to effectively address the commercial market even on a regional level, much of the marketing effort should be handled by technical people who are familiar with the complex technical possibilities, and not by marketing personnel.

Sixty-six percent of residents and 70 percent of commercial establishments purchase a system for its burglary detection feature. Fire detection is considered at best a byproduct of the system. However, as the calculations in Chapter 5 showed, personal and property damages from fire are substantial. Local fire detection is ineffective, especially for commercial establishments, when no one is within the facility. Alarm dealers could stress in their marketing efforts hard data on the benefits of fire alarms that are connected to central stations. Promoting the fire alarm feature can be a useful means of enhancing the sale of systems. Residential alarm owners find the following features most desirable: panic buttons, multizones, connection to a central station, and an interior audible siren.

Marketing research suggests that the potential success of a new product depends on the population group that is wealthy, well educated, and young (age of head of household 30 to 45). Widespread adoption by this group is indicative of acceptance of the product by the general population. Households in both Tredyffrin Township in Pennsylvania and in Greenwich, Connecticut, clearly satisfy the requirements of "early adopters." For example, in 1989 the median family income in Greenwich was $77,600, and per capita income was $46,070; in 1994 median family income was $78,000, median single-family home value was $499,900, 40.9 percent of adults 25 years old and over had at least a bachelor's degree, and the average age of the head of household was 39.9 years. Interestingly, our surveys did not detect success for home automation features with the early adopters group. It appears that home automation features such as emergency medical response, two-way voice communication, wireless remote or telephone disarming, and child tracking are not used much by the early adopters group, and will not be easily adopted by the general residential population.

THE SALE

Once a decision has been made to purchase an alarm, the question arises as to how an installer is chosen. Over half of residential yet fewer than 20 percent of commercial alarm owners who responded sought advice about a possible dealer. The majority of those who responded to the question about their source of advice in both groups turned to other alarm-owning residents or businesses, respectively, and some turned to the police for advice. The state alarm association is seldom consulted. It is obvious that the alarm associations are not visible to the public and do not serve a "natural" need that other product/service associations fulfill.

The referral basis for alarms reflects again the service- and experience-oriented nature of the product and industry. Referrals are the most important source of business. One needs to distinguish between active and passive referrals as the latter type is more effective. Localized and specialized dealers that excel in the provision of service enjoy passive referrals, and usually spend little more than a required Yellow Pages advertisement. Mass marketers cannot rely on passive referrals since they need to grow at a faster rate and because of their more anonymous relationship with their subscribers. However, such companies still recognize the merit of "warm" referrals and offer their subscribers monetary incentives to provide such referrals.

Success in getting referrals depends upon the level and quality of service provided. Many dealers perceive their role as installing systems, and then they passively enjoy the windfall of the long-term recurring revenues. They often play no active role in educating their customers, who generate large numbers of false activations. In the three years between our first survey in Pennsylvania in 1991 and the second in Greenwich in 1994, the false alarm problem appears to have become a much greater concern for both owners and nonowners of alarms. High valuation of dealers by customers and success in generating new business is closely related to perceived service and the delivery of prompt assistance in case of false activations. At the same time, many small dealers, electricians, and locksmiths that install alarms on a part-time basis have a limited short-term business view. They have little immediate monetary incentive to educate or service their customers when they falsely activate their system.

Based upon extensive observation of the industry and survey reports, the measures that are effective in both reducing false activations and improving the image of dealers are verification of activations and follow-up with the subscriber in the case of a police response. Verification of an activation is considered part of good and responsible service. Some of the more successful dealers respond to each activation with a phone call and, in case of need, send a technician to the site. Dealers sometimes hold keys to the property in order to gain entry in case no one is present. This situation exists in highly valued residential areas and commercial districts. Regular system maintenance and training of users are effective in reducing false activations and improve dealers' image. Another necessary element, which is mainly common in cases of highly valued commercial accounts, is private response. Some successful dealers, especially on the West Coast, respond themselves or through a special response company. Good, prompt, and reliable service yields promising referrals.

Much is discussed at the industry's conventions and in professional magazines about cold calls, newspaper and bulletin board advertising, and telemarketing. All our surveys clearly demonstrated that methods other than personal referrals are significantly less effective. Alarm installation is perceived by consumers as a service and, as such, a long-term relationship is established between the subscriber and the dealer. Effective customer generation methods can be determined by dealers in terms of the costs and revenues that accrue for each type of promotional effort.

Generation of referrals can be actively pursued, and some effective measures that we witnessed are outlined here. Salespeople are encouraged to cultivate in each neighborhood one locksmith and one insurance agent. Such contacts where mutual referrals are pledged need to be cultivated over time. When the first referral is made, the alarm salesperson should visit the referral generator and provide a cash reward. Also, if the alarm salesperson makes several referrals and receives none in return, a personal visit should be made, where continuing the relationship is questioned unless a mutually rewarding association is maintained. The locksmith and the insurance salesperson are requested to raise with their customers the issue of the possible need for an alarm system and to provide the name of the alarm salesperson who will contact them. Also, the alarm salesperson should be notified about homes where a burglary has occurred. Customers who have an alarm installed should be provided a monetary return for any referrals. A $10 reward per referral appears in many cases to be effective.

Telemarketing is claimed by many installers to be effective. Several companies that use telemarketing analyzed their own efforts. The following figures appear to prevail: 0.6 to 0.8 appointments per hour for one caller. Usually, one of two appointments that are generated in telemarketing ends up in an actual sale. One large company, however, claims that 10 appointments are necessary to generate one sale. Advertising in newspapers may not be cost-effective. It is most desirable to have an ad in the Yellow Pages. Advertising on radio and TV is often used by the mass marketing companies. The same large company reported that newspaper advertising in conjunction with other media is effective. Also, advertising must be done for a substantial period, for example, six weeks, to generate substantial sales. Data are not available on advertising by mass marketing companies such as ADT, Guardian Security, Westinghouse, or Brinks Home Security. Further, for any given company the amount spent varies significantly by region. As a result of extensive interviews in the industry we were able to derive the estimate of $100 to $300 per new account for direct advertisement. Adding indirect costs, which include corporate overhead as well as hidden hierarchal costs,[3] yields a total of $400 to $500 per new account.

Marketing alarms in high-income neighborhoods differs significantly from marketing them to lower-income groups. The 1993 mean and median installation prices in Greenwich, Connecticut, were, respectively, $2,898 and $2,000. Ten percent of homes had a system valued at $5,000, and one home had installed a $50,000 system. An average mass marketing installation in general costs the installer $600. Installation of a hardware system in an expensive home requires craftsmanship and much caution. Marketing efforts in high-income areas should stress the need for such care and the ability of the installer to conduct such work.

It is clearly difficult to define what a high-income neighborhood is. A wealthy suburban community in Iowa may be considered a middle-income neighborhood in the suburbs of New York. Not all homes in affluent areas are expensive. For example, in many wealthy communities large mansions include gatehouses, which have been converted to single-family homes or even apartments. Their residents' incomes are lower than their neighbors'. Some wealthy people may live in a nonwealthy community that has a special flair to it even though its average home value is relatively low. Often, elderly people with moderate incomes reside in expensive homes which happen to have risen in value over the years. Thus, not all residents of a wealthy community can be considered wealthy and all may not be potential buyers of expensive systems. In general, however, dealers may consider highly valued neighborhoods as those with average income or home value in the upper 20 percent of the metropolitan area in which they are located.

"Traditional" dealers of custom-made systems who concentrate in affluent areas[4] are usually more successful in attracting new customers than are the national companies. Our telephone surveys confirmed other findings,[5] such as that cold advertising is ineffective in such neighborhoods. Referrals play the most important role; subtle indirect marketing and public relations are most effective. Social gatherings for charities and cultural activities where the affluent society meets provide the base for networking. Participation in societies such as the Lions, Masons, and Rotary clubs provides connections that yield long-term business. Contacts with expensive home builders provide information on new home buyers. Later, a booklet that explains how to protect the home with no "hard selling" of the company's alarm can be mailed or delivered upon request. Packaging of security and home services is needed. On the security side, packaging includes private patrol, internal and external CCTV, access-control devices for various sections of the home, lighting control, and a large variety of sensors. Additional services available include servicing the home when the residents are away and emergency medical alert. In the first meeting with the potential customer it is important to conduct a comprehensive security check and to provide a written report suggesting a variety of managerial and hardware measures that will reduce the chances of burglary. It is essential to avoid a hard sales pitch and to present the company as a security provider and not merely as an alarm hardware installer.

Choice of installer by commercial firms is referral-oriented, and geographical concentration is evident. Forty-nine percent of respondents in our Pennsylvania survey knew that their security company serviced other businesses in the same area. At the same time, simply because other businesses have alarms does not motivate non-alarm owners to purchase a system. Where retail businesses are concerned, dealers do not acquire new customers just because they already have several other customers in the immediate area. Businesses, in general, appreciate, more than residential customers, quality of service over hardware. A dealer's good reputation, which results from reliable and consistent service, yields additional commercial customers. Also, high-end residential and commercial establishments need to be offered a whole gamut of services, including security checks, installation of preventive measures, medical alert, two-way voice communication, and severed-line monitoring. Services that may require entry into the premises to water plants, collect the mail, shut off the audible alarm, and perform a technical check of the system should be offered as options.

To conclude, referrals and knowledge about a dealer appear to be the most important reasons for the choice of a dealer. Good service to existing customers is the principal source for such referrals. Alarm buyers are usually unfamiliar with the technical aspects of a system. Thus, they rely for their choice of dealer on a person they trust or someone who owns a system. Neighbors, the police, and security professionals themselves are sources of information. As income level rises, direct anonymous sales calls or other types of cold contacts become less effective and positive information about the installer is of greater value. For high-end residential areas and for businesses, personal acquaintance with the owner is most effective. In our surveys, we asked what advice alarm owners can give to somebody who is interested in buying a system. The statement most often made was: "Select an installer who is reliable, comes well recommended, and has been around for a long time." Being good and reliable and promising continuing service are the principal ingredients that will bring the greatest business to non-mass-marketing alarm companies.

POLICY IMPLICATIONS

The perception of alarms as a luxury by both residential and commercial establishments needs to be altered. It is strange that even though standardized systems are offered for less than $200 and sometimes for free, consumers' perceptions have not changed much. The reason may be that companies in the industry until recently have advertised less intensively than other industries in the marketplace. Thus, the general public is less aware of the availability of inexpensive systems than they are about other electronic products. The increased emphasis on long-term advertising may change the public's perception. However, in view of the unfavorable reports in the mass media about the ineffectiveness of alarms and the problem of false activations, it is essential to improve the image of the industry.

The public should be aware of the benefits alarms yield to the community, to insurers, and to individual subscribers. This can be accomplished only by an industrywide public relations campaign. Such a campaign should be nationwide and last for an extended period of time. An effective public relations campaign requires hard data from reliable sources. As an example of the need for hard data to support a public relations drive, let's take the broccoli industry. Broccoli growers can advertise their product and state that it is very healthy. On the other hand, the results of a study on the benefits of broccoli published in the *New England Journal of Medicine* and quoted by media reporters will have greater impact and will cost a fraction of what the advertising entails.

The industry needs to divorce alarm purchase from its strong link to income. An effective industrywide public relations campaign is necessary to enlarge the pool of potential buyers. Industrywide research projects that constantly feed the media are the bases for effective public relations efforts. These efforts should be supported with full cooperation from the various bodies of the alarm industry. It is also desirable to tie the alarm industry marketing efforts into those of the home insurance industry. Insurers appear to enjoy a significant reduction in loss exposure because of alarm systems. Insurers can cooperate by circulating brochures that state the value of alarms, make reference to the association for further information, and provide a list of reliable installers.

Channels, methods, and timing of public relations and advertising efforts should be planned in order to effectively address the targeted non-alarm-equipped population. Our studies identified a strong link between alarm purchase and income, the value of the home, home ownership rather than rental, families with children in the household, and single-family homes. Further, it appears that alarm purchase is motivated by women. These facts suggest effective targeted marketing efforts that are directed at these segments of the population.

Targeting the market requires attention to one additional issue. Public relations efforts are aimed mainly at increasing the awareness of the product/service, and this in return will increase the pool of alarm owners. Such efforts are most effective when product ownership is "thin" in the appropriate segments of the population.

Once the market saturates, competition rises among dealers, and the method of marketing changes from industrywide campaigns to individual companies' efforts. For example, almost 100 and 94 percent of households own TVs and VCRs, respectively. Everyone is familiar with these products and the quality of each brand. For less product-educated buyers, a whole list of consumer reports is available. With respect to alarms, fewer than 50 percent of households own an alarm in Greenwich Township, where home ownership and value are very high. Nationwide, residential and commercial alarm ownership is below 15 percent for all establishments. Thus, industrywide public relations efforts are still most effective. Once saturation reaches the 60 to 80 percent range, direct advertising of individual companies will become more appropriate. Also, if alarm penetration exceeds some point such as 50 percent, establishments not alarm-equipped may become more vulnerable to burglaries. It is not clear that this possible vulnerability should be stressed.

One problem with industrywide marketing efforts is that some of the alarm installation business will spill over to nonmembers. Many alarm installers do not belong to the state associations. Many locksmiths and electricians also install alarm systems. Now that the reliability of wireless systems has improved, mainly in terms of false activations, we expect that many of these systems will be sold directly to end users through home improvement megastores. It is reasonable to assume that buyers of such systems will be offered the possibility of connection to third-party central stations. Clearly, members of the state and national alarm associations are not eager to support efforts that will benefit nonmembers. There is no quality control of nonmembers, and poor service may reflect on the entire industry. Indeed, alarm associations are currently involved to a limited extent in promoting industrywide public relation efforts; they do not initiate favorable media stories but mainly react to unfavorable media reports. We recommend stressing in all industrywide promotional efforts the existence of the association, the reliability of its members, and the fact that problems with an individual dealer can be addressed through the association, which will assure quality control over its members.

The strong relationship of alarm purchase to family size and the search for personal protection of the family were evident in all our findings. For residential alarms, the public relations efforts of the industry and the advertising of companies should capitalize on the personal protection motive. Industry and corporate marketing efforts should be targeted at families, mainly at the women in the household. In general, residential marketing measures that stress fear are less effective than those that are positively oriented, promising enhanced security and other home/business services. For example, advertising statistical facts about the effectiveness of alarms is more convincing than showing a scary break-in of a house.

Effective marketing efforts for residential, professionally installed, wired systems should be targeted at higher-income groups, homeowners, families with children, and preferably in neighborhoods where burglaries have occurred. The fact that owners of alarms who move usually install a system immediately provides a viable method of marketing. Owners of alarms are satisfied with their system and with their security company. Targeted marketing efforts are most effective when they exhibit satisfied buyers. Marketing research shows that such efforts should stress the positive attitude of buyers rather than a fear motive associated with the experience of burglary.

The importance of price in the purchase decision provides valuable marketing guidance. We found in our objective analysis of burglary patterns that an alarm is most effective when accompanied by at least three other security measures. Buyers of alarms, on the other hand, don't see alarms as a substitute for other security measures. Marketing of alarms should stress the provision of quality security services and not merely the sale of equipment. Thus, marketing efforts should stress the need for a customized security plan. This will differentiate the service of custom-made alarm companies from that of mass marketers. An alarm should be portrayed as an integral part of enhanced security and not as one aspect that can be replaced by other measures.

For those selling to commercial establishments, the sale of alarms alone should, and probably will, become a relic of the past. Technological innovations make the use of access-control systems and CCTV cost-effective for most establishments. Indeed, the professional literature suggests that integrated systems provide both better security and significantly reduce the labor costs of providing security.

Alarms appear to be effective in deterring intruders, and no other security precautions substitute for alarms (see Chapter 4). Most managers of commercial establishments that do not own an alarm are unfamiliar with these facts. Ignorance can be overcome by a continuous public relations effort by the alarm industry. Efforts aimed at commercial establishments should stress the unique property-protection features of alarms. Alarm companies that target commercial establishments need to be able to advise their customers about and provide them with other effective security measures. Marketing efforts need to address the affordability of new systems. Indeed, the vigorous competition in the industry and the significant reduction in the cost and prices of alarm products make alarms affordable to many more businesses. Marketing efforts that stress prices are the domain of individual companies and less the responsibility of the alarm associations. Integration of alarm, CCTV, and access-control devices improves the level of security of commercial establishments. Clearly, such integrated systems do yield higher costs of security even though prices of individual components are lower, and more competition will be evident. Stand-alone alarm systems of better quality will still be available at lower prices.

Alarms may indeed be less effective for commercial establishments than they seem to be. On the average, it takes an officer 15 to 20 minutes to respond to an alarm.[6] In many cases police response may not occur for two or three hours, a delay common in large cities. Added to this is a short 30-second delay for the signal to be sent to the central station. Accordingly, a burglar who operates in an isolated commercial district, such as an office park or a warehouse, on a weekend, has enough time to escape long before an officer appears at the site. A team of three burglars needs no more than five minutes to complete a burglary. In commercial establishments, the burglar may break through bars on a window or through the outside door of a two-door main entrance. The alarm is activated only when a window is broken or the inside door, which is easier to enter, cracks open. In simple terms, the burglar needs first to overcome the physical preventive measures and only then when he/she is already within the premises does the alarm kick off. Clearly, in such a case, an alarm is ineffective. Not surprisingly, 10 percent of non-alarm owners claimed in our surveys that alarm systems are ineffective.

This problem can be solved by physically reversing the preventive and detective measures in order to delay actual entry to the premises. In warehouses or in basements, the bars can be installed on the inside of the windows. The door contacts should be installed on the outside door while preventive measures such as dead bolt locks should be installed on the inside door. In such a case, more time elapses between the activation of the system and the actual unlawful entry. Thus, alarms can be made even more effective, the value of property stolen can be reduced even further, and the burglar may be apprehended.

The case above shows that difficulties experienced in marketing can be overcome by the redesign of security measures. It further suggests that alarm companies should not concentrate just on alarm installation but rather should provide their customers with the whole gamut of security services. Such a change in attitude and operation will enhance the image of alarm companies, improve service delivery, and also provide effective marketing tools.

Insurers provide discounts to homeowners and businesses who install alarms. In some cases, insurers require businesses that carry expensive merchandise to install UL-approved systems. The question is whether the discounts on premiums indeed yield sufficient reduction in loss exposure to be profitable for the insurance companies. Our detailed quantitative analysis in Chapter 6 suggests that alarm installation is financially beneficial to insurers. However, the discounts are not a motivation for alarm purchase, perhaps because nonowners are unfamiliar with their insurer's discount offering. Thus, under the present circumstances, insurers waste money by offering the discounts.

The discounts on premiums can be designed to both improve the effectiveness of alarm use and become an effective marketing tool. Higher discounts can be offered to homes and businesses where the chance of burglary is most diminished. The alarm associations could prepare literature for insurance underwriters, illustrating that research evidence shows the effectiveness of alarms in reducing loss exposure. The two industries could cooperate in promoting the sale of alarms to establishments where their effectiveness has been proven. Some cooperation exists in the marketplace with insurance agents and alarm companies jointly promoting the sale of systems. However, efforts should be directed at the underwriters to design their discounts to reflect the loss exposure for various types of establishments. It is possible to maintain the total dollar amount of discounts at the existing level, but the level of discount could be adjusted to accord with the degree of loss exposure. For example, higher discounts can be offered to expensive homes, where alarms appear most effective, and reduced for row houses, where they are least cost-effective for insurers.

Marketing of alarms to both the residential and commercial markets is based upon referrals and "hot" tips. There is no substitute in this industry for a customer who enjoys high-quality service and refers others based upon personal experience. Attempts are made by dealers to market alarms using mass marketing techniques such as telemarketing, cold calls, and mass media advertising. However, the survival principle suggests that the most profitable companies in the industry rely on referrals and appear to succeed on the basis of their long-term service record. Dealers who own their own central station and operate in or near high-income areas or highly valued businesses and effectively compete by offering good service have gained significant market share in defined geographical areas. It is also true that dealers who started in high-income neighborhoods or near highly valued commercial markets have flourished because of high-quality installation and service. Long-term survival in such difficult markets attributable to quality service may enable successful penetration in other segments of the market. Indeed our surveys show that in the residential market, as the income level of the neighborhood rises, there is more geographical concentration of particular companies. The signs, but mainly neighbors' referrals, yield business in such areas. Not surprisingly, the price matters less in the upper-income residential and commercial markets, and the quality of service is the most important ingredient in the choice of installer. Successful dealers' prices for both installation and monitoring are higher, and they keep growing. In middle-income neighborhoods, where the profit margins are lower, competition is stiffer, a large number of installers operate, and the rate of survival is lower.

The marketing of alarms has no uniform rules. Dealers' efforts should be directed at their particular markets. Methods need to address the characteristics of the particular markets. For example, marketing efforts aimed at high-income suburban homes differ from appeals to middle-income homeowners. Mass marketers are unlikely to succeed in high-income areas. The reasons are both the name appeal and the degree of professional service that are required. A subcontractor that works for a mass marketer cannot install hard wire in the extremely expensive windows of expensive homes because doing so requires special knowledge and care. Further, in our surveys of the affluent communities of Tredyffrin and Greenwich Townships, we asked for the name of the company that installed the system and the price paid. In less affluent communities a far greater percentage of alarms was purchased from the national mass market companies. High-income residents will refrain from responding to a $199 advertisement for an alarm but rather will contact a company that has a good reputation and has many visible signs in the purchaser's geographical area.

Our discussion so far clearly indicates that marketing efforts are closely linked to production specialization. The saturated dealer market requires product differentiation. Thus, a dealer needs to illustrate, in both his or her production practices and in the nature and level of his or her marketing efforts, that the firm specializes in the particular industry or region. Sectorial and regional specialization are necessary in order to survive in this saturated market. It is important again to emphasize that dealers may need to include access-control devices and CCTV if they specialize in the commercial market or in the high-income residential market.

Marketing efforts should be executed in a continuous fashion, should present empirical evidence about the product/service, and should be done in cooperation with the various segments of the alarm industry and with the insurance industry. Further, marketing efforts of installation/monitoring services should not be or even be perceived to be divorced from the production arm of the industry/corporation. For example, installers should make efforts to reduce false activations. Success in such efforts should be presented and supported with actual data in the marketing efforts.

What are the policy implications of these findings? There are three forms of marketing that need to be addressed in order to effectively penetrate the market:

> **Form 1:** Public relations efforts by the industry as a whole to improve the image of the alarms. The targeted population is wide, the effort is indirect, the effectiveness cannot be easily measured, and efforts are spread over a long period of time. These efforts increase sensitivity to alarms, and may raise modestly actual sales of various companies. The inability to measure effectiveness and the widespread impact on companies makes the actual spending seem unattractive. Industry and corporate executives are reluctant to

spend resources on such efforts because the effects may not all "hit" their organization, and may have a negative short-term effect on their "bottom line." A public relations campaign is similar to spending on research in that the positive impact on the organization may spill over beyond the tenure of the executive who initiated the effort.

Cooperation is required among the alarm associations, manufacturers, and dealers to establish or change the image of the product and introduce the associations to the public as a source of reliable information and support in case of need. The objectives should be to increase awareness of alarms and their role in improving personal protection. The image of the product should be changed from that of a luxury item to a necessity. The efforts should stress both the importance of the service element and the concept that members of the association do not merely sell hardware and enjoy recurring revenues but continuously serve their customers. Form 1 efforts are aimed at raising the market size for alarms. They can be compared to the efforts of the citrus industry, which stress the good taste of its products and their health attributes, aiming at raising business for all. The problem is that alarms are installed by electricians or locksmiths, or are sold in stores for self-installation. However, public relations efforts should differentiate between the services offered by members of the association from the "rest," and stress the public assistance role of the association. By so doing, it is likely that members of the associations will enjoy most of the fruits from these efforts. This appeal is aimed at the general population and is not aimed necessarily at consumers of the product. Much of the effort is generated through information provided to the press aimed at nonindustry elements, to improve the image of the product or the industry, or both.

Form 2: Mass advertising to the general population aimed at promoting the sale of alarms. Here the appeal is directly from the alarm associations or individual companies through TV and radio commercials, Yellow Pages, direct mail, and advertisements in magazines and newspapers. The effort is still indirect, as in form 1, in the sense that the targeted population is large and is not restricted merely to potential buyers. However, the impact of the effort is immediate and will directly benefit the initiating executive.

Form 3: Direct marketing through telephone or face-to-face contact with potential buyers of the product. Such contacts vary from "cold," where the contact is with an unaware person and with no referral, to "warm," where the contacted person is made aware beforehand of the expected contact through a referral. Cold calls are mainly through telemarketing aimed at selling the product. These efforts are done by individual companies and are popular in the alarm industry. Efforts appear to be most cost-effective in the retailing of alarms when the contact is warm.

Forms 1 and 2 are expensive because they need to both cover large geographical territories and be conducted over a significant period of time. A small amount of these two forms of marketing is engaged in by the alarm industry. Among alarm companies, ADT is perhaps best known for its appeals to the general public using the radio, TV, and newspapers to promote the sales of its product. Measurement of success determined by generated dollar sales per dollar of spending on each of forms 2 and 3 is possible only for individual companies. Effective marketing by the industry should incorporate efforts in all the three forms described above. In all three forms, measures of the effectiveness of alarms and the satisfaction of existing customers, such as the data presented in our reports, will improve the image of alarms and enhance sales.

How can the various segments of the industry improve marketing efforts?

Installers: "Traditional" installers of custom-designed systems should target the higher-income segments of their own market. Neighborhoods where burglaries have occurred are prime areas for alarm installation. Owners of single-family homes, townhouse owners, and women are the most promising parts of the market. The sale is successful if a woman in the residence desires an alarm. The sale should stress personal protection and should not build on fear. It should stress the peace of mind provided by an alarm. Savings resulting from insurance discounts could be explained and these savings calculated for each individual case. The public is quite aware of the false activations problem. The salesperson can discuss the efforts made by the company to deal with the problem, and its record versus that of other companies can be presented. In the sales presentation, the burglary, fire, audible, and multizone features of the alarm should be discussed. Generally, potential buyers are still not ready for the auxiliary features. For those who want such features, the companies should be ready to provide them. Emphasis should be given to the service provided and not merely to the hardware installation. Maintaining continuous contacts with the customer is important, and following up in case of false activation is appreciated. Upgrading of the system is an option that will attract potential buyers.

Another specific suggestion for an alarm salesperson is to build active cross-networks of references with a locksmith and a local insurance agency, where a monetary reward is given for each successful reference.

Manufacturers: Manufacturers should design user-friendly systems. Control panels should be simple to use. Manufacturers should establish direct and continuous communication channels with end users. Surveys of end users are desirable to identify both the weaknesses of existing systems and consumers' preferences. User-friendly systems can also serve to lower users' errors, which cause false activations.

Alarm associations: An association's main role is to make itself more visible. Thus, the associations should not merely provide services to their members but also carry the "message" about alarms to the general public. More specifically, the associations' objectives are to change the image of the product to that of a nonluxury item and to establish contacts with the press to increase the public awareness about the benefits of alarms. The association can strengthen its relationship with insurers and the police, since all three entities have common interests in promoting the installation of alarms. On a different front, the association should become a major source of information to those that wish to buy an alarm and should provide potential purchasers with a short list of installers. The association should both become a body for complaints about individual members and be able to effectively solve the problems.

In order to become effective in its relations with the public, the association needs to improve the reliability of its members. If the association becomes a mechanism to help potential buyers, more installers will wish to join the association. In order to raise the quality of its members, the association could and should require good business practices by its members. Those who adhere to such practices could be designated members in "good standing." Alternatively, the performance and complaint record of individual companies could simply be provided to interested potential alarm purchasers.

CONCLUSIONS

This chapter reviewed the motives for alarm purchase, the characteristics of buyers, installer selection, and the satisfaction of alarm owners with their system. The chapter provides marketing recommendations to dealers.

Income is the most important determinant for alarm purchase; as income rises, so does alarm purchase. In spite of the decline in installation prices, alarms are still perceived as luxury products. Experiencing a burglary oneself or having a burglary in the neighborhood are the important events in prompting alarm purchase. The woman in the household is usually the motivator for alarm purchase and makes the decision to buy a system. Single-family homes, followed by townhouses, are the type of housing with the highest probability of alarm purchase. In the case of residences, personal protection, and in commercial establishments, property protection, are the primary motives for purchase. The three most important motives for commercial alarm purchase in declining order are: insurance requirements, affordability, and having experienced a burglary.

In general, residential alarm owners have higher incomes, live in more expensive homes, and have families of three or more members. Alarm owners are more concerned with security and adopt significantly more security precautions.

The most important source of business for alarm companies is referrals. Alarm sale is not cost-effective if done by cold calls or by advertising in newspapers or on billboards. Passive referrals are more effective than active referrals. Dealers should provide reliable and quality service as a mode for further growth. Active referrals that are effective include an alliance of a dealer with either a local insurance agent or a locksmith to obtain mutual business referrals.

Marketing recommendations include "packaging" an alarm with other security measures or with other services, such as medical alert or emergency services, initiating a market niche for dealers. The chapter offers a wide range of marketing strategies for associations, individual companies, and salespeople.

NOTES

1. A survey of 3,000 dealers that was conducted by *Security Sales Magazine* in 1995 showed that the average contract with subscribers is 12.5 years. National alarm companies spend on advertising and other promotional expenses $400 per system sold. The average

monitoring fee is $25 per month. Thus, on the average, national companies spend about 10 percent of their revenues on product promotion.

2. The mass marketers have aggressively entered the market only since 1994. ADT, for example, installed 175,000 alarms in 1994, and over 200,000 in 1995, and Brinks installed 75,000 and Westinghouse, 60,000 in 1994 (Patrick O'Toole, "Profiles in Home Security," *SDM Magazine* [August 1995]: pp. 80-81). This may change alarm penetration significantly in future years.

3. Hierarchical costs include unseen marketing efforts by high officials in the company, which are not attributed to marketing costs. For example, at a board meeting at which the advertisers present their forthcoming plans, the time spent by the members discussing these issues is not an explicit item in the marketing budget.

4. For example, the Main Line in Philadelphia; Westchester County, New York; and Palm Springs, California.

5. For example, "Learn the Secrets to Garnering High-End Residential Business," *Security Sales* (February 1995): 26-34.

6. In our detailed survey for Philadelphia, we found that the total time spent by an officer responding to an activation is 16 minutes. See Simon Hakim and Erwin Blackstone, *Economic Cost of Alarm Response and Alarm Registration for the City of Philadelphia* (April 15, 1995). Report submitted to the Bureau of Administrative Adjudication.

9

False Alarms: Problems, Solutions, and Recommendations

INTRODUCTION

The Problem

The most pronounced problem with alarms is that of false activations. Each year, police officers nationwide respond to over 13.7 million activations. The total cost of false alarms in 1995 may have been as much as $6 billion. Local police departments report that 94 to 98 percent of all activations are false. A nationwide survey of 36,689 alarm panels by CSAA (Central Station Alarm Association 1994) showed an average of 1.44 false activations per system per year. The residential rate is 0.96 while the commercial rate is 2.75. Our survey in Pennsylvania showed that the third-party monitoring rate is 1.7 false alarms per year, while it is only 1.5 for large regional or national installers who monitor their own accounts. The national annual increase in alarm ownership is 11 percent, which leads to an almost equal increase in the number of false activations. The marketing technique of selling standardized systems for less than $200, or in many cases where hard-wired installation is done, for no charge, may raise the number of alarms even more in forthcoming years. A leading national company argues that the false alarm rate has been and will be reduced further so that the increase in alarm systems will not yield a proportionate increase in false alarm activations. It notes that its total false dispatches declined by about 10 percent between 1993 and 1995. At the same time, police budgets rise by only 3 percent annually. Already, the response to activations occupies about 10 percent of officers' on-duty time. Thus, in the future, the burden will increase because of the increase in alarm installations. Some large cities such as Las Vegas, have already ceased responding to central station dispatching. Other large cities, including Chicago, Los Angeles, New York, and Philadelphia, respond after a long delay. The priority of response to alarms and panic alarms is being reduced, a practice that can be unilaterally instituted by the police. Suburban police departments are still responding. If no action is taken by the alarm industry and police departments to curb the problem, and the number of false activations continues to rise, it is anticipated that many police departments will stop responding to alarms or that fines for false activations will rise. Consequently, alarms will become less effective, and the sales of systems will significantly diminish.

Municipalities across the U.S. have introduced alarm-related legislation aimed at reducing false activations. Such actions include fining users, licensing installers, reducing the number of free responses, suggesting that calls to the police be made over 900 lines (which results in charges to the security company), publishing lists of dealers with their false activation rates, and ceasing service to repeat activators. In some suburban communities crime prevention officers take the initiative and contact repeat activators to check the reason for the large number of activations. These officers even educate users on how to operate their systems. Then, installers are contacted and requested to manage these cases.

Cooperative programs between the alarm industry and the police, including the Model Cities Program, have achieved some reductions. Philadelphia reduced false alarm dispatches by 8,000 in 1995 compared to 1994; Elgin, Illinois, another of the three model cities, cut the false alarm rate per system from 2.57 to 1.63; and Bellevue, Washington, reduced the false alarm rate per system to 0.77 (*Security News* 1996). Some progress has been made on reducing false activations; the question is whether cost-effective methods are being utilized and whether other approaches may be superior.

Another possibility is for the police to provide the response service, but for alarm owners to pay the full cost. Another related question is whether alarm owners should be charged an annual fee for their system. These questions are discussed later in this chapter.

Analysis

An argument that we often hear is that the police are responsible for providing security to their constituents, and therefore police services are funded by the general tax; response to alarms is a part of patrol activities and therefore should not be separately charged. Further, the presence of alarms makes patrolling easier and therefore, arguably, police should provide response services. Two questions arise: (1) Is response to alarms indeed an appropriate function for public police? and (2) Should alarm owners be charged an annual fee for their systems?

Economic theory suggests the conditions under which the government (or in our case the police) should intervene in the marketplace. If any of the following conditions describe the service of alarm response, then government intervention and possibly public funding are required.

1. Existence of externalities: Externalities exist when the activities of one person produce effects on other(s) that the latter cannot avoid. For example, police intervention is needed to enforce a law prohibiting a person's playing high-volume music late at night, which adversely affects the neighbors. It is obvious that the neighbors who complain about the noise that keeps them awake should not be charged for the police response.

2. The "public good" nature of service: This is the case when everyone in the community enjoys the full benefit of the service. Further, it is impossible or very costly to prevent some people who do not share the financial burden from consuming the service. Everyone in the city enjoys the streets. Therefore a public agency plows the snow to prevent free riders from avoiding payment since they cannot be prevented from driving on the streets. Such a service will not be provided by the market even though it is beneficial to most constituents. Government intervention is required to assure that a public good is provided.

3. An increased level of service is possible with no additional cost: For example, suppose that the capacity of a municipal park allows additional patrons to visit without imposing any additional cost or reduced service. If the park is privately owned, then a price would be charged to all visitors, and the number of visitors would diminish. Thus, it is in the public interest that the service be provided at a price of zero dollars.

4. Monopolistic power: Monopolies usually exercise their power by lowering the quantity and possibly the quality of service and charging prices in excess of those that would be realized in a competitive market. Monopolies sometimes also exercise their pricing power to prevent the development of competition in their market. The government regulates monopolies and enforces anti-trust laws in order to provide consumers with greater

benefits from the product/service and to assure fair competition in the industry.

Clearly, the police service in responding to alarms does not meet any of these four conditions. When police respond to a false alarm activation, a private service is provided to the alarm owner. Nobody else in the community gains any benefit from the actual response to the alarm except the owner who falsely activated his/her system. In economic terms, response to false alarms carries no "public good" attributes. The patrol officer abandons other duties when faced with the requirement to respond to the alarm activation. Actually, patrol service may be reduced elsewhere in the community when an officer responds to somebody's false activation. In this case, there is no justification for the alarm activator not paying the full cost imposed upon the police. If alarm owners do not pay for this private service, then non-alarm owners subsidize the owners of alarms. For example, if 11 percent of homes/businesses own alarms and 90 percent of them activate their systems once a year, then 90 percent of the homes/businesses subsidize service to the 10 percent of the alarm activators.

REVIEW OF ORDINANCES AND IMPLEMENTED SOLUTIONS

Recommendations as to the preferred measures for a particular community need to be based upon three criteria: evaluation of experiences of cities which have adopted different measures, economic theory which suggests methods of efficient allocation of resources, and the particular attributes of the community in question. It is important to review and evaluate experiences of various cities since they tell us what measures are actually effective in the field. Economic theory provides a range of solutions that work in other industries under similar conditions. We do not need to reinvent the wheel; implementation of such proven solutions to the false alarm problem is likely to succeed.

Different solutions to the false alarm problem may be appropriate for different types of communities. Continued police response may be appropriate for a small suburban locality where the police have a strong commitment to the constituents and where direct personal relations exist. Private response may be considered in a heavily alarm-dense section of a large anonymous city, where the police are overwhelmed with other serious problems as well as large numbers of false activations and where the police already respond with great delay or not at all.

Six-City Case Study

We selected six cities and analyzed their alarm ordinances and activities. Emphasis was given to analyzing the impact of the enacted ordinances upon the levels of both activations and false activations. The selected cities satisfied all of the following conditions:

- The cities are of a substantial size.
- The cities have enacted an ordinance within the last five years, which has been enforced.
- The ordinances differ among the cities so that a variety of solutions can be analyzed.
- All but one of the cities have data available so that the impact of the ordinances can be analyzed.

Below is a summary of the selected cities' alarm ordinances:

1. Boston, Massachusetts (1992 population: 551,675).

   Boston's alarm ordinance went into effect in March of 1992. There is no registration of alarms or permits to have alarms. The first two false alarms are free, with a warning letter sent after each false alarm. The fine for the third false alarm is $50, for the fourth, $100, and for the fifth and additional false alarms in a calendar year, $200. At six false alarms in a calendar year, response is suspended until all fines are paid and the alarm owner can show that the problem causing the alarms has been corrected.

2. Montgomery County, Maryland (1990 population: 757,027).

   Montgomery County, Maryland, required all alarm owners to have their alarms registered by September 1, 1993. There is a one-time registration fee of $30. Police do not stop response for excessive false alarms; however, the fines for false activations are of a highly punitive nature. There is an escalating fine structure, with the first three false alarms being free, the fourth through the ninth costing $50, and fines continue to escalate to as high as $1,000 for residential properties and as high as $4,000 for commercial properties.

3. Milwaukee, Wisconsin (1992 population: 617,043).

   The original ordinance was enacted in July 1989. It required licensing of the alarm companies. A permit is also required of alarm owners. After two false activations in a calendar year, fines of $50 are imposed for each additional activation.

4. Portland, Oregon (1992 population: 445,458).

   The original ordinance was enacted in 1975. A major update was done in 1989/90, with additional updates in 1991 and 1994. The 1989/90 ordinance stated that a notice is simply sent out at the first activation. For the second and third false alarm, a $50 fee is charged, which increases to $100 for the fourth activation. Service is suspended after the fourth activation until a letter stating reasons for the false activations and solutions taken is sent to the alarm unit. In 1994 the policy was changed to a complete suspension after the fifth false activation.

5. Seattle, Washington (1992 population: 519,598).

   The program went into effect on September 1, 1993. Seattle does not allow any free false alarms. Fining begins with the first false activation. The fine is $50 for every false alarm. Police response is suspended after six false alarms in a 12-month period.

6. Toronto, Ontario (1991 population: 3,800,000).

The program went into effect on January 1, 1990. Service was suspended after the fourth false activation in a one-year period. Until September 1996 there was no fine structure or registration of alarms in Toronto. This is the only city that we studied that relied on suspension of service with no prior fines to reduce false alarms. Beginning in September 1996, the police charged 75 Canadian dollars for each of the first four alarms.

Findings

Table 9.1 provides the major details about the alarm ordinances. The number of "free" false alarms allowed per year ranges from 1 to 4, while fines range from zero to $4,000. Table 9.2 briefly evaluates the ordinances and activations. It provides the major advantages and disadvantages of the various ordinances.

Evaluation

Several methods have been adopted by localities to combat false alarms. The six case studies show that the most effective element in an alarm ordinance is the threat of ceasing response, usually after four or six false activations in a year. A system of escalating fines appears less effective. Of course, fines may be too low or their collection may be lax. The appropriate level of fines or charges will be discussed in a later section. In any case, Toronto, with the sharpest reduction in false alarms of 60 percent, has no fines but only ceases response to repeat activators. Portland, which had a 44 percent drop in false alarms and a 55 percent reduction in alarms per system, employed escalating fines and no response as well as alarm courses and much effort by the director of the alarm unit. Boston, which ranked third with a 33 percent reduction in false alarms, like Portland had escalating fines and no response to repeat activators. Seattle, which had a constant fine and the threat of no response, had a 24 percent reduction in false alarms. Milwaukee, which had only fines, experienced a 14 percent reduction in false alarms.

Table 9-1 Information About Alarm Ordinances

City and State	Alarm Regist.	Regist. Fee	No. of Free False Alarms	Fine Structure	No. of False Alarms Before Response Is Suspended
Boston, MA	No	n/a	2	3rd: $50 4th: $100 5+: $200	6
Montgomery County, MD	Yes	$30 One time only	3	Escalates from $50 for 4th to max $1,000 residential $4,000 commercial	No suspension
Milwaukee, WI	No	n/a	2	3+: $50	No suspension
Portland, OR	Yes	$12 Annual	1	2,3: $50 4+: $100	4
Seattle, WA	No	n/a	0	$50 each	6
Toronto, ONT	No	n/a	4	No fines issued	4

Source: "Canvassing the Neighborhood," Hakim and Blackstone, *Security Dealer*, February 1996.

Table 9-2 Evaluation of Ordinances and Activities

Cities, States	Inputs		Advantages	Disadvantages	Output
	Size of Alarm Unit	No. of Activ. 1992			%Decline False Activ.
Boston, MA	1	47,500	1) CAD system and alarm units are computer-compatible. 2) Database uses addresses supplied by alarm companies. 3) No discontinuation of response. 4) Alarm officer who runs unit.	1) Allows for two free false alarms. 2) Punitive fine structure, which may deter alarm ownership.	33
Milwaukee, WI	4	42,225	1) Alarm officer who runs unit. 2) Does not stop response for excessive false alarms.	1) Allows for two free false alarms. 2) CAD and alarm unit's computer are not linked.	14
Montgomery County, MD	5	48,000	1) Was successful in registering alarm owners. 2) Responsibility of alarm companies to register their customers. 3) Does not stop response for excessive false alarms.	1) Fines are excessive and punitive in nature. 2) Alarm registration is unnecessary. 3) Allows for three free false alarms.	NA
Portland, OR	9	22,676	1) Number of free alarms has been reduced as ordinance has been modified. 2) Alarm owners receive a service for their permit fee. 3) Single officer who heads alarm unit.	1) Allows for one free false alarm. 2) Alarm education should be provided by industry, not gov't. Alarm industry can provide education for alarm owners more efficiently and at less cost. 3) Alarm registration unnecessary.	44

Table 9-2 Continued

Cities, States	Inputs		Advantages	Disadvantages	Output
	Size of Alarm Unit	No. of Activ. 1992			%Decline false Activ.
Seattle, WA	2	34,435	1) No alarm registration. 2) Police utilize alarm companies' databases. 3) One officer in charge of alarm unit. 4) No escalating fine structure. 5) No free false alarms.	1) Police officer writes citations. 2) Response stopped after 6 false alarms in 12-month period.	24
Toronto, Ontario	3	56,758	1) No alarm registration. 2) Enforcement of ordinance makes it successful despite lack of fees or fines.	1) No fee or fine means that the cost of response is not recouped from those receiving the service. 2) Response stopped after 4 false alarms.	60

Source: "Canvassing the Neighborhood," Hakim and Blackstone, *Security Dealer,* February 1996.)

The no response policy obviously reduces the value of alarm systems. Most significantly, measures such as no response or escalating fines do not necessarily reflect well on overall effectiveness. One needs to consider the benefits of the measures compared to the costs they impose. It is not enough to consider the reduction in false activations. A no response policy may cause an excessive reduction in the use of alarms and consequently a reduction in security. Alarms reduce the number of break-ins, and an ordinance or police practice that forces alarm owners not to activate their systems and potential buyers to forgo alarm installation will reduce the security level in the community. Further, enforcement of ordinances is not cost free. Labor and other resources are expensive, reflecting their alternative uses. Portland's efforts have been successful; however, they impose significant costs on taxpayers. An effective ordinance is one where the benefit of reduction in costs imposed upon police from response to false activations is higher than the combined costs of reduced security and the enforcement efforts.

The major features of these cases are:

1. The most important factor in all these cases has been the diligent enforcement of the existing ordinance. Many cities that have high false alarm rates, such as Philadelphia and Dallas, have not aggressively enforced their local ordinances; the cities that are successful in lowering false activations have created systems that enable them to track the false alarms and promptly issue notices and fines. At the same time, their collection of fines and enforcement of no response is efficient but, as mentioned, may not reflect well on overall effectiveness.

   The system used to enforce the ordinances is somewhat dependent upon the ordinances themselves. For example, Seattle has its police officers issue citations that are the equivalent of parking tickets. The citation is issued by the officer at the scene. It is an effective, unproblematic way of issuing fines because the police officer at the scene knows the address of the offending alarm system owner. However, this system will only work in a city such as Seattle that does not allow any "free" false alarms. If free false alarms were allowed, then before issuing the citation, the attending officer would have to know how many false alarms the residence had prior to the current alarm. This would be impractical until software is developed that allows a Computerized Automated Dispatch (CAD) computer instant access to an alarm unit's database.

2. Localities differ in their willingness to employ sanctions to prevent false alarms. For example, Seattle allows no free responses, and Toronto formerly allowed the most, before action is taken. All cities send at least a warning notice after the first alarm. Many cities tried to be more lenient when they first started their programs, but these weaker ordinances proved unsuccessful. The general trend is to tighten ordinances. The number of free activations is reduced and the fines escalate.

Toronto's case proves that indeed more stringent sanctions lead to a reduction in false activations. In 1977, the ordinance required a warning letter to be sent after the fourth false alarm in a 28-day period. After another five false activations in a subsequent 28 days, police service was suspended. False alarms rose an average of 12.5 percent per year between 1977 and 1988. Toronto's subsequent more restrictive ordinance, which called for suspension after only four false alarms in a 365-day period, led to a 60 percent decrease in false alarms between 1988 and 1993. Not surprisingly, the less lenient an ordinance is, the greater is the reduction in false activations. Again, such an approach does not consider the adverse effects it causes to the level of security, and the high bureaucratic costs of managing the program. In the case of Toronto, as Table 9.2 illustrates, the administrative costs are low, but there is a great reduction in the level of security.

3. Much of the success can be attributed to the activities of the person who heads the alarm unit. Personal contacts with repeat activators, running special classes on alarm use, and cracking down on companies with a high false alarm rate appear to be most effective. Clearly, such personal contacts are possible in small communities or cities but cannot be employed in our big cities.

In Seattle a problem occurred with renters who owned alarms that produced a large number of false activations. The renters were not paying their fines, but instead were just moving to other apartments or houses. The alarm officer called Brinks, which sold many systems to renters. He discovered that these alarm owners, when they moved among rental units, not only weren't paying their fines, but also were breaking their contracts with Brinks. The alarm officer convinced Brinks to sell alarms only to the owners of the property. This way both Brinks and the Seattle police could hold the owners of the property responsible for alarm contracts and false alarms. This is one example of how having one person handle false alarms can alleviate problems that might otherwise go unnoticed. One might also observe that Seattle's alarm policy was so simple that the alarm unit director had the time to handle the problem with renters.

The alarm officer acts as a liaison between the police department, the end user, and the alarm and monitoring companies. In some cities, alarm officers conduct classes and/or personal sessions with the public on how to prevent false alarms from occurring. In Phoenix, alarm owners who attend these classes receive a $55 certificate to cover their next false alarm activation.

4. Many cities find alarm registration to be the cornerstone of their false alarm reduction projects; they are

able to keep track of all alarm owners through their registration numbers.

Montgomery County, MD, had new computer software designed especially for its alarm unit, which relies on alarm registration; the software stores all of the unit's information on alarm owners. All monitoring stations that serve the county are supposed to provide the registration number in each dispatch to the police. All of the alarm owner's information then appears on the police dispatcher's computer screen. Alarm registration also facilitates compatibility between a CAD system and an alarm unit's computer. If every address in an alarm unit's database has a corresponding registration number, and the CAD computer is designed to store alarm calls by registration number, then information can be easily downloaded by matching the registration numbers. Registration numbers do not vary with each alarm call. Addresses may be typed in incorrectly, or, as more frequently occurs, differently on each call, while registration numbers are easy to record.

Caution is required when making comparisons because the alarm units should be performing similar functions. For example, some units may be responsible for collecting fines, while others may not. Recognizing such issues, Boston's entire alarm "unit" consists of one alarm officer, and Seattle's two. Milwaukee's ex-director of the unit claims that registration fees are unnecessary and with the appropriate software, only one half-time person is needed. The Boston police did not have exact numbers on how many of the addresses ended up mismatched or how many had mail (fines or warning letters) returned as undeliverable. However, the number is low enough that the alarm officer can handle such problems as part of his regular duties.

It is too early to assess Montgomery County's registration system. However, the experiences of other places, including the City of Philadelphia, suggest that registration of alarms may yield more problems than benefits. Seattle's and Boston's decisions to forgo alarm registration and to treat activations as traffic tickets appear most effective. Registration fees may, however, be used to provide such services as education for alarm users, although such services can probably be provided less expensively by private companies.

5. A key to success in reducing false activations is open communication between the police and the alarm dealers. The alarm association in conjunction with the police can offer classes for repeat activators on how to use their systems. For example, in Milwaukee the alarm coordinator explained to dealers about the cost imposed upon the police by false activations. In a joint effort, a program using slides to show the proper use of a system was developed, which produced good results. Dealers respond to requests from the police and insist that alarm owners obtain any needed new equipment or they will stop serving them.

Recommendations

If recommendations follow strictly from the cases where the number of false alarms has been reduced the most, then Toronto's and Portland's ordinances and in particular the no response policy are to be recommended. Taking the solution a few steps further, to an absurd conclusion, the police should stop responding to alarms altogether, and the false alarm problem as such will clearly vanish. Such a conclusion would be totally incorrect. It is not enough to observe, as many in the industry do, the policies that lead to significant reductions in false alarms, but it is also necessary to consider the costs associated with the reduced level of security in the community. To stop responding after three or four false activations in the course of a year or to institute high fines may be detrimental. Non-alarm owners may consider not purchasing a system, or a large-scale trend of not arming the system by alarm owners may spread. Since our work has consistently shown that alarms are effective in reducing burglaries, such policies translate to lower security.

These cases do suggest that strong enforcement of whatever ordinance exists reduces false activations. However, the high cost of close monitoring by police can be avoided and more reliance on market forces is to be preferred. Seattle and Boston may not have reduced false activations as much as Toronto and Portland. However, the cost and effort of the Seattle and Boston police were much lower, and the level of security provided by alarms was preserved. Seattle and Boston do not maintain a file of all alarm owners. Indeed, it appears unnecessary to duplicate information that the dealers and central stations already have. In case of a false activation, a citation, which is similar to a traffic violation citation, can be issued by the officer responding to the activation. In addition, the problem of an inaccurate address cannot occur.

The types of ordinances and activities undertaken by the police vary with the size of the community. Portland has been successful in curbing false activations. Much of this success is attributable to the diligent efforts of the alarm unit director in working with individual alarm owners and dealers. In our surveys we witnessed similar activities that had much success in suburban localities such as Tredyffrin, Pennsylvania, and Greenwich, Connecticut. Such personal attention, however, is difficult when a large city is concerned, simply because of scale. A large city government cannot afford such involved personal relationships and must rely more on data management and strict automatic procedures. The police cannot overburden themselves by maintaining a large number of people in the alarm unit to deal with individual cases, for both efficiency reasons and because of the mere fact that the service provided is private rather than public in nature. Finally, large city police departments have greater demands on their resources than do most suburban departments.

When we started to analyze the alarm industry back in 1988, we met with many police chiefs in the Philadelphia area to learn about the issues. One thread was common in all conversations: frustration on the part of police with the problem of false activations. The industry's magazines have dealt with the problem, and committees were enacted by most state burglar and fire alarm associations, by the central station alarm associations, and by the International Association of Chiefs of Police to study and suggest solutions.

ANOTHER APPROACH TO THE FALSE ACTIVATION PROBLEM: MODEL CITIES

Another approach to the false alarm problem involves extensive cooperation between the police departments and the alarm companies. This approach, including the Model Cities Program, which was initiated in 1994, emphasizes intensive efforts by the police and the alarm companies to reduce false alarms by, among other things, working with and educating alarm users. The approach has yielded some reductions in false alarms and in false alarm rates per system.

Elgin, Illinois, a city with population of 85,000, had 2,086 alarm systems in operation in 1995. Through cooperation among the 95 alarm companies operating in Elgin, representatives of the alarm companies visited each customer, completed a 15-point checklist, returned the checklist to the police, and identified false alarm offenders. The false alarm rate was reduced from 2.57 to 1.63 per system, and total false alarm calls were cut from 3,488 to 2,556 between 1994 and 1995.

Bellevue, Washington, population 100,000, had 8,000 alarm systems in operation in 1995, and 11 alarm companies participated in the alarm task force's activities. In addition to escalating fines, questionnaires were given to alarm owners, classes were offered to alarm offenders instead of fines, and other measures such as verification and restricted response were utilized. Bellevue's false alarm rate was reduced to 0.77 per system in 1995 from 0.91 in 1994. Incidentally, the false alarm rate had been 1.02 in 1993, so it was declining even before the initiation of the Model Cities Program.

Philadelphia, Pennsylvania, the third and final Model City, in 1995 had a population of 1.4 million and 37,700 registered alarm systems. The Philadelphia program involved encouraging verification, canceling alarms, targeting false alarm abusers, and engaging in public relations efforts. The program was credited with reducing false alarms by almost 8,000 in 1995 compared to 1994.

Table 9.3 provides an additional view of alarm ordinances and activities for the six cities that we analyzed, and the three model city project. The table includes an annualized percentage rate of change from the time the ordinance was enforced to 1994/5. Then, the various activities were categorized and analyzed, and the cases ranked.

A few observations can be made. Enforcement of any ordinance reduces false activations. However, more restrictive ordinances, which reflect greater government regulation, are ineffective. In fact, Toronto and Seattle, which are less restrictive and spend the least per false response, are effective in reducing false activations.

Toronto achieved the greatest reduction in false activations, which is attributed to the practice of no response after the fourth false activation in a year. This same policy is common in five of the eight cities analyzed. An amateur economist will argue that the benefits of reduced false activations must be compared with both the cost of enforcing the ordinance and the adverse effect that ceasing response has on the level of security. If the net benefit is positive, then such a response policy (#1) is desirable. Observing merely the raw benefits side provides a biased picture and cannot lead to rational recommendations.

In comparing the alternative approaches of intensive efforts at educating false activators and modifying their behavior or simply relying upon market forces, our preference is toward the market-oriented approach. In an era where markets are increasingly relied upon as a less intrusive method for altering behavior, it seems most reasonable to utilize a market-oriented solution to the

Table 9–3 Measures Adopted and Effectiveness (in declining order)

City	Measures	Annualized Percentage Reduction	Number of False Alarms (before)
A. Survey Cities			
1. Toronto	1,6	17.6	127,143
2. Seattle, WA	1,3,6	14.0	33,540
3. Boston, MA	1,2,3,5,6,9,12	13.8	44,504
4. Portland, OR	1,2,3,4,5,6,7,8,9,12	11.6	34,848
5. Milwaukee, WI	3,5,6,8,12,13	9.7	45,149
6. Montgomery County, MD	2,6,7,9,10,11	8.7	44,000
B. Model Cities			
1. Bellevue, WA	1,2,4,7,14	29.0	7,280
2. Elgin, IL	5,7,10,12	26.8	9,682
3. Philadelphia, PA	5,14,15,16	9.4	129,317

Legend: The following are all measures directed at end users that police departments take to curb false activators. They are presented in order of declining effectiveness:

1. Suspending response after a certain number of false activations in one year.
2. Escalating fine structure.
3. Providing less than three free responses per year to false activations.
4. Mandatory classes for repeat activators.
5. Voluntary contacting of alarm dealers with names of repeat activators in order to identify the reasons for and solve the problem.
6. Sending computerized warning letters.
7. Mandatory registration of alarm ownership.
8. Aggressive involvement of alarm unit director at high level.
9. No response to alarm activation if fines are unpaid.
10. Mandatory inspection of alarm system.
11. After eighth false alarm requiring system upgrade to the county installation standards.
12. Police department contacts alarm dealers requesting them to deal with repeat activators.
13. Registration/licensing of alarm dealers.
14. Monitoring or encouraging verification of activations.
15. Cancellation accepted.
16. Public relation effects.

Source: A. Survey conducted by authors. B. International Association of Chiefs of Police, "Model Cities Progress Report," October 1995, Miami Conference.

false alarm problem. In a small city it is possible to deal with the false alarm problem by personal attention from the crime prevention officer. In many suburban localities the officer meets with repeat activators, checks the problem, and maintains contact with their alarm dealer. In a small- to medium-size city it is even possible to conduct classes for repeat activators.

As the size of the city increases, the relationship between the police and their constituents becomes more anonymous. Also, the magnitude of false alarms is large and difficult to manage on a personal basis. In large cities, alarm ordinances and activities need to rely on market forces using simple procedures that are less labor intensive.

We do not imply that other efforts are not useful or have been unsuccessful. Simply put, as long as alarm owners are willing to pay the cost for response to alarms, there is no problem. The problem arises because costs are shifted to others besides the false alarm activators. These other approaches may well be useful, but in any case they ought to be handled within the alarm industry—by producers and consumers of alarm services. Further, verification and cancellation of alarms are desirable and ought to be implemented. In any case, even if the industry can reduce the number of false alarms, society at large should not pay for them unless, of course, the number were reduced to a small level, an unlikely eventuality.

Despite all the efforts, the results seem to be modest. Many in the industry have the feeling that indeed a problem exists, but at the same time feel that this is "business as usual." Such an attitude is dangerous and unfounded. Even if business is good, it could be much better, and it may deteriorate significantly in the future if the problem is not solved. In our surveys we questioned non-alarm owners as to why they did not purchase a system. Our 1991 survey showed that 11 percent of households indicated the false alarm problem as such a reason. Three years later in 1994, 35.9 percent stated that "false alarms would be a nuisance to me," and another 17.5 percent said that "fines for false activations are too high." Public awareness of the false alarm problem had escalated in a three-year period and significantly impedes sales. It is no longer just a problem known to the police and the alarm industry, but it has reached the attention of the general public. The media only has to run some programs about the lack of police response to activations and the associated uselessness of alarm systems to hurt business.

"Business as usual" is incorrect from another angle. Most of the analyzed cities have tightened their ordinances in recent years. For example, the new Boston ordinance considers all burglary attempts to be false. Portland has stiffened its fine structure, raised the permit fee, and reduced the number of free responses. Measures are commonly made stiffer in most ordinances that are revisited. All this translates to a deteriorating demand for alarms in what could be in a more favorable environment. The industry should consider measures that are unpopular, may require them taking on some responsibilities, or may require changes in the way business is currently conducted, in order to achieve a substantial reduction in police involvement in response to false activations.

Economists have long been concerned about the effectiveness of deterrence measures against potential offenders. The two categories of deterrence measures are severity and certainty of punishment. The objective is to maximize the level of security in the community given its limited public and private resources.

Economic theory and empirical findings suggest that expending a given amount of resources on increasing the certainty of punishment is more effective than spending the same resources on severity measures. This fact has important implications to our case. Alarm ordinances and activities should center on a certain payment for all false activations, starting with the first. Escalating fees are less effective, and a prior knowledge of service suspension is most effective.

Taking the concept one step further, research suggests that simply requiring full payment for all false alarm responses to the activator site is most effective and has no punitive implications.

Fines for False Activations

Fines for false activations should be viewed as reimbursable costs of a private service rendered by the police. What should the level of the fee be? and When should it be imposed? Economic theory provides a clear answer to the level of this user's fee. There are two distinct services provided: public and private. Public service occurs when a real attempted or successful burglary has occurred; no fees should be charged. If a burglar is apprehended, then the entire community enjoys a reduction in potential burglaries. If, on the other hand, the activation is false, then this is a private service. No one but the activated property owner enjoys the benefits of the response. The price charged should be the real variable costs.[1] The fee will include patrol officer time devoted to the response,[2] the vehicle's variable costs, property and personal injuries associated with accidents in the drive to/from the scene, and the cost of the dispatching. In cases where patrol officers do not respond when they are dispatched, the cost of patrol officer time is not included.

The proportional cost of running a dispatching center is a significant part of the total cost of responding to alarms. The cost includes the share of the center's operating expenses that is incurred by alarm response, including labor, equipment, and imputed rent.

Some raise the idea that commercial establishments should pay higher fees than households. Unless response to commercial establishments is more costly than response to residential units, similar fees should be charged for both. Some believe that the fees should increase as more false activations result from an establishment. Again, since the fees should express real costs, there is no justification for raising the fees for false activations as their number rises. If the fee is above real cost, then there will be a greater decline in the purchase or use of alarms than is justified. Since alarms deter burglaries, they improve the feeling of safety of their owners, reduce the completion of burglary, and reduce both property loss and the number of assaults.[3] Thus, imposing higher than justified fines reduces the absolute and perceived security in the community. If the fees are below cost, then we encourage false activations and bring about subsidization of alarm owners by nonowners. Some suggest that all incoming calls for

response should be received over 900 lines. Monitoring companies will then automatically be charged for the fees and they will
be responsible for collecting the fees from the dealers or the activators. The International Association of Chiefs of Police has
opposed such stiff measures, which may penalize security companies for the faults of alarm owners and result in severe financial
consequences for them.

We suggest that the receipts of false activations be sufficient
to cover the costs of response by the police. The alarm-related
section of the police department will operate as an independent
profit unit. This will result in operating "profit" similar to corporate America, where each unit is responsible for all its activities
and needs to show bottom-line profits. Such a scheme will eliminate any inequities resulting from cross-subsidization between
owners and nonowners of alarms, and will encourage the alarm
unit to improve efficiency in providing the service. However, it is
important to note that if police monopolize the response to
alarms in a community, then they may charge higher fees and
may be inefficient in providing the service. Creating the environment for private response will encourage greater efficiency
and—if the police choose to continue to provide the service—
lower fees.

Registration Fees

Registration fees are collected in order to cover the fixed costs
of registering alarms, collecting fines, searching for unregis-
tered systems, enforcing the ordinances, and executing cases,
including court costs. Again, it is costly to manage alarm registration and enforcement, and there is no justification for such
costs being recovered through general tax receipts. If owners
of alarms do not pay for these costs, then all taxpayers bear
these costs.

For example, in the case of Philadelphia, since 11 percent of
households and 14 percent of businesses have alarms (Hakim
and Gaffney 1994, p. 69), over 85 percent of the funding for
alarm-related costs is borne by non-alarm owners, who enjoy no

benefits from either alarms or from the services provided to alarm owners.

It is obvious that the receipts from alarm owners should cover all these costs. Also, due to the private nature of the service we recommend users' fees. Allocation of funds from the general budget is unjustified since there is no reason to support cross-subsidization. Alarm owners should not subsidize nonowners and vice versa. Also, as in the case of the police response, creation of a profit unit for the registration of alarm ownership, fee imposition and collection, and managing court cases would result in increased efficiency in comparison to the case where funding and fee collection are accomplished through the general budget. There will be an increased incentive to improve fee collection and operate the unit efficiently. Indeed, the establishment of profit units has proven to be successful in both the private and public sectors, and the units could encompass all the alarm-related functions in the local jurisdiction.

CASE STUDY: CALCULATION OF POLICE RESPONSE COST, PHILADELPHIA, PA

In this section we demonstrate how to calculate the cost of response for the police department. It is based upon actual police practices and actual outlays. It does not necessarily represent the cost of response service that would result in a competitive environment. Private companies that respond to alarm activations typically charge in the range of $20 to $30. The higher cost of police operation is mainly attributable to higher per hour wages of sworn officers. The data for the calculation of both the response and the annual registration fees are based upon detailed data obtained for the city of Philadelphia. Economic cost estimation is distinct from accounting cost estimation and assumes that officers and other employees, and vehicles, can be utilized elsewhere in the city, yielding benefits at least equal to their paid cost.

Calculation of Police Response Costs, Philadelphia, PA

Alarm calls for January, 1995:[4]	11,183
Less calls of 5 minutes or less, and of one hour or more:	1,538
Responded to alarm calls:	9,645
Less real burglaries/attempts (2.6 percent):	251
False alarm calls for January, 1995:	9,394
Total number of minutes for officers' response to alarms, January 1995:	162,213
Minutes of false alarm activations ($\times$ 0.974):	157,995
Average response time for false activations (in minutes):	16.82
Officers' cost of time responding:	
Two officers responding to activation (in minutes):	33.64
Cost of two officers' response time:[5]	$18.80
Cost of sergeant's response time:[6]	$ 0.71
Patrol vehicle cost:	
Purchase cost of fully loaded patrol car:	$18,817
5.25 percent of service calls that are alarm related:	$987.90
Car amortization over five years. Annual cost:	$197.60
Per alarm call vehicle cost:	$1.95
Per activation driving costs:	
Total mileage patrol cars, 1994:	11,567,746
5.25 percent that is alarm-related mileage:	607,307
Cost of driving ($.30 per mile):	$182,192
Per alarm call driving cost:[7]	$1.20
Patrol cars accident cost:	
Patrol car accidents, 1994:	564
Alarm-related accidents, 5.25 percent:	29.61
Average cost of property damage:[8]	$3,810
Per false activation, property cost of accidents:	$0.74
Per false activation, personal injury cost of accident:	$1.81
Dispatching cost:	
Total cost, including salaries, equipment, and imputed rent, steady state:	$13,520,309
Per false activation, dispatching cost:[9]	$4.68
Summary, cost per false alarm response:	
Police officers' wages:	$18.80

Sergeant wages:	$0.71
Car expenses:	$3.15
Accidents, property:	$0.74
Accidents, personal:	$1.81
Dispatching:	$4.68
Total:	**$29.89**

The cost for police response to a false alarm was about $30 in 1995. If fees are collected only after the third false activation in a year, then the question is Who will pay for the police response to those who falsely activated their systems less frequently? If the system of three free false activations is retained, then the actual cost is shifted mainly to non-alarm owners.

As an alternative, these costs can be borne by the repeat activators of four or more a year. This is again an inequitable solution because the latter group subsidizes those who activate their systems three or fewer times. The following is the calculation of the imposed costs on repeat activators:

From October 1, 1994 through February 23, 1995, there were 10,068 eligible activations for fines. In addition, there is a reject file, which extends back to July, 1994, of 38,000 activations. From the reject file we arrived at 23,750 total activations for the period of October 1, 1994 through February 23, 1995, of which 3,938 were the fourth or higher activations.

Calculation of Fines for Repeat Activators

For the period October 1, 1994, through February 23, 1995:

Identified fourth or higher activations:	10,068
Imputed fourth or higher activation, unfinished file:	3,938
Total number of activations eligible for fine:	14,006
Activations not eligible for fine:	46,712
Total number of activations:	60,718

The share of alarm owners who activate four or more times per year is 0.2307. Therefore, the complementary group, which consists of alarm owners who activate three or fewer times per year, is 0.7693. If all police response cost is imposed upon repeat activators, their per activation fee will be $130.

Calculation of Annual Alarm Registration Fees

Annual alarm registration fees should be based upon the annual costs of administrating the program. It should include the expenses borne by the Bureau of Administrative Adjudication, the hearing expenses for alarm violations, and the imputed rent for the police dispatching center. However, the initial establishment of an efficient software and hardware system to handle the administrative response to alarms and fine imposition and collection would probably entail additional costs, which are unknown at this point.

Estimate of Alarm Registration and Violation Tracking Expenses

In this category we include labor, computer, and office expenses. The total cost now incurred by the Bureau of Administrative Adjudication is $455,834.

Estimate of hearing expenses for alarm violations:

Salary:	$ 15 per hour
Benefits (40%):	$ 6 per hour
Clerical staff (30%):	$ 4.50 per hour
Total per hour, labor:	$ 25.50

Three hearings are conducted per hour. One thousand hearings are expected to be conducted per year. Total annual costs for hearings are estimated at $8,500.

Estimate of dispatching center's imputed rent:

The area is 5,300 square feet, and the imputed rent is $15 per square foot. The share of alarms in the total calls for service at the dispatching center is 5.25 percent. Thus, 5,300 × $15 × 0.0525 = $4,174.

> Summary, registration cost per alarm owner:
>
> | | |
> |---|---|
> | Bureau of Administrative Adjudication Code Unit: | $455,834 |
> | Hearing expenses for alarm violations: | $ 8,500 |
> | Dispatching center's imputed rent: | $ 4,174 |
> | Total costs, administering alarms: | $468,508 |

Since the total number of registered alarms is 32,000, the annual fee per alarm should be $15.

Inflation-Adjusted Alarm Response and Registration fees

Fees for alarm registration and response to false alarms should be adjusted annually (or, theoretically, even more often) to reflect changes over time in the costs of providing the services. For example, in the most recent 10-year period consumer prices increased in the Philadelphia Metropolitan area by 56 percent. Not adjusting for the higher prices means that the $30 response charge at the end of the next 10 years (assuming for illustrative purposes the same rate of inflation in the next 10 years as was experienced over the previous 10 years) in real terms would be only $19.23; the $15 annual registration fee in real terms would be $9.62. Adjusting for inflation for a 10-year period would require a response fee of $46.80 (1.56 × $30) and an annual registration fee of $23.40 (1.56 × $15). Since we assume that alarm fees will not be reconsidered for 10 years, we recommend establishing fees based upon modest inflation adjustments. For example, an annual CPI increase of 4 percent for 5 years, and then charging that flat price for the entire 10-year period. This procedure would involve a response fee of $36 and an annual registration fee of $18. Over the entire 10-year period such a procedure would yield fees that in the first 5 years would be slightly high and in the last 5 years would be somewhat low. Certainly, if at all possible, it is preferable to annually adjust the fees for the previous year's inflation rate. However, annual readjustments for inflation create administrative difficulties and costs, which makes their implementation questionable.

Recommendations

Fees for alarm response and annual registration should reflect the real cost. Imposing fees that do not reflect cost is both inefficient and inequitable. If the fee is below the cost, then alarm owners will not do their utmost to avoid false activations. Fees that are less than cost further shift the burden of payment mainly to non-owners of alarms. If the fees are above the cost, households and businesses will reduce their purchase and use of alarm systems beyond what is desirable. Since alarms are proven to reduce burglaries and are complementary to police operations, reduced use of alarms will reduce security and the feeling of safety in the community.

The private nature of the alarm response service means that users' fees are appropriate. Such users' fees will create an implicit profit center and will encourage efficiency in the provision of the service. For Philadelphia, for example, the following current real fees are suggested: $15 for the annual registration and $30 flat rate for each false activation. Registration and response fees, adjusted for inflation, assuming a 10-year revisitation period for the ordinance, would be $18 and $36, respectively. If three false activations per year are free, then a decision should be made as to who should bear the costs associated with the free activations. Imposing these costs upon repeat activators of four or more a year would yield $121 per activation for all activations in excess of three. However, it may be considered inequitable and inefficient to impose these additional costs upon the latter group.

PRIVATE RESPONSE

Feasibility of Private Alarm Response

Another alternative is shifting to private response to alarms. Indeed, in the beginning of the alarm industry, alarm response was originally done by alarm company personnel (Shanahan 1995). The company personnel would notify the police if signs of a break-in were evident. Eventually the police took over response to alarms and provided the service at no charge to alarm owners.

Incidentally, when alarm response was performed initially by alarm company personnel, alarm owners in effect paid for the service and the costs they caused. There was no subsidy from non-alarm owners to alarm owners.

The key question is whether the market is large enough to provide a reasonable return to a private company. In fact, private firms are already providing response to alarms in some areas. For example, in Ft. Lauderdale, Florida, GSI Tactical Response provides armed response to alarm activations. The firm employs off-duty police officers who meet the state requirement for private citizens to carry guns. The firm responds to activations with two armed officers who notify police if a real burglary is occurring. The police then respond promptly to what they know is an actual crime.

To learn more about the feasibility of providing private response we have conducted many interviews with firms currently providing such services. We are reporting the results of a few such interviews conducted in 1995 to indicate the feasibility of private response. Another example of a firm successfully providing private armed alarm response comes from Los Angeles, California. The firm Golden West K-9 has experienced very rapid growth since 1988. It contracts with numerous alarm companies to provide response to alarms. It also provides patrol services and standby guards to ensure security for enclosed (by gates) residential communities. Its 92 employees use 26 patrol cars to cover 65 square miles. In 1995 Golden West K-9 responded to about 1,000 alarm activations per month. The typical residence paid $20 per month to the alarm company, which then paid the private response firm $12. Businesses were charged $30, of which $18 went to the alarm response provider. The firm had about 5,000 customers in 1995. The monthly fee included two responses at no additional charge. A fee of $25 was charged for each response in excess of the two provided as part of the monthly fee. The number of responses for businesses and residences was far different.

On the average the firm responded 15 times per month per 100 homes. For business, the response rate was 45, or three times as great as that for residences. Therefore, the firm collected most of its response fees (penalties) from businesses. The California private response provider paid its patrol officers in 1995 at least $8.50 per hour. Some earned $10 per hour, plus bonuses for good performance of an additional $4 per hour. Health insurance and profit sharing were also offered.

Substantial training is required for patrol officers. The training involves qualifying for a state gun license, and baton and mace training. Golden West K-9 requires its armed patrol officers to requalify every three months whereas California only requires requalification once a year. The firm even has some K-9 units. Insurance expense is 6.3 percent of base wages for armed and K-9 officers, and 4.5 percent for unarmed officers. One or two officers respond to an alarm activation on the average in under 15 minutes. The modal response time is 10 minutes. Similar to the usual situation, 97 to 99 percent of all alarms are false. In responding to alarms the usual procedure is to watch the premises and notify the police if a real incident is occurring. The firm will try to avoid using weapons and will do so only if a customer is in danger. The officers often surprise burglars, and they will then make a citizen's arrest. Golden West K-9 has in fact been quite successful. The chief executive, Jerry A. Usher, noted that alarm response is a highly profitable component of the guard industry but that successful participation in the industry requires well-trained personnel.

Another interview with a Philadelphia, Pennsylvania, firm, Fetzer Protection Services, Inc., provides support for the notion that even a small firm can successfully provide private response to alarms. The firm began 14 years ago. It has four part-time officers, and it works in a high-crime area of Philadelphia. The officers have all completed a police academy training course and are either off-duty patrol officers or retired officers. Fetzer Protection provides its services directly to its 50 to 70 commercial clients. It charges $75 per alarm response. The officers carry 9 mm guns, wear bulletproof vests, and are radio-dispatched. If there is evidence of an actual burglary, one officer enters the premises and another guard or police officer will provide backup. If, for example, an open door is visible, the officers will remain at the location and will request police backup. Incidentally, the firm's officers must obey traffic laws, even when responding to an alarm. The firm's officers have made more than 2,000 apprehensions in the 14 years of its operation, or an average of about 144 per year. Indeed in a two-week period in 1995, the firm's officers apprehended 17 burglary suspects. The firm also provides patrol services in warehouses. The company has keys for its clients' premises for both its alarm response and patrol services. The firm finds that essentially all the burglaries are committed by drug addicts, who will do thousands of dollars of damage just to obtain a few dollars' worth of merchandise. Also, many of the addicts are "high" on substances, such as PCP and cocaine, that seem to increase their strength so that apprehending them is difficult. The apprehension record of Fetzer Protection Services is even more remarkable when the drug use status of the suspects is considered.

Another interview, with First Response, Inc., a Portland, Oregon, firm, also demonstrates the feasibility of private armed response. The firm has been in operation since 1989 and in 1995 had 14 officers and 7 vehicles. First Response provides both alarm response and patrol services. The company has a contract with one alarm company but mainly contracts directly with the end users of alarms. Ninety percent of its customers are businesses, and the remainder are residential. The firm has keys for 80 percent of its customers' premises. It derives much of its business from alarm owners who have experienced large numbers of false alarms that resulted in stiff fines. In 1995 the firm provided a simple response to an alarm for a $20 per occurrence charge. That response was limited to walking around the premises. For $45 per month the firm will respond to as many as three free activations per month and will reset the alarm, and even do identification checks on occupants. A flat $20 fee is charged for each call in excess of three per month. The officers are reserve or volunteer police officers, and they have completed extensive firearms training. The firm itself provides six hours of additional weapons training and 120 hours of alarm response and patrol training. The firm provides 24-hour radio-dispatched service. Each patrol vehicle is equipped with a laptop computer to provide pertinent information on the account when the officers need to respond. The firm's officers will notify the police if there is an actual burglary, and they will enter the premises only with the police or with another officer. The officers make citizen's arrests. Officers earn between $9 and $13 per hour. The firm has an insurance expense of $2,500 per month. First Response was ranked in the top 100 area companies in growth in 1994. Its annual revenues exceed $500,000 and its profit ranges from 5 to 10 percent of gross revenues.

Another southern California firm providing private response to alarms stressed its rapid growth. In five months in 1995 the firm increased its employment of armed guards from 30 to 100 and utilized 41 vehicles. The company makes 2,200 alarm responses per month for its 20,000 commercial monitored accounts. Its coverage area involves 5,000 square miles and includes five regional offices so that no customer is more than 15 minutes away. The business has grown so much because police place a low priority on alarm calls, often not responding for 2.5 hours. The firm responds within 15 minutes in marked patrol vehicles. The patrol officers do not try to apprehend burglars but rather notify the police, who then respond within 10 minutes. About 95 percent of its calls are false. The firm charges different prices for different levels of service. For example, for $45 per month for non-UL systems the firm will respond three times at no additional charge. Beyond three responses per month, $25 is charged for each response. Another pricing plan involves a $25 per month charge and a $25 per response fee. These prices are for alarm response and are in addition to monitoring charges. The firm requires that its officers pass the state licensing test for armed patrol, which involves 40 hours of training. In fact most of the officers have attended a police academy or have served in the military.

The firm stated that entry into the private response field involved a minimum investment of $20,000 to $30,000, which includes training for three officers, a car, and a radio system. The minimum efficient size of a response company is five cars. In addition, alarm response has to be provided along with patrol service in order to be profitable. The company stated that alarm response alone was not feasible.

A firm in Virginia offers armed response to alarms. The firm has 50 percent residential and 50 percent commercial clients for its alarm response. This firm stressed its ability to obtain reasonably priced insurance. It did so by documenting its training program for its officers and its drug screening process for employment applicants. Its officers are trained by police officers; each undergoes 100 to 150 hours of training. The firm maintains relations with community colleges and other institutions to ensure high-quality trained officers. The firm provides for a fee a 24-hour response to alarms service for its alarm monitoring customers. One officer is on duty all the time. The firm guarantees a 15-minute response to alarms. Alarm response is provided in conjunction with patrol and vacation watch services. For example, some residential customers want their mail picked up, their pets fed, and lights turned on and off. This vacation watch is particularly popular during the Christmas and summer vacation seasons. Some commercial accounts want their country clubs, golf courses, and fenced lots patrolled. The typical charge for such patrol visits is $10 to $15 per visit, with the usual rate of one visit per day. Residential accounts pay $19 per month, which includes unlimited response calls, or $9 per month and $15 per response. Commercial accounts pay from $23 to $100 per month, depending on their size, for unlimited response. The firm reported that its breakeven point, where it just covers all costs, is seven patrol visits per day and 125 alarm response accounts. Officers are paid $8 to $10 per hour, substantially in excess of the $6 industry standard. They also receive benefits, including health insurance and sick leave, worth an additional 20 percent of their wages. The firm has been sufficiently successful that it is planning to expand its coverage to another geographic area.

A firm in Wisconsin also provides private armed response to alarms. Like most of the others, this firm stresses the role of training. It has 18 officers, eight of whom are off-duty police officers from neighboring communities. The remainder are criminal justice students and professional security officers. The firm's officers have at least 24 credits of police science, 40 hours of training in defensive arrest techniques, 40 hours of police firearms training, and an average of 20 hours training in first aid and CPR. Nongraduates of the Wisconsin Police Academy are provided training by the State of Wisconsin Department of Justice. The firm also requires twice per year recertification on firearms. Initial training costs approximate $800 per officer. The firm pays its experienced officers $10 per hour and provides health insurance. The officers generally carry 9 mm revolvers and have two-way radios. The company's liability insurance coverage entails an expense equal to 5 percent of its payroll. The company provides private detective, on-site security services, and patrol services in addition to alarm response. In the case of alarms, the police usually arrive before the security officers do because private security officers are not allowed to use sirens. If the company's officers are first on the scene, they will apprehend, search, and handcuff the suspect, then wait until the police arrive. The firm's officers will not enter a building until the police arrive unless someone is in personal danger. Officers will guard the doors of the establishment until the police arrive. The company has been in existence for 2.5 years and in the alarm response segment for only two months. It responds to alarms at over 100 businesses. The firm charges $40 per response but does not charge for response if the business has a patrol contract with the firm. It also offers a monthly response contract for $40, which includes two responses per month. After two responses, each additional is priced at $25. If an officer has to remain at a site for a substantial period, the first hour is priced at $40 and additional hours at $25. Contract subscribers receive one hour at no additional charge. The firm's total revenues in 1995 were about $450,000 with 15 percent gross profit after paying for equipment.

A firm in New York City provides armed alarm response to its highly valued commercial monitoring customers mainly located in a restricted geographical area. It attributes its rapid growth to the fact that police often take about three hours to respond to burglary alarms. The firm has 10 guards and three vehicles. In a test for UL rating, the firm was able to respond in three minutes, far below the allowed 15 minutes. The firm noted that a properly installed system is important in preventing false activations. Further, the firm tries to differentiate a system problem from a burglary. Since sensors are zoned separately, the firm can determine how the burglars move through the premises. Sometimes burglars chain the doors or jam the locks to prevent their apprehension. The officers will break through the door if they cannot otherwise gain access. The firm's officers have never confronted burglars. Burglary gangs generally use radios and leave when the guards arrive. The firm employs licensed guards with prior security experience. Applicants take a polygraph examination and are required to have pistol training and a class 100 license. The firm utilizes licensed instructors to provide daytime classes for its officers. The officers tend to be better educated than the average security officer. The firm has been able to obtain reasonable liability insurance. The chief executive of the company could only recall one or two occasions in his many years in the business when officers had to use their weapons. The officers have keys to the protected premises. The firm pays its experienced officers, who are called response agents, $600 per week. High-quality officers are the crucial ingredient in the successful provision of armed alarm response.

Benefits of Private Response

The above cases show the feasibility of private response. The many benefits of private response include freeing the police from responding to calls they almost always find not to involve a criminal event. The police in large cities generally treat alarm calls as a low priority, almost like a nuisance. By the time they arrive at the scene of a real intrusion, the burglar is long gone. In a commercial break-in, a three-person burglary team can complete their "duty" in five minutes. Police rarely arrive at the scene in less than 15 minutes. Thus, only rarely does a police officer confront and arrest a burglar as a result of alarm activation.

Response to alarms is a frustrating experience for a college-educated officer who is trained to deal with security incidents. On the other hand, private response forces will reach the scene in a shorter time period with a greater chance of interrupting the burglary. Police then will respond with high priority to the private response call. Accordingly, private responders may well apprehend more burglars because of the more timely response. The performance of Fetzer Protection Services Inc. of Philadelphia in apprehending suspected burglars shows the possible benefits in this area. Further, since the trend is to reduce the number of free responses and require a fee for false activation, substituting private firms for public response may be less expensive.

Wages of even well-trained private guards are substantially lower than those of the police. For example, the median 1992 wages of skilled private security officers were $23,192 compared to $32,000 for police officers. Since most of the cost of responding to alarms is wages, substantial savings, on the order of 25 percent, could be achieved through the substitution of private responders for the police. Private provision means that competition may start in the alarm response service. Reduced priority of response and increased response time by police, higher fees for false activations, the reduced number of free responses, and the suspension of response for repeat activators are all factors that make private response more attractive to alarm owners. Entry of such providers introduces competition into the response service. The result is lower costs and fees, and better service than the "traditional" monopolistic police service.

Competition will result in two ways: First, several providers could be allowed to serve the same geographical area. Second, the municipality may provide a franchise for a limited time period to a company that wins a bid. It might seem a little strange to talk about competition in alarm response when few firms have as yet entered the industry. However, given the declining reliability of police response and the worsening for alarm owners of ordinance provisions, it is quite likely that private response will turn out to be a profitable venture.

The question is not whether alarm owners will have to pay for the costs they cause by false alarms. Rather the question is to whom—the police or a private company—and in what form— fees, fines, or no response—will the payments be made. It is important to recognize that private response may be both less expensive and superior to public response. Indeed it is likely that in some localities private responders and the police could compete for the business of responding to alarms.

The Quality and Training of Private Responders

Successful private response requires well-trained officers. The case reports show that firms have been able to attract such skilled personnel, usually off-duty or retired police officers from adjacent communities. Insurance expenses are not an overwhelming obstacle, even in the case of armed officers, provided that their training and quality are good. The interviews suggest that armed officers are indeed required for effective response to alarms. State licensing of private security agents may be helpful in raising standards. Licensing may also help attain greater status and recognition for private security officers. For example, licensing may help facilitate private security personnel's being able to go through red lights in emergency response situations. Licensing, however, often raises entry barriers unnecessarily, to the detriment of consumers. This occurs because the interested group gains control over licensing and uses that control to restrict entry, which raises prices and the income of the group.

A possibly better solution is certification, which means that an industry group examines the qualifications of applicants and certifies that certain applicants meet the standards.[10] Certification is used in such occupations as accounting, medicine, and automobile repair. Certification does not prevent other individuals from working in the industry but simply indicates that they do not meet the requirements of the industry for certification. In the case of private responders to alarms, firms are likely to want to hire individuals who are certified because that would probably mean lower liability insurance premiums and greater consumer acceptance. For example, automobile repair companies advertise the use of certified mechanics. The industry should consider the establishment of certifications, which would raise quality and status, and probably reduce liability insurance premiums, yet would not have the adverse consequences of licensure.

In general, we recommend maintaining power in the private market via certification instead of the unnecessary government control of licensing. Consumers will eventually recognize the merit of using companies that employ certified responders if indeed the industry acts responsibly in its quality control. The less the government intervenes in the marketplace and the more that is left to consumers' free choice based upon experience, the higher will be the quality of response service.

Other Conclusions from the Interviews

The interviews also indicate that alarm response is often more economically provided in conjunction with patrol services, stationed guard services, and possibly vacation and medical services. The industry is thus likely to have alarm response provided by firms offering a package of complementary services. In addition, there are economies of density; namely, it is cheaper to serve subscribers with a variety of services in an area where the firm has a large number of subscribers. Further, small firms can be quite successful in providing private response. The use of highly sophisticated technology is possible, as evidenced by First Response, Inc., in Portland, Oregon. Finally, response to alarms is an activity that does not require public provision, and, indeed, the service may be provided better and cheaper by private firms.

Private response is not a general prescription for all communities. In many suburbs, elimination of police alarm response service may bring into question the need to maintain an independent police department (which is already providing the service quite efficiently). Further, the number of alarm owners may be too small to justify private operation economically. Local officials need only to assure that the pricing of response is set at average total cost. On the other hand, as the size of the city rises, response to alarms becomes more of a burden to local police, and the density of monitored alarms is great enough to justify private operation.

Some of the following conditions need to be satisfied in order for private response to exist:

1. Threshold entry requires an investment of $20,000 to $30,000, three officers, a car, and a radio system. The minimum efficient size is five cars. The service area must be sufficiently small that response is possible in 15 minutes.
2. An alarm response service needs to be packaged with other security or miscellaneous services in order to be profitable. Such services include patrol, on-site guards, and detection. Overseas, private response is often packaged along with medical alert and other emergency and miscellaneous services. These include feeding pets, picking up the mail, and turning lights on/off.
3. Local ordinances or police practices should allow for priority response in case of a private response service dispatching a bona fide activation.
4. Private response usually succeeds in affluent neighborhoods or commercial districts where valuable merchandise is involved and insurance companies require UL certification or the like.

POLICY ALTERNATIVES

The Public Option:

1. Set Prices at Average Total Cost

   If police response is to be retained, then the police must be sure that they charge the average total cost for alarm response. The average total cost is the total cost of responding to alarms (including wages and benefits for officers, covering their response and paperwork time; the pay for the dispatchers who call the police; equipment and automobile costs; and normal profits) divided by the total number of false activations. This fee should be charged to the alarm user for all false responses. There is no reason or justification to stop responding for multiple activations through the year. The fee should not go up for additional responses unless the cost of response indeed rises. We calculated the response cost and the appropriate fee in Philadelphia to be $36 for 10 years starting in 1995. We also calculated an annual registration fee of $18 to compensate the Bureau of Administrative Adjudication for managing the alarm registration database, the collection of fees, and the court expenses.

2. Shifting Responsibility to Alarm Companies

   A city should consider shifting as much of the burden of false alarms as possible onto the alarm companies. Many police departments complain that the alarm companies are making a profit from a service the police provide. This claim is at least partially supported by the fact that alarm companies become very upset when large city police departments talk about no longer responding to alarms.[11]

   A possible way to share the false alarm burden is to have the police continue to respond to alarms, but to shift the burden of collection of false alarm fines from the police department to the alarm companies. The alarm companies always have the correct addresses and are in a contractual relationship with the alarm owners. The contract should specify that the alarm owner is obligated to reimburse the alarm dealer for false alarm response fees. The police should charge the dealers, who would then bill the end users for the false alarms. This requires modification of existing practices in that the name of the dealer would appear in a special field in the message and in the central station dispatches to the police. The police can more easily work with a relatively small number of alarm dealers than the large number of alarm owners. In case of nonpayment, service can be discontinued by the dealer. The city could also maintain the power to enforce action against alarm owners for nonpayment while using the dealer only as an agent to collect the fees.

Another possibility would be to have the central stations collect the response fees. The central stations are few in number, so administrative costs would be low, but central stations often do not enjoy a contractual relationship with the end users. In any case, the ultimate financial responsibility rests with the alarm owners, who can contest their fees similarly to contesting a parking violation.

3. Eliminate Free False Alarms

    The first step to shifting the burden to the alarm companies is to eliminate all free false alarms. Police response to false alarms should not be viewed as a free good by either the alarm owners or the alarm companies. Now it would be a service provided only to the activators; no one else enjoys the benefits. Currently, however, all taxpayers bear the cost of response to false activations, which is, by all means, a private service, and as such should be entirely paid by the false activator.

    If the police are going to respond to alarms, then response should be treated as a chargeable private service. When an alarm company signs up an alarm customer to have a monitored alarm, the company should be required to inform the customer that by signing up for the monitored account, he/she is agreeing to receive a private service from the police, for which a response fee will be charged, in the event that the alarm is activated. Alternatively, a separate response contract can be negotiated between the dealer and the alarm owner, which sets down the response procedure. In any case, the customer should also be informed that the police will waive the fee if the activation is valid.

4. Register All Alarm Companies

    The next step is for a city to register all alarm companies. It is much simpler to register the relatively small number of alarm companies that operate in a city than to try to register the tens of thousands of alarm owners in the city. All alarm companies would be required to be licensed, and they would all get a registration number. An activation that does not bear a registration number may not receive police response. There need not be any requirements for obtaining a license. The purpose of the license is to make sure the city knows the companies with which it is dealing and can contact them when information is needed about an alarm owner. The license fee or application process should not be so onerous as to deter companies from entering the alarm installation or monitoring field. A small one-time fee should cover administrative costs for processing the license application. However, as in Milwaukee, a failure to register should result in fining the appropriate dealer

5. Have Alarm Companies Collect Fines

    When a monitoring company calls in an alarm, it should be required to give the name of the alarm owner, the address of the alarm, and the permit number of the alarm company. The city would then keep a record of all the alarm calls by each alarm company, and by name and address of the alarm. Every month, the police would send a printout to all of the alarm companies showing their customers who had false alarms, how many, and the total amount owed by the alarm companies for the police response to those alarms.

The amount that the alarm companies would be charged for police response would be a set fee that, ideally, would be equal to the fully loaded cost of response, times the number of false alarms to which the police responded. Alternatively, each registered dealer would be able to connect to the city's computer system and download its own customers' activations. Presumably, the alarm companies would collect this money from their customers. However, it would be the responsibility of the alarm companies to pay the police. The process is not unique to alarms, but rather similar to the imposition of sales tax, where merchants collect the taxes for the government.

If an alarm company's customer refused to pay the fine, it could discontinue monitoring and also place the customer on a list of delinquent alarm owners so that the customer could not receive monitoring service from another monitoring facility. This list could be disseminated by the city. This shifts the entire burden of collecting fines to the alarm companies from the police departments, with the exception of the minimal amount of effort necessary to send bills to the alarm companies. If a dealer refuses to pay the bill, then the police would have a reason to revoke the dealer's right to operate in the city. The city may choose, however, to maintain the collection responsibility and take enforcement action to collect the fees from the end users in a manner similar to the collection of parking ticket fines.

The monitoring company can be the agent or the party responsible for the collection of the fees for false activations. The name of the monitoring company is part of the message sent to the police and thus the message format requires no changes. Further, there is a smaller number of monitoring companies than dealers, which makes the city's administrative efforts easier.

If alarm or monitoring companies collect the fees for false activations, they may choose to offer service contracts to alarm owners. A service contract could include a number of free responses to false activations for which the customer pays a set annual "premium." Such a policy could specify provisions for technical failure of the system and/or a specified number of user's errors. The service contract could incorporate prices set according to the extent of the services provided.

This form of service contract is similar to others offered for business and home appliances and equipment. The service contracts for alarm equipment should incorporate the same business practices as contracts for similar systems such as heating services.

Advantages of the proposed method for curbing false alarms:

1. The city will not be required to maintain a costly database, either of all alarm owners or of alarm activations by alarm owners. The city would have to maintain only a small database listing alarm or monitoring companies, which could be easily stored and accessed using the companies' license numbers. The city would have to maintain information only about unpaid fees. There would be no problem with address mismatches because all of the information would be stored under the company's license number, along with the customer's name and address. The police could just have the computer print up all names and addresses with the false alarms from each company, or these data could be downloaded at any time by the alarm/monitoring company. Even if an address were not input exactly the same way every time, the alarm company would still have enough information to send a bill to the customer responsible for the false activation.

2. Under this system the costs of response to false activations are borne by the activators instead of the uninvolved taxpayers. Further, the responsibility of collecting false alarm fees is shifted to the alarm-monitoring companies who enjoy the monthly fees. The police will still be providing a service, but they will be able to cover their costs. The police are now expending much of their resources on false alarm response. With false alarms now paying for themselves through those using the service, the police will be free to expend the resources they were previously using to answer false alarms on services of a public nature. This suggested shift of responsibility is termed *user fees* and is expanding in a variety of government services. Wherever the beneficiaries of the service are few and can be easily identified, direct payments as suggested above are frequently implemented in the public sector. This is a non-punitive means of requiring those who benefit from a quasi-private service to pay for that service.

3. This system is simple compared to a full-blown false alarm reduction program. For example, Multnomah County, Oregon (Portland), has what is widely acknowledged to be a successful false alarm program. It has managed to cut false alarms down to .48 per system per year, which is well below the national average. However, in order to do this, all alarm systems must be registered, which requires database maintenance; a false alarm unit that employs nine; radio and TV ads for community education; and also community education classes taught by members of the police alarm unit. This involves an enormous commitment of resources by the police. Utilizing our suggested approach, once the database is set up, it might require only one person to run the whole operation. For example, the ex-director of the alarm unit in Milwaukee claims that using advanced software and a similar process to our suggested one

enables one half-time person to handle the entire operation. The city would not need to run commercials or hold classes to reduce false alarms, because it would not be losing any money from false alarms. On the other hand, alarm and/or monitoring companies would have a strong "built-in" incentive to reduce the number of false alarms. Every time an alarm company has to bill a customer for a false alarm, it will incur administrative costs. Also, false alarms often are caused by equipment malfunction.[12]

Many companies will absorb some of these fees. An alarm customer will not be very pleased to receive a bill from an alarm company for a false alarm caused by shoddy equipment installed by that alarm company. Also, it is quite possible that customers will start holding alarm companies responsible for false alarms when they no longer receive a fine in a city envelope but a false alarm fee from their alarm company. All of the above will prompt alarm companies to install higher-quality equipment, and also to better educate their customers in how to use their alarms. One further benefit will be that some of the sales will be directed away from competitive dealers who simply offer the lowest price to dealers who provide quality equipment and strive to reduce the number of false alarms that their customers have.

4. There is no reason why there cannot be both private and public response to false alarms. As stated earlier, the tightening of ordinances and the diminished quality of police response will attract private companies to this market. If the police charge for false alarms and an alarm company feels that it can provide the service at a lower cost than the police and still make a profit, then it is likely that that company will offer its own private response service. However, this will happen only if the police charge a fee that recoups all costs for every false alarm. If the police do not charge for every false alarm, or if they charge a fee that does not recoup all costs, then there will be little or no incentive for

private response services. However, if the police do charge the fully loaded cost for all false activations, then it is likely that private response will develop. Police will charge a monopolistic price that may attract private contractors to offer the service at lower prices. For example, in September 1996 Toronto police began to respond to only four activations in a year and charged 75 Canadian dollars for each activation. The police, however, continued to respond to actual break-ins reported by a private security company. The pricing of police response led to an immediate increase in the private response business.

If the police do not respond to alarms at all, the demand for private response will rise along with a significant decline in the purchase of new systems. This reduced demand is expected mainly in the middle-income portion of the residential market. The mass marketing companies are apt to lose the most in such an event. The only factor that may inhibit private response under these circumstances is if the public values police response more than private response to the point where the public will be willing to pay the higher price for police response, eliminating the demand for private response. Such an outcome is unlikely based upon experiences in other places.

The Private Option:

In order to minimize the burden of false alarms on police departments, the current trend is to shift responsibility for responding to alarms from the police department to private response companies. Under the current system that is used in most cities, a sworn officer responds to every false alarm call and must fill out a report detailing the event. In Philadelphia, for example, officers respond to 3,000 false alarms per week. This represents a tremendous commitment of resources for the department; at least 10 percent of the police officers are devoted to alarm response. Private armed response should be seriously considered by the security industry. There are two ways to initiate private response: competitive and franchised.

Competitive Private Response:
Competitive private response is the desired form of private response. With competitive private response, each company would either hire its own private response teams, or more likely, would contract with companies that provide private response. These companies would have various schedules of charges, varying from a fixed amount per subscriber to a charge for each response. Alarm owners could be offered pricing plans including a certain number of responses for a specified monthly fee, or a fee for each response. If a situation at the premises needed a police response, they could get a priority dispatch.

With private response to activations, there would be no false alarm "problem," because the response teams would be getting paid for, and making a profit on, each response. The police would retain the responsibility for apprehending burglars and providing support for their incarceration. Most likely, response companies will have contracts with more than one alarm company or directly with alarm owners, covering an area with sufficient alarm density to make possible profitable operation. There are few, if any, economies of scale in alarm response, so a competitive environment is likely to exist. Las Vegas is the first city to legislate no police response unless a private response unit is at the site. Many other major cities, including New York, Chicago, and Los Angeles, have sufficiently delayed police response that it can be construed as no effective response.

Franchised Private Response:
If competitive response is tried and is found to be undesirable, then an alternative is to franchise private response. A system of private response districts could be set up that is similar to cable TV franchises. The city could be divided into districts, and private response companies could bid to serve all interested subscribers in each district in the city. The companies would answer all alarm calls from all monitoring companies in their district. Alarm owners would not be required to contract with a private response company. However, police will either not respond to direct dispatching from central stations or will respond at low priority. Alternatively, police

may set higher fees for response to discourage direct dispatching. The companies should have time-limited contracts, with bidding for each district every few years. This will help to keep the prices for the companies' services at a competitive level since the price that will be charged will be part of the bid. Although the franchisee will have a monopoly on the district for the period of the contract, it has to provide high-quality service and competitive prices in order to be able to bid at the conclusion of the contract.

The response company will serve all subscribers in their district. The set fee for response will be part of the bidding process, and will be specified in its contract. It will be up to the response company to respond to all central stations' dispatching calls. In the case of a real event detected at the scene, the response company will be able to get priority dispatching of the police.

Advantages of Private Response:

To reiterate, if police maintain the alarm response, the price is higher than under a nonregulated market where private response exists. There are two reasons for this:

First, police are in effect a monopoly and have no incentive to be as efficient as a competitive response business will be. Alarm ordinances often set fees at higher than cost to punish repeat activators. In fact, the police chief can, at his discretion, stop or change the priority of a response. As long as one of the three following conditions exists, a monopoly power persists: three free responses a year, response fees that are set below the level of the competitive market, and reasonable police response time. Under these conditions, there is little chance for private response to emerge.

Second, from a cost viewpoint, wages of trained police officers are 25 to 33 percent higher than those of well-trained guards. Fringe benefit differences are even higher.

Fees in a nonregulated competitive environment, where police response does not enjoy legislative advantage, will be significantly lower. The community will not need to subsidize property owners who use the alarm system less than three times a year. In many local jurisdictions, fines for additional activations over a year escalate rapidly even though actual cost per response remains constant. Thus, in a competitive environment, repeat activators will also benefit from private response. In addition, employment and business opportunities will be created in the community.

Indeed, as the previous discussion suggests, private response companies have been successful in achieving lower fees and response time than the police. Not surprisingly, private response has been successful in large cities where the problem is particularly acute and where response time is excessive. Lower fees combined with quicker service on the part of private response companies could encourage more people to acquire alarms, raising the level of perceived security and reducing the number of burglaries. Thus, the alarm industry in the long run will be better off with private response

Another advantage of the shift to private response is that police officers are better trained than private guards to deal with crisis situations and are frustrated with frequent false alarm response. Further, in case of an actual break-in, the officer who often responds to false activations is psychologically unprepared in the rare case of a burglary in progress, leading to serious and, in some cases, catastrophic consequences.

CONCLUSIONS

Response to false alarms occupies 10 to 30 percent of officers' time and is estimated to occupy the equivalent of 120,000 officers nationwide. If the problem persists, police in many major cities will either stop responding to alarms or response time will rise. Either of these effects will reduce the effectiveness of alarms and adversely affect their sales.

Efforts to reduce false activations by the police and the industry have produced moderate results, especially given the rapid increase in alarm installations, resulting from mass marketing efforts by several companies. This chapter offered an easily applied model, involving little administrative effort, that relies on both economic theory and the evaluation of alarm reduction programs in some large cities.

The recommended model has the following features: There would be no registration of alarms and no annual registration fees. Citations for false activations would be sent to the address dispatched by the central station and would be handled like traffic tickets. There would be no escalating fees for repeat activators and no ceasing of response. Fees for false activations would approximate average cost and would stay constant unless marginal cost rises. Dealers would be responsible for paying the fees for false response and could turn to their subscribers for reimbursement. This chapter also describes the merits of private response and the imminent replacement of public with private response.

REFERENCES

Central Station Alarm Association. 1994. *1992-1993 False Alarm Committee Report.* Bethesda, MD.

Hakim, S., and Mary Ann Gaffney. 1994. *Commercial Security.* Washington, DC: Security Industry Assoc.

"IACP Convention Receptive to Model Cities Presentation." *Security News.* January 1996.

Shanahan, Michael J. 1995. "Surviving the Policing Paradigm Shift." *Baretta USA Leadership Bulletin.* April.

NOTES

1. Usually, the police department is the only "company" that responds to false activations. Thus, as a monopoly its price may be higher than what it would have been had there been many companies providing the service. Economic theory suggests that the fee should reflect normal cost, including normal profit, which would have existed under competitive market conditions.
2. We assume that officers are providing security services to the community, which they must abandon when responding to activations. Further, the benefit of their services to the community is at least equal to their income.

3. See, for example, S. Hakim and Mary Ann Gaffney, *Commercial Security* (Washington, DC: Security Industry Assoc., 1994): Chapter 5.
4. Data include calls on robberies and burglaries for the nine police divisions of the city. Accuracy and consistency of data were examined by comparison with data on alarm activations for 11 months in 1994.
5. Average annual salary of a patrol officer is $36,385. Fringe benefits are $25,314. The total including fringe benefits is $61,699. In order to calculate the per hour cost of an officer we used 230 working days, 8 hours of work per day, resulting in per hour cost of $33.53. Multiplying by the average response time of 16.82 yields two officers' costs per response of $18.80.
6. A sergeant accompanies the response team in approximately 1 of 15 alarm response cases, or in 10,120 cases. Average annual salary for a sergeant is $41,075. Fringe benefits are $27,391. The total including fringe benefits is $68,466. A sergeant works 225 days per year, 8 hours a day. Thus, per hour salary is $38.04. Average response time is 16.82 minutes, which yields 170,213 minutes, or a total cost of $107,915; 151,795 alarms are responded to per year, which yields an added cost for sergeant time per false activation of $0.71.
7. Total cost of alarm-related driving is $182,192. Dividing by 151,795 alarm-related annual calls yields a driving cost of $1.20 per response, or four miles average driving per response.
8. Cost of property and personal losses due to accidents are calculated, based upon national data derived from the *Statistical Abstract of the U.S., 1994*. Total property damage was $38.1 billion for 10 million cars, which yields an average cost of $3,810. The Philadelphia P.D. reported 290 civilian and police injuries, or 15.225 alarm-related injuries for 1994. National data show that the average economic loss per person from injury is $18,016. Thus, the average cost of injury per alarm response is $1.81.
9. The total cost of the police dispatching center is multiplied by the share of alarm-related costs of 5.25 percent and divided by the number of false alarm calls of 151,795, yielding an average cost of $4.68.
10. See, for example, Jim Mundy, "Certification," *Security Line* (July 1995): p. 8.
11. For a discussion of the shift to private response in Canada, see Paul A. Hallam, "Visions of the Future," *Canadian Security* (November/December 1995): p. 35.
12. According to a survey of eight central stations by the Central Station Alarm Association in 1992, 10 percent of false alarms are attributable to system malfunction.

10

Legal Issues[*]

ALARM COMPANIES AND THEIR EXPOSURE TO LIABILITY

As the ability of law enforcement agencies to respond to requests for assistance becomes more limited, individuals and businesses are increasingly contracting with private entities such as alarm companies, private patrols, and guard services to provide for their security needs. The obligation of these private security services to respond and their duties to their customers and others once they have responded have become increasingly important issues. This chapter will address some of the legal issues that arise regarding the relationship between a private security service and its customers.

---

[*] This chapter was written by Lessing E. Gold, Stephen D. Marks, and Joshua L. Rosen of the firm of Mitchell, Silberberg and Knupp in Los Angeles, California. Some editing was done by the authors of the book.

Of course an alarm system alone can only detect and warn of an intrusion; it cannot prevent it. Nonetheless, such systems in general provide early detection of possible intrusion far superior to any that can possibly be provided by law enforcement authorities. While in the majority of cases, a customer relies on the law enforcement authorities to respond once an alarm signal is received, in many cases, customers have alarm systems that are monitored by a guard service or private patrol response team. These private guards are generally capable of responding to emergencies far more quickly than overburdened law enforcement agencies. However, private security services are not protected by the same legal immunities enjoyed by governmental agencies. Generally, governments are protected from liability with regard to the provision of police and fire-fighting services pursuant to the doctrine of sovereign immunity. For example, California Government Code Section 845 provides:

> Neither a public entity nor a public employee is liable for failure to establish a police department or otherwise provide police protection service or, if police protection service is provided, for failure to provide sufficient police protection service.

California Government Code Section 846 provides:

> Neither a public entity nor a public employee is liable for injury caused by the failure to make an arrest or by the failure to retain an arrest of a person in custody.

Thus, under the sovereign immunity doctrine, governmental agencies and their employees will generally not be liable for failure to provide police and fire services, or for negligently providing such services (see, *Antique Arts Corp. v. City of Torrance*, 39 Cal. App. 3d 588 [1974]). However, because private security companies do not enjoy these immunities, their potential liability is theoretically unlimited.

Although on rare occasions the relationship between a private security company and its subscriber is based on an oral agreement, in virtually every instance, the relationship is governed by a written contract. As a matter of practical reality, written contracts are in fact mandated, because state and local consumer protection laws and/or insurance companies issuing errors and omissions coverage to private security companies require that the relationship with a subscriber be governed by a written agreement. Further, because without a written contract the potential liability of private security companies is enormous, a written contract clearly stating the obligations of the alarm company and limiting its potential liability is a business necessity. To do business in the private security industry without a written contract that limits the liability of the security company to an agreed-upon sum, or relieves it of liability entirely, is to invite disaster. Only the most foolhardy businessperson would agree to provide alarm protection for a relatively nominal rate, entirely unrelated to the value of the customer's property, when the customer's premises could hold property valued at $100 or millions of dollars, a factor over which the security company has no control. Therefore, a written contract is fundamental to the legal relationship between a private security company and its customers.

Because burglar and fire alarms act as detection devices and cannot in and of themselves prevent burglaries or fires, because of the perceived increasing crime rate, and because the criminal mind can find a way to circumvent even the most sophisticated system, some customers will suffer burglary and fire losses notwithstanding the detection and deterrence capabilities offered by an alarm system. When such losses occur, the customer and/or the customer's insurer often seek to hold the alarm company liable for such losses, asserting a variety of claims, including breach of contract, breach of warranty, negligence, strict liability, and fraud. The alarm industry has dealt with such claims almost since the invention of the alarm system. While a few courts have taken iconoclastic views, the vast majority of both state and federal courts addressing these issues have agreed on the general parameters of alarm company liability. Although the reasoning of these courts may differ, the result is generally the same. See, for example, *Better Food Markets v. American District Telegraph* 40 Cal. 2d 179 (1953); *Schreier v. Beltway Alarm Co.*, 533 A.2d 1316 (Md. 1987); *First Financial Ins. Co. v. Purolator Security, Inc.*, 388 N.E.2d 17 (Ill. 1979); *E. H. Ashley & Co., Inc. v. Wells Fargo Alarm Services*, 907 F.2d 1274 (1st Cir. 1990).

An analysis of alarm company liability must begin with the duties owed by the company to its subscribers. Although the terms of any written contract between parties will likely override the theoretical common-law duties owed by the company, an examination of the relationship between the company and its subscribers in the absence of a written contract provides a helpful starting point.

The liability of the company to its subscribers in the absence of a contract depends to some degree on whether or not the alleged wrongful act of the alarm company falls into the category of "nonfeasance" or "misfeasance." The former category can generally be described as the failure to act, while the latter can generally be described as acting in an improper manner. In most instances, the claims of subscribers against an alarm company will fall into the category of nonfeasance, that is, the failure of the alarm to send a signal upon an intrusion, or the failure of the company to respond to the alarm signal. Under classical tort theory, an individual or company is only liable for acts of "nonfeasance" if an affirmative duty to act existed. Generally speaking, an affirmative duty to act exists only when there is a "special relationship" between the parties, for example, if one party acts in a fiduciary capacity to another. If no "special relationship" exists, classical tort analysis concludes that an individual or company is not liable for acts of nonfeasance, and no liability will attach unless the individual or company commits acts of misfeasance, that is, is actively careless.

A good example illustrating the presence or absence of a "special relationship," the difference between misfeasance and nonfeasance, and the liability that would attach to each, depending on the presence or absence of a special relationship, is the doctor/patient relationship. If a patient comes to see the doctor in his or her office, a special relationship will be held to exist under which the doctor owes affirmative duties to the patient, and the doctor is potentially liable to the patient for both acts of nonfeasance (doing nothing) and misfeasance (acting carelessly). On the other hand, if a doctor drives by the scene of an accident involving injuries, no special relationship will exist between the doctor and the injured persons. The doctor has no duty to stop and provide treatment to the injured parties, and he or she cannot be held liable for failing to stop and provide treatment. However, if the doctor stops and provides treatment, and does so in a careless manner, this would constitute misfeasance, for which the doctor would be liable.

Since an alarm company's relationship with its customer is an ordinary commercial relationship, it has generally been held that there is no "special relationship" between the alarm company and a customer giving rise to an affirmative obligation to act, without a duty provided for in a contract.[1] The courts have also held that a contract for alarm services is not a contract for an essential or "public" service such as medical, legal, or housing services, such that an affirmative duty would be imposed on the alarm company, without assumption of that duty in a contract.

ALARM CONTRACTS SHOULD SPECIFY LIABILITY

As noted above, in the vast majority of cases, the relationship between an alarm company and its subscriber is based on a written contract between the parties. Where there is a written contract, general tort principles regarding duties and negligence do not apply, but rather the terms of the contract are the exclusive measure of the alarm company's duty. As the California Supreme Court stated in *Better Food Markets v. American District Telegraph Co.*, 40 Cal. 2d 179 (1953), the seminal case in the United States in the area of alarm company liability:

> Although an action in tort may sometimes be brought for the negligent breach of contractual duty, still the nature of the duty owed

and the consequences of its breach must be determined by reference to the contract which created that duty...

Thus, a carefully drafted contract will explicitly set forth the duty of the alarm company with regard to service, maintenance, and repair of the system, and with regard to the company's monitoring and response obligations. The contract should set forth those duties narrowly and with particularity, and should explicitly state that the alarm company is assuming no duties and makes no warranties and representations other than those specifically set forth in the contract. The contract should also make it clear that the alarm company makes no warranty that the type of system purchased is necessarily the best available for the customer's particular security needs and assumes no ongoing obligation to advise the customer of new technology that would provide the customer with a greater level of security.

The contract should include affirmative statements that the company is not an insurer, that the fee paid for the alarm system or service is solely related to the value of the system or the service and not the value of the subscriber's property, that given the relatively small amount of consideration paid by the customer, far less than insurance premiums and totally unrelated to the value of the customer's property, the alarm company is not assuming liability to indemnify the subscriber for burglary or fire losses, and that the customer's remedy is limited to a return of the fee paid to the alarm company. The contract should also contain clauses exculpating the company for any burglary or fire losses suffered by the customer and liquidating or limiting the amount of any liability that does exist. It should also contain third-party indemnity provisions, providing that the customer is responsible for, and will hold the company harmless against, any liability for personal injury and property losses suffered by third parties.

These clauses, taken separately and together, will properly limit both the duties of the alarm company and its potential exposure for an alleged breach of those duties, and should protect the alarm company from exposure to liability far in excess of that contemplated by the parties at the time of execution of the contract, and entirely out of proportion to the compensation received by the alarm company.

Although the legal issues relating to these contract clauses will be discussed in greater detail later, the reader should be familiar with the meaning and effect of some of the types of clauses commonly found in alarm company contracts.

EXCULPATORY OR ASSUMPTION OF RISK CLAUSE

An exculpatory or assumption of risk clause relieves a party, generally the party that is rendering performance or providing a good or service (the "performing party"), from liability to the other party, generally the party who is paying for and receiving the good or service (the "receiving party"), for any act of negligence or breach of contract by the performing party. In other words, the receiving party is assuming the risk that would ordinarily fall on the performing party of any loss that results from the performing party's failure to properly perform. Such clauses are often found in contracts for recreational activities such as skydiving or river rafting, but are also found in commercial contracts. The courts have generally found that such clauses should be enforced as long as the contract clearly informs the signer of the effect of signing the document, and unless enforcement of the clause would defeat the reasonable expectations of the parties under the circumstances. See *Paralift, Inc. v. Superior Court*, 23 Cal. App. 4th 748 (4th Dist. 1993). Courts have refused to enforce such clauses only where the service involved is an essential or "public" service that must necessarily be used by members of the public, since the purveyors of such services necessarily have a decisive advantage in bargaining strength. In such circumstances, the consumer is left with a Hobson's choice—sign the contract, regardless of the terms, or forgo the service. Therefore, the courts have refused to leave the public at the mercy of the purveyors of such services and have refused to enforce exculpatory clauses in such contracts. See *Tunkl v. Regents of University of California*, 60 Cal. 2d 92, 101 (1963).

LIQUIDATED DAMAGE CLAUSES

A liquidated damages clause is a contract provision pursuant to which the parties agree in advance to the precise amount of damages that will be paid if the contract is breached. Courts will enforce such clauses where, under the circumstances involved, it would be impracticable or extremely difficult to fix the actual damage suffered, and the amount stated represents a reasonable endeavor by the parties to estimate the probable damage that would result from a breach. In the event of a breach, the injured party need only prove the fact of the other party's liability, not the amount of damage, since the injured party will recover the amount stated in the contract regardless of whether the actual loss suffered is more or less than the amount stated.

LIMITATION OF LIABILITY CLAUSE

Limitation of liability clauses are akin to exculpatory clauses, but rather than entirely relieving the performing party from liability, they set a maximum amount of damages for which the performing party will be liable in the event of a breach. These provisions can be distinguished from a liquidated damages clause in several ways. First, the courts do not require that the actual damage be difficult to estimate in order to enforce a limitation of liability clause. Second, there is no requirement that the amount stated in the contract represent a reasonable endeavor by the parties to estimate the amount of the actual damages, or that the amount stated bear any relationship whatever to the actual damages suffered. Third, a limitation of liability clause does not fix the amount of damages as does a liquidated damages clause. Rather it merely sets a ceiling on damages. If the amount of actual damages is less than the amount stated in the contract, recovery will be limited to the amount of the actual damages. If the amount of actual damages is greater than the amount stated in the contract, the nonbreaching party will recover the amount stated in the contract.

THIRD-PARTY INDEMNIFICATION CLAUSE

A third-party indemnification provision provides that if a nonparty to the contract makes a claim against one of the contracting parties for losses suffered as a result of an alleged breach of contract, the nonbreaching party will indemnify the breaching party for any liability for such claims. The rationale for enforcement of such clauses is that generally the third party will have some relationship to the nonbreaching party (that is, a customer, a guest, or a tenant for example), and thus potential injury to the third party will be foreseeable to the nonbreaching party, who can take necessary action to prevent against it, while the existence of and the risk of injury to the third party is not foreseeable to the breaching party, who is thus incapable of protecting or insuring against it.

JUDICIAL DECISIONS

As noted above, liquidated damages/limitation of liability/exculpation clauses found in most alarm contracts have been subject to innumerable attacks on a variety of grounds, and are the subject of hundreds of published decisions regarding this issue, coming from the courts of virtually every state. These clauses have been challenged on virtually every ground imaginable, including, but not limited to, the relationship between the amount stated in the contract and the actual damages; the reasonableness of exculpating the alarm company or liquidating or limiting damages in alarm contracts, particularly since the clauses are generally contained in preprinted contracts prepared by the alarm company; whether the clause applies to the particular alleged wrong committed by the alarm company; and whether the subscriber is bound by the clause if the subscriber failed to read the contract. While the reasoning may differ, virtually every court that has faced this issue has upheld the validity of clauses in alarm contracts that exculpate the alarm company from liability, shift the risk of loss to the subscriber, or limit or liquidate the subscriber's damages.

Some jurisdictions, including California, uphold these clauses as liquidated damages clauses. These courts have reasoned that given the inherent uncertainties as to the types of losses that might result upon a breach of the contract (i.e., the variety of possible consequences of the alarm company's failure to perform, the amount of the loss, and what portion of the loss, if any, could have been avoided had the alarm company performed properly) there was no reasonable basis on which the parties could have predicted the nature and extent of any loss that might result from the alarm company's failure to perform, and that therefore, "it was impracticable or extremely difficult to fix the amount of actual damage," and that the amount stated in the contract represented a reasonable endeavor by the parties to estimate the damage. See *Better Food Markets v. American District Telegraph Co.*, 40 Cal. 2d 179 (1953).

The majority of jurisdictions have analyzed these clauses as exculpatory/limitation of liability clauses rather than as liquidated damages clauses, and they have been universally upheld as such. The courts have universally rejected the argument that alarm services were "essential services" or "public services" so as to require invalidation of such clauses in the alarm context as contrary to the public interest. See, for example, *Schreier v. Beltway Alarm Co.*, 533 A.2d 1316, 1323 (Md. 1987); *First Financial Ins. Co. v. Purolator Security, Inc.*, 388 N.E.2d 17 (Ill. 1979); *Wedner v. Fidelity Security Systems, Inc.*, 307 A.2d 429, 432 (Pa. 1973).

Numerous cases have upheld provisions that totally exculpate the alarm company from any liability. See, for example, *Steiner Corp. v. American District Telegraph Co.*, 683 P.2d 435, 439 (Idaho 1984); *Pick Fisheries v. Burns Electronic Security Services, Inc.*,

342 N.E.2d 105 (Ill. 1976); *Shaer Shoe Corp. v. Granite State Alarm Co.*, 262 A.2d 285 (N.H. 1970); *L. Luria & Sons, Inc. v. Alarmtec International Corp.*, 384 So. 2d 947 (Fla. 1980); *West Side Loan Office v. Electro-Protective Corp.*, 306 S.E.2d 686 (Ga. 1983); *Sue & Sam Mfg. Co. v. United Protective Alarm System, Inc.*, 501 N.Y.S.2d 102 (1986).

In other cases analyzing such clauses as limitation of liability/exculpatory clauses, the courts have enforced the clause to limit the subscriber's damages to the small amount stated in the contract, rather than to completely exculpate the alarm company, either because the contract did not contain language completely exculpating the alarm company, or because the alarm company, for the sake of judicial efficiency, conceded liability up to the amount stated in the contract. See, for example, *Rollins, Inc. v. Heller, 454 So. 2d 580* (Fla. 1984); *General Bargain Center v. American Alarm Co.*, 430 N.E.2d 407 (Ind. 1982). The cases upholding these clauses as limitation of liability or exculpatory clauses have done so even though the contract generally refers to them as liquidated damages provisions, finding that the label placed on the provision by the parties is not determinative.

Many of these courts have found that clauses limiting or exculpating the alarm company from liability for a burglary or fire are valid and reasonable because the alarm company is not an insurer, and it contracts to provide an alarm system, not to insure the physical security of the premises. See, for example, *St. Paul Fire & Marine Ins. Co. v. Guardian Alarm Co.*, 320 N.W.2d 244 (Mich. 1982). These courts have uniformly found that these clauses represented an objectively reasonable risk allocation, within the expectations of the parties, given the small compensation paid to the alarm company, which is completely unrelated to the value of the subscriber's property. As the court stated in *Guthrie v. American Protection Industries*, 160 Cal. App. 3d 951 (2d Dist. 1984):

> Most persons, especially operators of business establishments, carry insurance for loss due to various types of crime. Presumptively,

insurance companies who issue such policies base their premiums on their assessment of the value of the property and the vulnerability of the premises. No reasonable person could expect that the provider of an alarm service would, for a fee unrelated to the value of the property, undertake to provide an identical type of coverage should the alarm fail to prevent a crime.

The courts have also found that the subscriber, rather than the alarm company, is in a better position to protect against the loss, since the subscriber is aware of the value of the property in its premises, while the alarm company is not; the subscriber is in a better position to obtain the appropriate amount of insurance than the alarm company, and is in a position to take appropriate additional security measures if necessary. See, for example, *E. H. Ashley & Co., Inc. v. Wells Fargo Alarm Services*, 907 F.2d 1274, 1278-80 (1st Cir. 1990); *Leon's Bakery, Inc. v. Grinnell Corp.*, 990 F.2d 44 (2d Cir. 1993); *Fireman's Fund American Ins. Cos. v. Burns Electronic Security Services, Inc.*, 417 N.E.2d 131 (Ill. 1981); *Lo Bianco v. Property Protection, Inc.*, 437 A.2d 417 (Pa. 1981).

In the face of these decisions, subscribers have attempted to attack the limitation clauses based on assertions that the contracts are adhesion contracts, that is, that the clauses are contained in preprinted form contracts, standard in the industry, and thus the subscriber had no choice but to agree to the contract language or forego the service, and thus the subscribers were in an unequal bargaining position, and the contracts violate public policy. The courts have uniformly rejected this argument. See, for example, *Continental Video v. Honeywell Protection Services*, 422 So.2d 35 (1982); *E. H. Ashley & Co., Inc.*; *St. Paul Fire & Marine*. Akin to the adhesion contract argument is the argument sometimes made that the contract language is oppressive and unconscionable because it is one-sided. The courts have universally rejected this argument. Courts have held, in general, that contract unconscionability turns not only on a "one-sided" result, but also on an absence of "justification for it." The courts have found that since a contract is largely an allocation of risks between the parties, the risk reallocation accomplished by an exculpatory/limitation of liability/assumption of risk clause can be unconscionable only if it reallocates the risks in an objectively unreasonable or unexpected manner, or if it shifts a risk to a party, the avoidance of which is either largely or solely within the control of the other party. Where the risk of loss is at least in part dependent on factors outside the control of the party who would bear the risk without the contractual provision, such clauses are not unconscionable. In the alarm context, the courts have held that the contract is not unconscionable since, given the fact that the compensation paid to the alarm company is relatively small, and far less than a theft insurance premium, a subscriber could not reasonably expect that it was purchasing the equivalent of theft insurance, and thus the clauses provide for commercially reasonable risk allocation within the reasonable expectations of the parties. See, for example, *Morgan v. Minnesota Mining & Manufacturing Co.*, 246 N.W.2d 443 (Minn. 1976); *Fretwell v. Protection Alarm Co.*, 764 P.2d 149, 152 (Okla. 1988); *Ostalkiewicz v. Guardian Alarm*, 520 A.2d 563, 565-66 (R.I. 1987); *Stefan Jewelers, Inc. v. Electro-Protective Corp.*, 288 S.E.2d 667 (Ga. 1982); *H.S. Perlin Co. v. Morse Signal Devices*, 209 Cal. App. 3d 1289 (4th Dist. 1989). The court in *Fireman's Fund American Ins. Cos. v. Burns Electronic Security Services, Inc.*, 417 N.E.2d 131 (Ill. 1981) expressed the reasoning of these cases most cogently:

> The terms of the contract belie unconscionability. The chance of a burglary and the potential loss depend not only on the quality of the alarm, but on many factors peculiar to Henry Kay and within Henry Kay's knowledge and control. For example, the type and quality of the merchandise in the store, perhaps the prime motivation for a break-in, was for Henry Kay to determine, not Burns. It is not unreasonable for Burns to feel that the jeweler was better able than itself to buy any desired amount of insurance at appropriate rates. Burns could properly insist on the exculpation clause to make sure that the risk of burglary lay on the jeweler, not Burns. It should also be noted that the product was designed to outwit the ever advancing burglary profession. The risk that the protection

provided by the alarm system would not be enough was substantial, regardless of how good the particular alarm was.

Allocating the risk to Henry Kay was thus not a bargain which no man in his senses not under delusion would make and which no fair and honest man would accept. On the contrary, the exculpation clause was a commercially sensible arrangement and the plaintiff is bound by it.

In fact, some courts have held that these clauses provide a valuable social benefit by keeping the price of alarm services affordable. See *Sommer v. United Protective Alarm System, Inc.*, 583 N.Y.S.2d 957 (1992). Courts have noted that if the clause was not enforced, the availability of reasonably priced alarm services would decline because the company's exposure would far outweigh its potential economic benefits. Indeed, the Pennsylvania court in the Lo Bianco case stated that not to enforce these clauses would represent a less, not more equitable allocation of the risks, since even if the alarm company was aware of the value of the subscriber's property at the time of the contract, the subscriber could purchase valuable additional property without the alarm company's knowledge, making it impossible for the alarm company to effectively insure against the loss. The court also stated that if the clauses were not enforced, alarm companies would be forced to charge much higher prices across the board, resulting in the cost of alarm service for the rich being subsidized by subscribers with modest property.

It should be recognized that in the cases discussed above courts have upheld liquidated damages/limitation of liability/exculpatory clauses as they relate to claims made for breach of contract or warranty and for negligence. On a few occasions, subscribers have sought to avoid the contractual provisions limiting liability by bringing actions in strict products liability. Newer contracts have dealt with this issue by expressly stating that the limitation provisions apply to actions brought on a theory of strict liability. In any event, the theory of strict product liability is inapplicable to the rendering of services, and courts have uniformly refused to apply it in the context of alarms. In addition, strict product liability only applies where the purchased product itself causes the injury. Alarm company liability cases generally do not involve this circumstance since it is not the product that causes the harm (i.e., an exploding panel) but rather the allegation that the failure of the system or of the alarm company to respond failed to prevent the burglary or fire, which was the cause of the loss. Finally, it is noteworthy that many courts have held that strict liability does not apply to merely economic loss. Although this would not be applicable to circumstances where the subscriber or others allegedly suffered personal injury as a result of the failure of service, it does apply to circumstances where the customer is making claims that relate to the loss of property.

Because the law relating to the enforceability of limitation of liability/exculpatory/liquidated damages provisions in alarm contracts between the company and its subscribers is relatively well settled, the most troublesome area for alarm companies today relates to the obligations to and potential liability to nonsignatory third parties. It is not unusual for the property of third persons to be stored on the subscriber's premises, or for subscribers to take property of third persons on consignment, and to have that property stolen or destroyed during the course of a burglary or fire.

LIABILITY TO THIRD PARTIES

In such circumstances, alarm companies in some cases have successfully argued that there is no liability to the third party because the third party is a third-party beneficiary to the contract between the company and its customer, and thus the third party is bound by the contractual clauses limiting liability. In addition, companies have successfully argued that there is no duty to the third party because the company has no duty to take affirmative steps to protect someone from harm arising out of the unlawful conduct of others, or that the company has no duty to the general public and that its duties are limited to persons with whom it has contracted. See *H.R. Moch Co., Inc. v. Rensselaer Water Company,* 247 N.Y. 160. (1928). In this regard, in the recently decided case of *North River Insurance, Co. v. Jones,* 655 N.E.2d 987 (1995), the Illinois Court of Appeal held that an alarm company's duty and the limitation of liability provisions of the contract relate to the premises protected and the property located thereon, regardless of who may have legal title to the property, and held that the limitation of liability clause in the contract applied to limit the liability of the alarm company for the theft of property from the premises, even though the owners of the property were not parties to the contract.

In most cases the alarm company has no reason to know, and indeed does not know of the subscriber's agreement to take merchandise on consignment or to otherwise have the property of others in the protected premises. Since the alarm company generally has no such knowledge, it may be argued that it has no duty to protect such property from the unlawful acts perpetrated by third parties or from fires started without the company's participation. Without a duty by the alarm company to the third-party owners, they cannot successfully make a claim against an alarm company. As a result, where there is no relationship at all between the alarm company and the third party, there is no logical reason to impose a duty on the alarm company to persons with whom it has no relationship.[2] To hold otherwise would be to enlarge the zone of liability of alarm companies to an unlimited number of people, and to cover them to an unlimited extent, liability far beyond that to which any other industry has exposure. Such an extension of the concept of duty would, to quote Justice Benjamin N. Cardozo, extend such liability to an unacceptable degree and create relationships with parties that neither party expected or desired. It would effectively make the alarm companies something that the contracts explicitly state that they are not, that is, insurers of the property of people with whom they did not, nor ever had, the opportunity to contract.[3] As a result, such third parties are in essence unforeseeable, and no duty of care is owed to them. In this regard, the alarm companies are in no different position than the water company in *H.R. Moch Co., Inc. v. Rensse-laer Water Company*. In that case the New York court held that a company that contracted to supply water to a city and its residents was not liable to plaintiffs for the damages to plaintiff's property resulting from a fire that the fire department was unable to bring under control because the water company failed, through care-lessness, to maintain adequate pressure in the water main. The court noted that imposing liability for unforeseeable harm is unlikely, therefore, to evoke greater efforts at preventing acci-dents. Similarly, in *Edwards v. Honeywell Inc.*, 50 F.3d 484 (1995), the plaintiff, the widow of a fireman killed in fighting a fire, sought compensation from the alarm company, claiming that the alarm company had failed to promptly notify the fire department of the fire, and that if it had, the fire department would have reached the fire before it got out of control. Therefore, there would have been less risk to the fire-fighters, and her husband would not have been killed. The court refused to find the alarm company liable, holding this consequence of the alarm company's negligence to be unforeseeable, and stating that the alarm company had no duty to the fire-fighter. The court held that alarm companies have no knowledge of the risk of fire in their subscriber's premises and no practical ability to reduce that risk. Alarm companies also lack the knowledge of the risk to the firemen summoned to extinguish any fire. Such risks depend not only on the characteristics of the par-ticular premises, but also on the particular techniques used by each fire department, the training and qualifications of the fire-men, and the quality of the department's leadership. The alarm company knows nothing about these matters and has no power to influence them.

In general, the courts have held that the alarm company has no common-law duty to third parties, and thus the question of whether a third-party indemnity clause in a written contract will be enforced does not often arise. However, a well-drafted contract should contain such a clause for two reasons: First, the presence of such a clause in the contract would require the subscriber to pay for the defense of any claims brought by a third party, even if the claim itself does not succeed. Second, the presence of the clause is crucial in the event that a court finds that the alarm company owes a duty to the third parties. There is a paucity of authority on the question of whether such a clause is enforceable. However, logically, it should be enforced for the same reasons that the liquidated damages/limitation of liability/exculpatory clause is enforced. The alarm company simply cannot anticipate such losses and cannot effectively act to prevent or insure against them. The alarm company's fee is not based on the value of the property on the premises; the alarm company is not acting as an insurer, and allocating the risk of third-party loss to the subscriber is a reasonable allocation of the risk in light of the circumstances.

A final question merits some discussion. Even assuming that the alarm company breached its contract or acted negligently, the question remains as to whether or not the act or omission on the part of the company was the cause of any loss. Some cases have held that the customer can never, as a matter of law, prove that the acts of the alarm company caused the loss, since the direct cause of the loss is the burglar or the fire and not the failure of the alarm company to prevent it. These cases have also held that determining whether the burglary or fire would have been prevented if the alarm had functioned, or if the company had properly responded, is a matter of pure speculation, since as one court stated: "[w]hether that would have been the result had the apparatus been in working order can never be known. It would depend upon contingencies without number, any one of which would have been sufficient to disappoint it." And, as the court stated in the *Antique Arts* case:

> Whether the immediate presence of police on the scene of a robbery could have prevented it and/or resulted in the recovery of the loot after the consummation of a robbery, or whether immediate police response to a concurrent transmission of the alert could have prevented the robbery or recovered the loot is a subject replete with speculation and conjecture. On either assumption, concurrent and aggressive police action to abort a robbery or prevent a loss could be unsuccessful and could result at best in the escape

of the robbers, but also in personal injury or death to those involved and to innocent persons in the vicinity.

Other cases have held that the subscriber is entitled to produce evidence in an attempt to establish that the loss would have been averted had the alarm company acted properly. However, these cases have set up a burden of proof that is difficult, if not impossible, for the subscriber to meet. They require the subscriber to establish at minimum: (1) how long the crime took to commit; (2) evidence of how long it would have taken for emergency response units to respond had the alarm been working and sent a signal, including specific evidence of "average response times" and "worst-case scenario times"; (3) to what extent the loss or damage would have been eliminated or lessened if the alarm system had functioned as represented. Even if the subscriber, using average response times, can establish that the police would have arrived prior to the departure of the criminals, the alarm company can still defeat the element of causation by establishing that under the circumstances at the time of the actual burglary, it would have taken the police longer to arrive.

ISSUES INVOLVED WITH PRIVATE RESPONSE

Most of this chapter has been devoted to issues relating to the liability of alarm companies. A brief consideration of the potential liability of security guard and patrol companies is also warranted.

Several issues arise with regard to the potential liability of such companies:

- The liability of such companies to their customers and third parties for nonfeasance, that is, the failure to perform.
- The liability of such companies to third parties for misfeasance, that is, acting in excess of what is reasonable under the circumstances, that is, false imprisonment and use of excessive force.

- The liability of such companies for acts of their employees that may be outside the scope of their employment.

With regard to the first issue, the liability of such companies to their customers and third parties for nonfeasance (i.e., the failure to perform), the governing principles should be the same as those discussed above with regard to alarm companies. As with alarm companies, the relationship between security guard and patrol companies and their subscribers should be governed by a written contract containing the types of limitation of liability, liquidated damages, and exculpatory language discussed in reference to alarm company contracts. Moreover, the principles discussed above in relation to alarm companies' lack of any duty to the customer to prevent a crime or other incident, the question of whether a causal relationship exists between the failure of the company to perform and the injury or loss suffered by the subscriber, and the absence of any contractual duty of any kind to third parties, appear to be fully applicable in the security guard/patrol company context. This is true in that, in the context of failure to perform, there is no meaningful distinction between the relationship between an alarm company and its customers and third parties, and the relationship between security guard/patrol companies and their customers and third parties.

However, with regard to the second issue, the liability of such companies to third parties for misfeasance (acting in excess of what is reasonable under the circumstances), patrol/security guard companies face issues not present in the alarm company context. Patrol/security guard companies are often called upon to detain or arrest third parties and to use force to do so. While governmental law enforcement authorities have the right to arrest a suspect on probable cause (a reasonable belief that a crime has been committed), private citizens generally have no right to arrest or detain other private citizens unless they actually observe the crime being committed. Further, as stated above, private entities are not protected by the doctrine of sovereign immunity. Law enforcement authorities will be immune from liability for false arrest/imprisonment, even if probable cause did not exist, as long as they acted reasonably under the circumstances. If an employee of a security guard or patrol company improperly arrests or detains a third party, the security guard or patrol company is potentially liable to the third party for false arrest or imprisonment (and also possibly for libel and slander). The contract between the company and the subscriber will not immunize the company from such liability, as the duty of a private citizen not to falsely arrest or imprison another private citizen arises from common-law and statutory principles entirely independent of any contractual relationship between the company and the subscriber.

The same principles apply with regard to the use of excessive force by an employee of a security guard or patrol company in effecting an arrest, even if the arrest is otherwise proper. Although, of course, law enforcement authorities do not have the right to use excessive force to effect an arrest either, the parameters for the degree of force that may be used by a law enforcement officer to effect an arrest are broader than those that may be used by private citizens. Generally, the laws relating to self-defense, the defense of others, and the defense of one's property should be applicable in the context of the activities of security guard and patrol companies. Common-law principles generally provide that one may use only that force that is reasonable under the circumstances to defend oneself, to defend others, and to defend one's property. As such, under general common-law principles, an individual would not have the right under principles of self-defense to shoot someone who was about to punch him, if he or she knew the other individual to be unarmed—although he or she would probably have the right to punch the other individual in return. Thus, if an employee of a security guard or patrol company uses force that was not reasonable or warranted under the circumstances in effecting an arrest, even if the arrest was otherwise proper, the security guard or patrol company is potentially liable to the third party for assault and battery. Again, the contract between the company and the subscriber will not immunize the company from such liability, as the duty of a private citizen not to assault and batter another private citizen and the limits of the self-defense privilege arise from common-law and statutory principles entirely independent of any contractual relationship between the company and the subscriber.

Finally, brief consideration should be given to the issue of the liability of security guard and patrol companies for the actions of their employees that are outside the scope of their employment duties. Generally, an employer is not liable for the misdeeds of an employee if those misdeeds are not committed in the course and scope of employment. However, it is often much more difficult to determine whether those misdeeds are committed outside the course and scope of employment than may appear at first blush. The difficulties in making these determinations may be even greater in the security guard/patrol officer context, given the fact that security guards and patrol officers are often in uniform, armed, driving in official-looking vehicles, and have the aura of authority. Certain courts have held governmental entities liable for the actions law enforcement authorities committed while in uniform, even though those activities (for example, rape) clearly are not within the bounds of the officer's official activities. These courts have reasoned that, because of the uniform, the police car, and the weapon, the law enforcement authority has a greater level of authority than do ordinary citizens and that private citizens will submit to that authority more readily than they will to the authority of someone who is not a law enforcement officer. Since the law enforcement agency provided the officer with the uniform, the police car, and the weapon, these courts have held the law enforcement agency liable for such actions of its employees. This is because the agency provided the instrumentalities that enabled the officer to exert a greater level of authority and influence; thus the agency facilitated the commission of the wrongful act even though the wrongful act itself is clearly outside the course and scope of the officer's duties. The same principles would likely apply in the case of security guard and patrol companies. However, no general principles can be set forth here, since the law of what is and what is not within the course and scope of employment, and the liability of the employer who provides the instrumentality that facilitates the commission of a wrongful act even though the wrongful act itself is clearly outside the course and scope of the employee's duties varies widely from jurisdiction to jurisdiction.

CONCLUSIONS

Private response companies do not enjoy the same legal protection for inadequate or nonresponse to a call for assistance as that enjoyed by police and other government agencies. Further, contracts specifying the amount of liability or the maximum liability are especially useful.

The emerging field of private response raises both the usual liability issues, and in addition questions arise concerning liability for injury to third parties. Contractual specifications, for example, will not eliminate liability for the actions of private security officers who use excessive force.

NOTES

1. Indeed in *Antique Arts v. City of Torrance,* discussed above, the court rejected an argument that a "special relationship" existed between the plaintiff and the police, obviating the operation of sovereign immunity.
2. On the other hand, some courts have relied on the very fact that there is no contractual relationship between the alarm company and the third parties to hold that the third party is not bound by the limitation of liability provisions in the contract with the subscriber. These courts reason that the third party cannot be bound by a contract to which it was not a party. They further suggest that an alarm company cannot have it both ways, that is, argue that it has no duty to the third party because it had no relationship with the third party and that a loss by the third party was unforeseeable, yet still argue that the third party is bound by the limitation of liability provisions in the contract.

3. Moreover, to impose this duty and liability on the alarm companies would lead to an absurd result. The alarm company would have greater duties and liabilities to the third parties who had not paid for the service than they would to the subscriber who had compensated the alarm company.

11
Success Stories

This chapter will discuss individuals and companies that have changed the landscape of the security industry. Some have changed the nature of marketing, others have pioneered technical improvements, and still others have emphasized filling untapped segments of the market for burglar alarms. Some have offered services such as response to alarms, which others have eschewed. This chapter examines some of these success stories and suggests some recommendations drawn from the experience of these entrepreneurs and innovators.

MANUFACTURING: NAPCO

An individual who certainly improved the landscape of the alarm industry is Richard Soloway, who in 1969, along with his partner, Ken Rosenberg, founded Napco Security Systems, Inc. The multi-divisional, multinational firm began with five workers, including the two founders. In 1996 it employed more than 1,300 and had annual worldwide sales in excess of $50 million.

Napco has emphasized research and development as a mechanism for growth and success in the industry. (Incidentally, Richard Soloway was trained as an electrical engineer, which may in part explain the firm's early and continued emphasis on research.) An indication of its R&D emphasis is its obtaining of about 20 patents. Its initial patent involved an automatic tape dialer employing an electromechanical solenoid that pulled tape into the tape deck instead of having the tape under constant pressure. The development permitted Napco to introduce a reliable tape dialer—the Mark 1000 Series—that allowed a call to be made automatically to a neighbor or the police indicating a possible burglary. Soloway states that, until this development, reliable communication was a problem for the industry. Napco also developed nonsupervised wireless transmitters and receivers in the late 1960s and early 1970s.

Napco was successful in the mid-1970s in adapting audio technology for the alarm industry. For example, it obtained a patent for an automatic siren cutoff after a 10- or 15-minute period. Prior to Napco's work on adapting sirens, the industry had relied on bells for alarm-sounding purposes. Even in 1996 sirens were still overwhelmingly used for this purpose.

Napco's developments during the 1980s included the Magnum Alert® Series, a microprocessor-based control panel, totally integrated with a digital dialer, siren, and keypad. The circuitry was all matched, permitting smooth operation. The company sold substantial quantities of this equipment. Napco also developed various improved versions of its Magnum Alert® control panels and keypads during the 1980s.

Napco's emphasis on research and development continued in the 1990s, including the introduction of multiplex and modular control panels for both residential units and commercial establishments. It introduced keypad readouts in English. For example, the control panel might note that a sensor in the basement had detected a possible problem. It has also produced many types of improved motion detectors, keypads integrated with locks, two-way voice technology, and Adaptive® dual technology designed to reduce the incidence of false alarms. For example, Napco sensors can adapt to changes in the environment such as the random burst of space heaters or the sudden introduction of an animal/ pet and are "forgiving" of owner errors, protecting against unnecessary alarm dispatches.

The 1990s have also witnessed the development of improved microprocessors and equipment that is "more intelligent." Napco has drawn on advanced microprocessor technology, along with its experience and expertise, to reinvent the product genre, notes Soloway. This was marked by the successful introduction of the firm's fully supervised Gemini™ Series Hybrid Hardwire/Wireless Multi-Tasking Line systems, which save on installation cost without compromising system dependability.

Napco's emphasis on R&D is illustrated not only by the products and patents it has produced but also by its employment in the 1990s of about 70 engineers, its research expenditure of almost $10 million over a three-year period, and its devotion of about 7 percent of its sales revenue to R&D. In the 1990s it constructed a 2,500-square-foot research laboratory to investigate how sensors could be improved to reduce false alarms. It recreates alarm-producing factors in the laboratory. Napco's clear research emphasis is important for the long-run position of the company and the industry.

Soloway mentioned that producing reliable and quality products was most important. Along those lines the firm has employed substantial automation. Regarding Napco's circuit board production, for example, Soloway notes that 80 percent of each printed circuit board's assembly in 1996 was automated while the balance was handcrafted. The firm also tries to help its dealers and employed in 1996 about fifteen training representatives and three course instructors who held classes in numerous cities nationwide.

The quality of alarm equipment has improved substantially over time in no small measure because of Napco. Soloway notes that because of market pressures and other factors prices of equipment have declined as well. For example, the price for dealers for improved entry-level control panels in the mid-1990s was approximately $75 instead of the $150 price in the latter part of the 1980s. Passive infrared (PIR) prices declined from $40 to under $20. Manufacturers' price reductions have helped make alarms more affordable and contributed to the industry's growth.

The firm has also been a "good citizen." It has been especially active in trying to reduce the false alarm problem. As mentioned, the firm has succeeded in producing equipment that overcomes many of the causes of false alarms. It has also been active in trying to inform the industry about the serious consequences of false alarms, especially as they impact the industry's image, retarding its growth. Accordingly, Soloway has been an active board member of the industry's prestigious Alarm Industry Research and Educational Foundation (AIREF), among other activities.

Napco has certainly made a substantial impact on the industry, becoming one of its leading manufacturers. Its consistent and long-term growth shows the importance of an emphasis on research and development and the importance of innovation. Napco's past performance along these lines bodes well for its position in the industry.

MANUFACTURING: ADEMCO

Ademco is an example of a highly successful alarm equipment manufacturer.[1] The company was founded by Maurice Coleman in Brooklyn in 1929 to produce mechanical alarms that produced a loud clanging from a bell in case of intrusion. By 1963 the company had been purchased by what is now Pittway. When Ademco's chief executive Leo Guthart started with the company in 1963, it had 27 employees; by 1992 it had 1,400. Today Ademco produces highly sophisticated alarms, many of which are wireless. It has become one of the leading alarm manufacturers, and its parent corporation is also the owner of the major distributor of alarm products. A rival alarm manufacturer has referred to Ademco as the "General Motors of the alarm industry."

Guthart attributes Ademco's success to the design of good products that are high in quality but low in price. The products, Guthart notes, must be reliable and consistent in quality. Specifically, the firm has invested in substantial engineering and product development, using technology drawn from the electronics and computer industries. The firm employs modern production techniques and has focused on customers' needs. For example, the firm utilizes focus groups of end users and dealers to try to determine what consumers want. The industry in general has not employed wide surveying of users to achieve a direct, continuous, and structured flow of information from end users and installers. Almost all of Ademco's manufacturing is done using robots, which can produce a wide variety of products with low cost for altering production lines. Such technology clearly gives it a competitive advantage over other American manufacturers.

The central reason for the firm's success can be attributed to Leo Guthart, whose innovative behavior and willingness to take risks led to its rapid growth. The firm has devoted much effort and investment to engineering and product development. Like the other manufacturers of alarm equipment, in the 1980s Ademco was producing systems that relied upon wires and telephone lines. Sensors that detected movement were connected by wire to a control panel that utilized the telephone lines to reach the central monitoring station. Burglars could cut wires or telephone lines, or a telephone system breakdown could render the alarm system ineffective. For example, burglars severed the cables connecting a Chicago jewelry store with Wells Fargo's central station and stole $2 million. It would be inconvenient to try to report a burglary and hear "I'm sorry, all circuits are busy. Try again later." Further, a wired system is sometimes difficult and expensive to install. A skylight in a commercial establishment or doors and windows in both residences and commercial establishments would be examples of problem spots. Also, installation of wired systems generally requires more time than wireless systems, and skilled installers are costly.

During the 1980s Ademco saw the advantage of wireless, or radio alarm systems. It began work on both short-range radio (connecting sensors to the central panel) and long-range radio (connecting the alarm system to the central monitoring station). Others like I.T.I. also expected wireless radio to become an important technology and began to develop reliable wireless systems. Ademco recognized that successful wireless development required assessing the probable progress in battery technology; in the 1980s batteries usually lasted 9 months. In 1995, batteries' lifespan extended to years, and they provided 30 days' warning prior to depletion.

Ademco committed itself to improving long-range radio for alarm systems and employed 50 engineers in that endeavor. As part of long-range radio use, in the 1980s the firm applied for F.C.C. licenses to operate a cellular-like communications network in the unused 900 MHz range. The firm succeeded, and today wireless products are a significant portion of its business. In 1995 Ademco operated AlarmNet in 19 cities, a radio network used by most of the major alarm companies in those cities. For example, in the Philadelphia area AlarmNet had 15 or 16 receiving towers, which provided a very high degree of reliability over a coverage area for the cellular-like system of 35 miles. Short-range radio devices were included in about 15 percent of all burglar/fire alarm systems, and in 1994 AlarmNet increased its subscribers by 50 percent. The AlarmNet system was expanded in 1994 to include more suburban areas, and new networks were established in Las Vegas and Northern New England. An indication of Ademco's commitment to improving technology is given by the following statement in the corporation's 1994 Annual Report:

> Over the last eleven years we have spent over $30 million developing short and long-range wireless products and systems. We believe that we are one of two clear cut leaders in the short-range

wireless product market and the undisputed leader in product and system development in the long-range wireless market.

The willingness to invest in developing new products explains part of Ademco's success. For example, as late as 1995, the substantial investment requirement meant that AlarmNet had not yet become profitable. A similar willingness to expend resources on R&D is occurring in the case of its Cylink subsidiary, which produces encryption products designed to ensure the security of information sent electronically. Cylink is spending 30 percent of its sales revenues on research and development.

Another element in Ademco's success is its pricing and product strategies. Ademco introduced a new one-way radio device to be sold to installers for $100; this in turn is expected to increase demand for AlarmNet. The product is priced well below other one-way radio devices. In fact, Guthart noted that the AlarmNet monthly charge is low. The charge is about $5 per month per subscriber. The firm also has tried to differentiate its products, and it devotes considerable resources to marketing its products.

Ademco's success derives from its emphasis on innovation and its concern for producing high-quality, low-price products. It is willing to invest substantial resources in developing new products. That strategy has been, and is likely to continue to be, successful. For example, AlarmNet development required substantial investment and obtaining F.C.C. licenses, but now entry by other firms is likely to be difficult. The first-mover advantage Ademco gained is likely to be important. Ademco is thus positioned to do well in its wireless products and in AlarmNet.

DISTRIBUTOR: ADI

ADI, which began in 1985, is like Ademco wholly owned by Pittway Corporation.[2] It is nationwide, and even continentwide, with 80 branches including Puerto Rico, Mexico City, and Canada. Senior executive of ADI, Steve Roth, attributes its success to having the right products at the right places and to establishing a personal relationship with its customers. As discussed in Chapter 7 on the structure of the alarm industry, the function of distributors, or wholesalers, is to get the products from the manufacturer to the installer promptly and as efficiently as possible. Further, "just in time" inventory strategies employed by installers demand prompt order filling. In the competitive distribution segment, margins are low, so firms must keep costs down. ADI innovated by developing supermarket-like operations at the wholesale level. Installers, especially the smaller ones, who want to shop directly at the store can do so. Larger installers rely more upon ordering merchandise through ADI's computer system. The firm also provides pick-up service at the store or ships merchandise, usually for next day delivery. Roth mentions that shopping at ADI is a good experience. The supermarket concept saves on labor expense since buyers can perform much of the search process for themselves. For buyers who want advice, ADI has service representatives, who provide technical service and support. The firm states that it provides a very high level of service, the most crucial element for a distribution firm.

The ability to get the items to its customers "just in time" and its local availability are important in ADI's success. The firm, which utilizes a hub and spoke system of supply, is able to provide overnight service for many of its customers. An example of ADI's emphasis on next day delivery is its opening, in 1994, of a new shipping hub adjacent to the principal UPS hub in Louisville, Kentucky. Local availability and merchandise pick-up are important, and they are made possible by having 80 branch locations. ADI's large size and resulting purchases may also provide some bargaining power with manufacturers. However, large firms (and ADI certainly is large) on occasion become too bureaucratic and lose their ability to compete with smaller firms. According to Steve Roth, each of the ADI branches is in effect a small company that enjoys the advantages of being supported and assisted by an integrated and sophisticated computer system. Local branches maintain independent initiatives in a quite decentralized management style. The management hierarchy is thin and follows the concept of Total Quality Management. Further, Roth maintains that in spite of its size, the company still enjoys a personal relationship with its customers. Another issue is ADI's relationship with its sister firm Ademco. Whether the vertical relationship with Ademco yields advantages for ADI is not clear.

Other factors in ADI's success are its marketing and promotion activities. The firm utilizes catalogues which have a large readership. Manufacturers find the catalogues sufficiently useful that they purchase advertising space in them. ADI also has monthly promotions. It holds about 20 expositions a year in which 50 to 70 manufacturers participate. Roth states that these trade shows are highly effective. Direct mail is also used to promote its products. Finally, the large number of branches is itself a marketing tool that facilitates purchase of products from ADI.

One indication of its success is its relatively large and growing market share in the highly competitive distribution segment of the alarm industry. Also, as reported in the corporation's 1994 Annual Report, ADI was chosen "Preferred Distributor by over 49% of the respondents to SDM's annual industry poll, an increase of 7% over a poll taken a year earlier." Further, ADI even handles purchases from manufacturers and the associated money management for some of the largest firms in the industry. ADI seems to have provided the right combination of price, availability, and service to succeed in a competitive environment.

DEALERSHIP—MONITORING RESPONSE

Norman Rubin is an example of a pioneer and innovator in the alarm industry. He has succeeded in establishing a number of firms, has grown them, and then sold them. Norman Rubin began in the industry in 1939 and has been active ever since. His father, who formed Supreme Burglar Alarm Corporation in the Manhattan borough of New York City, had been in the business since 1913.

Rubin's work provides an interesting insight on the development of the industry. Early alarms were of two types—those that rang on site and those that were monitored at a central station. Grinnel, which owned ADT, Holmes, and AFA, was found by the U.S. Supreme Court, in 1968, to have monopolized the "accredited central station protective service business." About the same time, in 1969, Rubin purchased the Central Office Alarm Corporation, which had central stations on West 32nd Street in New York City and in Long Island City, and bought Owl Protective in Philadelphia. When the acquisition occurred, both acquired companies were losing money.

Mr. Rubin had previously, in 1965, formed a group to establish his first central station, the Mutual Central Station Alarm Corporation, a UL-approved central station. Ray Adams was an integral member of this group. In an interview Rubin stated that his firm provided superior service and charged somewhat lower prices than his larger competitors. Thus, at the time of the acquisition of Central Office Alarm Corp. and Owl Protective, Rubin already had experience operating a central station. He simplified the operations of the newly acquired central stations and improved their profitability. In 1972, he sold what was now a UL-approved central station company, including Owl Protective, Central Station, and Mutual, to Honeywell for $11.5 million. He said the sale was motivated by an insufficient depth of management, which seemed to imply that he was spreading himself too thin. At the time of the sale, Mr. Adams stayed on to manage the Honeywell operations in New York, New Jersey, and Pennsylvania. Rubin retained a small local alarm dealership, the Supreme Burglar Alarm Corporation, but he no longer had a central station. Accordingly, in 1973 he established Vari-Guard Central Station Alarm Corp., which obtained, in 1975, UL approval. This firm, Rubin stated, stressed service. The firm provided high-quality installation, which enabled it to maintain a low rate of false activations.

An example of Rubin's ability to tap unserved markets occurred with his formation of an alarm company in 1962, Peerless Alarm Systems, in Westchester County, New York. This county is, and was at the time, one of most affluent in the entire country. He believed that the residential alarm segment of the market was a potentially high-growth segment that was not being tapped. There were 8 to 10 other local companies but they were not aggressively pursuing the residential alarm market. Rubin induced the police to install monitoring facilities in their stations. At the time there was only one accredited or approved central station in all of Westchester County. Originally, the Scarsdale Police department had no desire to monitor alarms. Rubin installed a console with 20 connections, which grew to a capacity of 2,500 connections. Rubin was also involved when the towns of Ossining, Harrison, and Mamaroneck obtained alarm monitoring facilities. Rubin stated that the police knew that his company installed high-quality alarm systems and provided good service after the sale. He said his firm was always concerned about false alarms and tried to reduce them, a policy that helped it gain acceptance with police departments. One factor, then, in Norman Rubin's success was his emphasis on quality installation, which helped reduce false activations. In the 1970s in Westchester County Peerless charged $3 per month for connecting the subscriber to the police department. For that $3 price, Peerless provided and maintained the monitoring equipment. The firm leased alarm systems to businesses and sold them outright to households. Peerless' average price for installed alarms during the 1970s was about $2,500. In 1985 Rubin sold Peerless after many years of operation.

Rubin, together with Ray Adams, also established Jeweler's Protection Services Ltd. in 1975 with a UL-approved central station. Rubin states that the firm installed quality alarm systems and was very responsive to customers. Jeweler's Protection, not surprisingly, went after the niche market of the jewelry district with a potential customer base of 3,000 within a six-block area. The firm also provided private response to alarms. Rubin now owned two central stations in Manhattan and proceeded to pursue the niche market of furriers, jewelers, and art galleries. For highly valued operations like jewelry stores, insurance companies required UL approval and guard response. Rubin's firms did well, and in 1983 he sold his companies to British investors for $28.5 million. Rubin states that a financial stake and interest in the company are important in encouraging good performance. He, along with three others of his top managers, remained with the new company, Rubin as a consultant and member of the board of directors and the other three as employees.

Rubin left the company in December 1987 and in 1988 formed a new company in Manhattan, Mutual Central Alarm Services. In 1989, the new company became a UL-approved central station. Mutual Central, Rubin notes, continues to follow the strategy of pursuing niche markets. In this case the firm is concentrating on high-level customers interested in quality. Mutual Central uses the most modern equipment, does not purchase accounts, and achieves quality installation, all of which means that the firm has a low rate of false activations. Mutual Central follows a policy of covering direct labor and equipment costs from its installation prices. The firm also provides private armed response to alarms. Rubin stresses the importance of quality and of having employees who have a financial stake in the success of the company. Mutual Central, for example, has many employees who are stockholders, and who therefore have a strong additional interest in the firm's success.

Norman Rubin's experience shows that room still exists for individual initiative and entrepreneurship in the alarm industry. He seems to be adept at starting firms and moving on to other opportunities. He has been successful in tapping niche markets that have not been pursued aggressively by larger firms.

DEALERSHIP—MONITORING

Commonwealth Security is an example of a successful installation and monitoring firm that has achieved substantial growth through a policy of emphasizing high-quality service and focused internal growth and acquisitions.[3] The company, which was formed in 1971 and incorporated in 1973, has its headquarters in

Lancaster, Pennsylvania, and operates one UL-approved monitoring station. In 1990, it had 7,500 subscribers and 100 employees; in 1996 it had 30,000 subscribers and more than 200 employees. The principal person behind the company's growth and success is Patrick Egan, about whom more will be said shortly.

Commonwealth has concentrated on small markets like York, Pennsylvania, and Virginia Beach, Virginia, because national companies were not fully exploiting the opportunities in small markets. For example, the company had only two competitors in Altoona, Pennsylvania, in 1985, reflecting the lack of involvement of large companies. Richmond, Virginia, was the only large city where Commonwealth Security competed in 1995.

Acquisitions have played an important role in Commonwealth Security's growth. In August 1995, the firm completed its 22nd acquisition with MGI, Inc. of Hampton, Virginia. Its average acquisition has involved 1,000 to 1,200 subscribers. All the acquisitions have occurred in its Mid-Atlantic area of operation. Commonwealth has made acquisitions in Virginia in part because the company noted that no other companies were actively acquiring companies in Virginia. The company identified the Mid-Atlantic corridor along Interstate 95 from Philadelphia to Virginia as a high-growth area and has focused its acquisition efforts in that region.

In terms of internal growth, Commonwealth Security has focused on high-income residential and business consumers. It does not compete against the large discounters and sells about 98 percent of its systems at list, or book, prices. The firm in 1995 installed about 200 systems per month.

The company employs both telemarketing and personal sales people. It calls on insurance agents, builders, and police chiefs to try to obtain referrals. It also contacts architects and stresses the use of yard signs.

An indication of its emphasis on service is its activities on the problem of false activations. The company contacts customers who have had two false activations during some time period. It uses a custom video, a private label instruction book, and customer training to stress the importance of the false activation problem. Commonwealth has an automatic call distribution system that permits a customer to abort a call. The firm has achieved a false alarm rate of .8 alarms per system per year, which is well below the national average.

Commonwealth Security has also tried to keep its costs down, a necessity in the competitive alarm industry. It is a shareholder of one of the largest alarm groups in the U.S. The group, Security Network of America, in 1995 comprised 25 UL-approved central stations, including Guardian Alarm in Detroit and Alarm Detection in Chicago.

Patrick Egan, who directs the successful operations of Commonwealth Security, has been an important figure in the security industry's activities. He was a founder of the Pennsylvania Burglar and Fire Alarm Association, a past president of the National Burglar and Fire Alarm Association, and a board member of the Central Station Association, among his other responsibilities.

Commonwealth Security has been successful by following the niche strategy of servicing untapped markets and emphasizing service. The company has avoided having to deeply discount its prices to compete with the large mass marketers.

DEALERSHIP—MONITORING RESPONSE

Protection One[4] effectively began in 1991, when its current management participated in the purchase of the security business of Paci Corp. Protection One increased its monitoring subscribers from 32,000 in 1991, to 98,000 at the end of 1994, and to 130,000 in September of 1995. Earnings before interest, taxes, depreciation, and amortization increased 760 percent over that same period.

In 1995 the company was the fifth largest in the U.S. in terms of subscribers and was the largest in its five-state area of operation, which includes of Arizona, California, Oregon, Nevada, and

Washington. Protection One has 85 percent residential and 15 percent small commercial subscribers. It is vertically integrated: it installs and services alarms, monitors accounts, and provides armed response to alarms in Las Vegas, Nevada, and Southern California.

Protection One has achieved such rapid growth largely through the purchase of subscriber accounts. It operates one central monitoring station, which has a low incremental or marginal cost so that the marginal or extra profit from monthly recurring revenues from its existing and acquired accounts is high. The current capacity of its central station is 250,000, so the firm has substantial room for growth. Further, the firm notes that if it can increase its subscribers to 500,000, the cost per subscriber will decrease further, to perhaps $3.50 per month. The combination of a large and efficient central monitoring station and an aggressive acquisition program is an important part of its success.

In acquiring subscriber accounts, Protection One usually pays 20 to 30 times monthly recurring revenues. Because of its efficient central station, its margin is higher than many competitors, and it can afford to pay higher prices for acquisition. The firm looks at every single subscriber contract to determine the worth of the acquisition. Further, it limits its subscriber acquisitions to areas where it operates in order to try to achieve sufficient density of accounts. Density means lower cost and an enhanced ability to provide armed response. A minimum of five years is required to break even on acquisitions.

The firm has emphasized growth by acquisition because the firm claims that acquisition is cheaper than internal growth. It notes that local companies are well-known in their communities and can generate accounts with lower marketing expenses. Interestingly, some have become Protection One dealers after selling accounts to Protection One. Sometimes service technicians come to Protection One along with the acquired accounts.

Protection One attributes its success to a number of factors. In particular, the firm stresses its acquisition program, noting that it only buys accounts with good technology or technology that can be easily upgraded. It has developed a strong network of 32 dealers (as of September 1995) from whom it buys accounts.

Its emphasis on service is another factor explaining its success. For example, it will repair a subscriber's system within 24 hours. Its operators answer calls within 20 seconds and verify alarms and respond to alarms within one minute. Protection One has a training program for all employees, which is an important component in its effort to provide quality service.

The company also tries to control all aspects of customer service. For example, each new subscriber acquired is visited by a Protection One employee, the monitoring is emphasized as being by Protection One, and yard signs with the Protection One logo are installed. The whole concept is to create "brand loyalty."

A regional strategy has also been important in its success. Having thousands of subscribers in an area can lead to greater efficiency, better service, and economies of scale. Accordingly, the company has made acquisitions and encouraged growth only within its five-state area of operation.

An important niche marketing strategy is its decision to offer private armed response to alarms. In Las Vegas, private response is required, but the firm believed that such a service was also important in Los Angeles, where police response takes one hour. Protection One has established a goal of responding within 10 minutes. Accordingly, it needs a high density of subscribers to achieve that response time. In any case, the firm believes that the packaging of monitoring, service, and response gives it a competitive advantage.

Another factor in its success is its selling of enhanced services to its subscribers. Over 40 percent of its subscribers have two-way voice communication. Many have an extended warranty and a cellular backup; the latter is priced at $10 per month.

In general, Protection One has achieved so rapid a rate of growth because of its having followed a sound business strategy. Its management is young and knowledgeable about the industry.

MONITORING AND INSTALLATION: INNOVATION IN THE FORM OF MASS MARKETING

An individual who transformed the electronic security industry from one of custom installation and relatively high prices to standard systems employing the techniques of mass marketing certainly qualifies as a success story.[5] Peder Kolind pioneered this approach in 1983 with Brinks Home Security. Prior to that time, electronic security systems were primarily sold to businesses and affluent homeowners.

A brief discussion of Kolind's background is helpful in understanding his contributions. Peder Kolind was working for a security firm in Denmark when he developed the idea of mass marketing alarm systems. The Danish firm rejected the concept (a common occurrence in the case of innovation) because the firm was committed to the traditional method of custom installation. Kolind worked on his own concept for awhile, but he realized that he required the financial support and recognition provided by a well-established company. However, that company would almost certainly not be a traditional alarm company since changing long-established methods of operation is difficult. He enlisted the support of the largest insurance company in Denmark, and the rest is, as they say, history.

Kolind brought this idea to the United States and convinced Brinks, which, at that time, was not in the alarm industry to try mass marketing alarm systems. Brinks established Brinks Home Security, and in 1983 the firm began its alarm activities. The firm charged low prices for a standard system (for example, one standard panel and one standard sensor) and made profits from the monthly recurring revenues. It lost money on installations but made profits on monitoring since monitoring prices exceeded the cost of monitoring. The initial losses on installation were substantial, probably requiring an investment of as much as $50 million dollars by Brinks Home Security. The mass marketing strategy was not without some risk, which explains why Kolind wanted the participation of a large, well-established, nontraditional alarm company. The company had to have adequate resources, a recognized and respected name, but not be committed to the ways of the past. Further, consumers have to be sufficiently sensitive to the low installation price to be willing to purchase substantially more systems.

Under Kolind's leadership, Brinks emphasized radio, television, and newspaper advertising to stimulate inbound telephone calls about its low-price standardized system. Kolind stressed that the cities chosen for promotion had to be of adequate size to make the strategy work. The practice was so successful that in 1995 Brinks Home Security had 320,000 subscribers and a large number of imitators. A sufficient number of consumers were obviously interested in low price to make the strategy profitable.

Kolind left Brinks in 1988 and repeated his success with companies in other countries, including England, France, Portugal, Spain, Sweden, and Pakistan. In each case, he used a leading non-security company, including telephone, electric, natural gas, and insurance firms. He later worked with Westinghouse and was bound through July 1996 by a noncompetition agreement with Westinghouse.

Kolind was an innovator in other ways as well. At Brinks, he began the concept of open offices, whereby the chief executive simply has a desk in an open area with many other executives. Kolind learned about the concept of open offices from his previous work with a real estate firm. In effect, the system helps break down the hierarchical order normally employed in most organizations. When the hierarchical order is loosened, top executives are more accessible to employees. This fosters an entrepreneurial atmosphere, where employees are free to communicate with upper management, not only about the current business of the firm but also about any new ideas or innovations. Today, if one visits Brinks Home Security's main office one cannot help but notice the unusual arrangement of desks and the absence of enclosed offices.

Kolind mentions a number of aspects he considers important in his success. He always had a minority equity interest with a put option—namely, he could sell back his stock shares at a prea-greed-upon formula. He also believes that the infrastructure must be set up for mass marketing. Kolind stressed that copying his idea is difficult because success requires copying all the various aspects. He likens his approach to that of "McDonalds."

Peder Kolind shows the importance of an innovator, someone willing to depart from the conventional approach. He has certainly been adept at building and creating. He also has exhibited flexibility and the ability to adapt to changing circumstances. All selling activities at Brinks were done over the telephone using credit cards. Six years later at Westinghouse, consumer reluctance to provide credit card information over the phone required a change in operation. Interestingly, Kolind mentioned that not everything proved successful; for example, at that time, Minnesota had too low a crime rate to make mass marketing successful.

Kolind offers some advice to potential entrepreneurs in the alarm industry. He recommends that security companies maintain professional installers to ensure high-quality installation and a reduced false alarm rate. He further recommends developing technology that can be installed by the salesperson, combining the functions of the salesperson and the installer as a solution to the infrastructure problem.

When we interviewed Mr. Kolind he was working at his latest project, the largest entertainment center in Central America, which has a restaurant, bar, and nightclub, and nightly attendance of 2,000. This entrepreneur certainly changed the landscape of the alarm industry.

DISCUSSION

The seven stories that we described provide general pointers, which may help other companies in their pursuit of success. However, certain conditions are required for success, and they do not usually exist.

First, behind each successful company there is usually someone who makes the difference. Management science has recognized this element, and in many universities, programs and courses have been created to determine how organizations can be structured to be innovative. In one word, this person is termed an entrepreneur. We find such people in government, universities, businesses, and religious organizations. Entrepreneurs are future-oriented thinkers. They look forward, toward the future of the industry in which they are involved, in order to identify opportunities or market niches that have not been developed. Entrepreneurs are able to use their innate creativity and flexibility to implement their ideas. In doing so, entrepreneurs are the decision-makers.

All business environments are fraught with uncertainty. For the nonentrepreneur, uncertainty and the risks created by uncertainty can be a source of anxiety, indecision, and discontent. One of the characteristics that sets entrepreneurs apart from nonentrepreneurs is that entrepreneurs use uncertainty to their advantage; they are willing to take risks. Entrepreneurs do not take unwarranted risks. Rather, they are able to identify the inherent risks in a project, and define methods so that they can control those risks. In some cases it is their own money that they risk. In all cases, it is their reputation that is at risk. Within the framework of a company, the entrepreneur's job may be at risk.

Ademco's Leo Guthart looked forward in order to identify a solution to the problems created by the reliance of alarm systems on telephone wire transmission. He innovated, using a new technology, creating wireless or radio alarm systems. Like a true entrepreneur, Mr. Guthart was able to view problems as an opportunity for success.

Napco and Richard Soloway have made many innovations to solve industry problems beginning with improved communications through an automatic tape dialer through work in the 1990s on sensors designed to reduce false alarm occurrences. Napco is an excellent example of a firm whose growth is attributable to an emphasis on research and innovation.

Norman Rubin's formation of Peerless Alarm Systems was the result of his ability to identify market niches, which, at that time, were not being served by the alarm industry. Most entrepreneurs have a sense of their own limitations. This was the case for Mr. Rubin; he clearly recognized that he was spreading himself too thin and sold Owl Protective, Central Station, and Mutual to Honeywell. In addition, Rubin was able to identify and serve an existing unserved residential alarm market segment. Peder Kolind innovated, applying the mass marketing concept to the alarm industry. As is the case with all successful entrepreneurs, he was not simply a risk-taker, but a risk manager. That is, he was able to identify the risks inherent in mass marketing alarm systems and manage them through his affiliation with Brinks.

The commitment and the energy of the entrepreneur spills over to other areas of interest that may produce little or no monetary return but reflect his or her commitment to success. Back in 1991, Patrick Egan, the founder and president of Commonwealth Security, served as the president of NBFAA. He wanted one of the authors of this book to give the keynote talk at NBFAA's convention in Nashville, Tennessee. The author met him, his associate, and a few others in a restaurant off the Pennsylvania Turnpike. Obviously the meeting leader, Mr. Egan wasted no time; he clearly and succinctly stated his point. He had another meeting before ours and one after ours. His associate stated that they basically lived in the large van they owned, and that they were constantly on the move. At the convention, Patrick was ever present; it was obvious that, as a true entrepreneur, he was capable of making and indeed did make most of the decisions.

When he built Brinks Home Security, Peder Kolind was also involved in a joint venture with British Telecom and was commuting between England and the U.S. His plans constantly changed as circumstances changed. Undaunted by the ongoing change and uncertainty in his environment, Mr. Kolind continued to act on new ideas and identify key aides, who helped structure and then implement those ideas. People who worked closely with Kolind at that time claim that without Mr. Kolind's creativity, flexibility, and expert decision-making capabilities, the venture would have been impossible to accomplish.

Research shows that entrepreneurship is a gift built into one's character and cannot be easily acquired. In addition to the previously mentioned characteristics, entrepreneurs are self-confident and outstanding leaders. They are committed to their ideas, enjoy their work, are energetic and strongly determined to succeed. Interestingly, some of the entrepreneurs we interviewed did not see their ideas as special. In our frequent conversations with Mr. Rubin, and in the telephone interview with Mr. Kolind, they both stated repeatedly that theirs was a simple concept. However, the nonentrepreneur lacks the insight and determination to make such an impact in an industry. Further, Peder Kolind noted that his employer turned down the original idea of mass marketing alarm systems. A true entrepreneur, Kolind was not willing to abandon an idea simply because one company did not believe in his vision. He continued to pursue support for an idea in which he believed. The rejection of innovation is common, and happened in the case of such concepts as the supermarket and xerography.

In addition to the aforementioned attributes, there are two distinct characteristics found in most entrepreneurs. Since most of their energy is focused on creativity and innovation, they are usually incapable and uninterested in managing the day-to-day operations of their companies. Their strength as well as their expertise often lies in the development of an organization. Truly successful entrepreneurs understand their limitations and choose someone else to manage their creation. Mr. Kolind successfully designed and built the Brinks and Westinghouse operations; then, after completing his job, he delegated the structure and management functions to an accomplished organizational person. It was that person's responsibility to structure and manage the routine operations. Kolind, recognizing that his strength was in building, delegated responsibility and moved to his next entrepreneurial project. Norman Rubin relied to a large extent on Ray Adams' expertise in managing the structural aspects of the companies they developed. A well-known entrepreneur, Henry Ford, tried to run the day-to-day operations of the Ford Company. He met with far less success than he had when he built the company.

All the entrepreneurs whose stories are presented in this chapter rely on an organizational person to implement their ideas. The Catholic church provides a good insight into successful organizational structure. The Pope, when elected, is usually old, which limits the time he presides over the large Catholic organization. There is usually a rotation from an entrepreneurial to a structural pope. An entrepreneurial pope introduces innovations to the church, opens new markets, and promotes new ideas (e.g., John XXIII). After his death some years later, a structurally oriented pope is elected to structure all the envisioned changes and make them an integral part of the church. In order to avoid stagnation, the next pope is again an entrepreneur, who make changes that fit his special views. The lack of an entrepreneur means that the organization stagnates. Yet, if innovations are constantly introduced, and they are not built into the routine of the organization then the organization is due to fail.

Recommendations and Policy Implications

Companies should be careful about turning down new ideas. When an entrepreneur approaches with a new idea, careful considerations should be given to it. While some companies have established venture capital departments to prevent their too hasty rejections of new ideas, other companies have become trapped into executing only routine operations and have stopped innovating. When innovation stops, a company usually stagnates and may fail. Causes for rejecting innovation vary; however, in many of the cases rejection originates in signals transmitted from top management. Companies should consider changing or infusing top management with new talent sufficiently often to refresh the company. Also, an entrepreneurial president is desirable for a limited time period in order to bring new ideas and innovations into the company. It any case, companies should attempt not to resist change.

A frequent problem with alarm dealerships is that they are a family business. In many cases, a person built a successful dealership and keeps managing it until retirement. Stagnation often develops, or the potential of the company is not achieved since the people manning the various positions remain there for long periods of time. It is often quite impossible to replace the owner/ president who started the business and managed it for many years. True, such a person is most familiar with the company and resists being put aside. However, new management can help these companies, and the entrepreneurs who started them can use their skills for new ventures. Many such successful efforts have been achieved in the alarm industry when children have taken over the business while their parents were still active. The secret is to transfer the power of daily operations and related decision-making, while the entrepreneurs shift to their comparative advantage, initiating new ventures.

The Israeli army is a good example of a successful, constantly refreshed structure. The Chief of Staff and his top commanders are all replaced every four years. Commanders who are not promoted as a result of the vacancy created are shifted to parallel jobs. This way the entire command structure is refreshed. Commanders are exposed to new responsibilities, preparing them for the possible next promotion. Commanders unqualified for the next level are forced to retire. The system is not hampered by stagnation. Indeed, frequent rotation is a main reason for the new thinking and innovation attributed to the Israeli military establishment and to its success in most military confrontations.

Not all companies will make changes. Nevertheless, all should remain alert for opportunities. One secret is niche marketing. Production and marketing efforts might be directed at providing something that does not exist in the marketplace or that satisfies an unfulfilled demand. We dare to say that niche marketers to business or affluent cliental should not enter mass marketing, which may lead to a disruption of their main line of business.

Alarm industry participants must maintain a desire and inclination to improve their performance. Although most will not become a Rubin, a Soloway, or a Kolind, they can maintain the attitude and outlook of an entrepreneur. At the least, they will be less likely to reject the next major innovation.

CONCLUSIONS

This chapter presented seven individuals and companies in the areas of manufacturing, distribution, dealership, monitoring, and response activities whose ideas and activities changed the landscape of the electronic security industry. The individuals discussed are all energetic entrepreneurs who have put forth new ideas and modifications of the conventional industry practices.

These success stories suggest that companies should be careful before turning down new ideas. To prevent such errors, large companies form capital venture departments, which are supposed to analyze all new ideas before turning them down. Entrepreneurs among the dealers started their businesses themselves, made them a success, and maintained full control of their companies for many years. Entrepreneurs' power is usually in developing unconventional ideas and successfully implementing them.

NOTES

1. Information was obtained from (1) an interview with Leo A. Guthart, (2) an article by N.R. Kleinfeld, "This Long Island Industry Is Beating the Recession," *New York Times* (April 8, 1992): pp. B1 and B2, and (3) The *1994 Pittway Corporation Annual Report*.
2. Information was obtained from an interview with Steve Roth and the *1994 Pittway Corporation Annual Report*.
3. Information was obtained from an Interview with Patrick Egan and Steve Firestone of Commonwealth Security.
4. Interviews with John Mack and John Hess and company-supplied material.
5. Information came from an interview with Peter Kolind and from Patrick O'Toole, "Profiles in Home Security," *SDM* (August 1995): pp. 80-82.

12

The Present and The Future of The Industry

It is usually quite risky to predict the changes that will occur in the economic, legislative, and technological environments and their effect upon the operations of firms in the security industry. Clearly, it is very difficult to predict all the relevant changes that will occur, and how they will combine to affect these businesses. However, some effort at prediction is required in order to avoid situations where firms find themselves unprepared in a changing environment and cannot adjust to the new realities.

We will try to be safe by indicating the changes that are known to occur and analyzing their effects upon the industry. Then, we will make suggestions for effective business strategies. In order to make the analysis flow, we will be brief in describing the changes. Interested readers may refer to other chapters of the book for more details.

REGULATORY ENVIRONMENT

We are now in the midst of a global era, where government activities are questioned, and governments often even initiate an easing of regulation, a transfer of service provision to the private sector, and a general reduction in their role in the marketplace. The objective is to increase competition by shifting from a public or private monopoly to multiple service providers in order to improve quality and increase the availability of service while reducing prices to consumers. Governments are perceived as being inefficient in providing services because of their monopolistic power, while similar arguments are made against private monopolistic powers that are regulated by government. The objective is to at least shift producers' profit to the consumers of the service.

In the telecommunications industry, all legal barriers to entry confronting the telephone and cable TV companies are likely to be dissolved. The regional Bells are being allowed to enter the long-distance service, cable TV, and other businesses. Long-distance carriers and cable TV providers, among others such as local utilities, are expected to enter the local exchange market. Lobbying efforts to limit entry into the alarm industry or increase regulation are very unlikely to be successful. Ameritech is already the second largest alarm company in the U.S., and other telephone companies are studying entry.

The auctioning of the portions of the frequency spectrum by the federal government enables greater use by cellular and radio communication, which will tend to lower prices and increase use.

POLICE OPERATIONS

Many police departments in the large North American cities have reduced the priority of response to alarms or require private physical verification. In Los Angeles, New York, Philadelphia, and Chicago response to alarm activations is ignored or delayed, in many cases for over an hour. Police in Las Vegas will not respond unless a private guard company has visited the target. In Boulder, Colorado, police stopped responding.

It appears that community policing will spread, while conventional centrally oriented activities such as patrol will diminish. This trend may entail judgment concerning alarm response to the local officers, who will probably feel less obligated to respond given the high rate of false activations.

TECHNOLOGICAL ENVIRONMENT

This is the one area that is likely to undergo the most changes. We will witness the wide use of wireless systems, both within premises and as a communication mode to the central station. Technology has significantly improved the reliability of internal wireless systems, and battery life has increased to 10 years. Indeed, reliable wireless systems are already being sold in a variety of chain retail stores and are expected to become a significant share of all alarms. We do expect that security of wired lines will improve; however, wired systems will still lose market share to wireless systems.

Use of cellular, satellite, and broadband radio linkage in two-way supervised systems, digital dialers, fiber-optic lines, derived channel multiplexing, and various combinations of the above will replace traditional telephone connections. The increased availability and lower cost of radio and cellular eliminate the need to protect wired lines and improve the reliability of alarm systems' connections. Already, cellular technology is used to track missing vehicles, a related security service. Cellular connection is expected to spread significantly to other uses at much lower prices. Lower cellular prices can be attributed to intense competition, both among cellular companies and with hard-wired telephone services. It is also attributable to the low, almost insignificant, marginal cost of cellular connection.

Technological improvement in personal alarms will affect the industry. Individuals will be able to carry small two-way communication units, which include some or all of the following capabilities—telephone, paging, and a panic button for security and medical response. The central station will be able to locate the individual in a manner similar to the location and identification of missing vehicles.

Wireless systems can be integrated with wired telephones in a manner where one telephone number can be responded to simultaneously by both devices. Further, the wide spread of personal communications makes it possible for a person to perform an effective first verification of his business or residence alarm activation.

Automation is evident in central station operation. The problem of false activations associated with the openings and closings of businesses is improving with the introduction of smart features, and so is the identification of users. The labor-intensive central stations, where operators attend to every call, is about to change as well. The use of improved software will require operators' intervention only in exceptional cases.

Access-control devices will be adopted in businesses and are expected to penetrate into the residential market, starting with high-income homes. Fingerprint and voice recognition technology and retinal scanning will improve, and their prices will go down. Smart-card technology is improving and holds much hope for wide applications, including pass cards with coded entry and interactive and talk-back capabilities. Access-control devices are tied into security systems. Some very interesting commercial applications have been installed in universities and colleges. One such application has taken place at the University of Pennsylvania.[1]

Technological development leads to improved integrated access control, closed-circuit television, and data security. Software enhancements make these systems accessible to unsophisticated commercial end users. Stand-alone security systems may change; large commercial establishments may build on interactive broadband capabilities to receive, store, and analyze information about their operations. For example, timing the exit of trucks from a facility can be recorded by CCTV for accounting purposes, and the information can be transferred to the accounting file. Further, an unknown truck leaving the facility can be fully recorded, including information about the driver, for possible action.

Integration of devices can take another form. All the products that protect the door and the premises can be integrated. The locking of doors, access control, and the burglar alarm will be controlled together and will be supplied by a single manufacturer and sold and installed by one dealer. The home or business computer will be connected to the alarm system, CCTV, locks, and cellular or radio connections, and will be provided by a single supplier.

BUSINESS ENVIRONMENT

Competition among long-distance carriers will intensify with RBOCs' having received permission to enter the long-distance market. On the local level, local utilities, cable TV operators, and possibly long-distance carriers will provide local telephone service, which was monopolized in the past by the RBOCs. Competition will result in lower prices on local and long-distance calls, which will benefit central stations. Large central stations will in particular enjoy significantly lower prices because of quantity discounts.

Cellular telephone use is spreading, and the competition among providers will lower the price to a level competitive with the wired telephone. The use of wireless communication to connect to the central station is preferred since there is no wire to cut. Development of software that results in the more efficient use of operator time and more prompt response will affect mainly large central stations. The 1995 auction of additional spectrum by the Federal Communications Commission will permit increased use of wireless at lower prices.

Interestingly, we are witnessing the entry into the alarm business of large heating oil companies, which find the industry complementary to their main line of business.

The effects of future changes upon the segments of the alarm industry are:

Manufacturing

The big problem in the manufacturing segment of the alarm industry is the absence of direct communication between end users and manufacturers aimed at product improvements. Partial information is provided through focus groups and by the distributors. A direct and continuous flow of information from residential and commercial end users is needed in order to design more user-friendly systems. Such an effort will further serve to reduce the number of false activations.

The following factors are likely to affect manufacturers of alarm equipment: Economies of scale in central station operation may raise market share for large stations and reduce the absolute number of small operations. This phenomenon will coincide with a reduction in the number of small dealers, who do not supply well-differentiated products/services. Thus, production will have to be reoriented to satisfy the needs of large central stations and be less oriented toward small ones.

Electronic security will be bundled with other security measures such as CCTV, access control, locks, electrical sensors, and more. As a result, all components will need to be compatible with each other and the software. To further complicate matters, security systems will become part of home and business automation, environmental and facility control, and more. All that will provide more opportunities for alarm manufacturers, while at the same time exposing them to competition from other electronics and computer manufacturers.

Central Stations

In a large segment of the market, the sale of standardized systems has reduced the price of installation to a level where profits have been eliminated. Many dealers install alarms at or below cost, anticipating adequate compensation from future recurring revenues from the monthly monitoring charges. Also, the sale value of a dealership is determined by the number and value of its subscribers. The introduction of standardized systems by Brinks, ADT, Westinghouse, and many smaller dealers has brought down the price of installation. However, monthly charges remained unchallenged in the residential market, ranging from $20 to $30. The contract is usually between the end user and the dealer. In the case of third-party central station use, the dealer contracts with the third party. In such a case, the dealer's share of the monthly fees is assured. Because of this, the price of monitoring has remained rigid.

Now that wireless alarms have improved technologically and are offered by chain retail stores, the nature of competition will change. Such self-installed systems cannot be offered for less than the standard price range of zero to $300. Market penetration of wireless systems is therefore possible only by lowering the monthly monitoring prices. Further, if indeed cable TV providers or the RBOCs are about to enter the industry, they will need to satisfy a significantly high threshold, which is possible only at lower prices. The only competitive frontier that can sustain a price war is the monthly fees. Indeed, in the case of the retail sale of wireless systems, the monitoring contract can be drawn up directly between the customer and the central station, avoiding the "commission" to the dealer. Thus, the absence of the dealer's share enables price cuts by the wireless system seller. Monthly charges can be reduced to $15 assuming $400 marketing cost per system.

Lower monitoring prices from newcomers to the industry seems inevitable. It will adversely affect existing dealers and central stations. Vertically integrated large companies that offer both installation and monitoring will be able to absorb the reduction in prices. This is indeed true for large companies that exploit economies of scale in monitoring, with average residential cost per subscriber substantially less than $10. Dealers who contract with third-party monitors and share the revenue with them will have difficulty competing with vertically integrated large dealer-monitoring companies.

Economies of scale in monitoring exist for the following reasons:

- Software becomes more efficient as the number of incoming calls rises, resulting in lower cost per subscriber.
- In large central stations, operators will be needed only in extreme cases. Since 60 percent of central stations' cost is manpower, this attribute will significantly benefit large centers.
- Large central stations are flexible in the location of their facilities. They can locate in places where unskilled labor wages and real estate costs are low.
- Competition among long-distance carriers will result in even lower charges for large centers with high volumes of calls. Indeed, lower telephone charges have permitted monitoring from a distance, which has facilitated attaining greater economies of scale.

Conventional wisdom in the late 1980s suggested that 1,000 residential subscribers were sufficient in order to start a central station. Our computations as of 1996 suggest that the minimum threshold has risen to 3,000 subscribers and is likely to rise further. Significant economies of scale extend to over 60,000 subscribers, and no increased costs are evident up to one million accounts.

Competition is further evident in the packaging of services. As noted in Chapter 9, the problem of false alarms is already known to potential alarm buyers and hinders sales. In most large North American cities, there is no effective police response to activations. Las Vegas is the first major city to institute a policy whereby police respond only after a bona fide break-in has been verified by a private guard service. This trend will undoubtedly expand to many other major cities. Telephone companies, and not necessarily RBOCs, may choose to enter the security as well as other electronic home and business service industries. In this era of deregulation and increased competition, the only way that large players can gain sufficient market share is by cutting prices or offering a package of attractive services. In high-income regions of metropolitan areas that are hit by crime, and in the wealthy neighborhoods of major cities with a high density of alarm owners, newly merged companies will offer monitoring and private response for a price compatible with the price for monitoring only from existing companies. These companies may be able to shield themselves from litigation by contracting out the response service.

The era of small monitoring companies may have passed. Even subscribers with particular needs can be successfully served by large central stations that use sophisticated software. Existing software can provide a differentiated level of service.

The means to achieve growth in the industry has been the acquisition of accounts. Over time, the price of accounts has been rising and in 1996 reached a level of 25 to 30 times monthly recurring revenues. However, if successful entry of wireless and other "packaged" providers does indeed occur at lower monthly fees, then acquisition prices will drop to reflect the decline in profits.

Distributors

Consolidation of central stations and dealers may change the distribution segment of the industry. As larger players install alarms and monitor accounts, some vertically integrated companies will purchase directly from the manufacturers. However, the opening of the industry to other related security, electronics, and facility management services provides new opportunities for alarm distributors.

It seems that industry consolidation will weaken the supermarket concept that became popular in the mid 1980s. Distributors' role will be to provide "just in time" products. Large companies operate nationwide and need to supply certain locations whenever demand rises. Distributors will need to maintain adequate and prompt service using on-line computer connections and overnight service. Manufacturers do not maintain distribution channels and will need to rely on distributors for the service.

Dealers

Installation of "traditional" residential alarms has minimal threshold, involves no special expertise, is labor intensive, and exhibits no economies of scale. Due to stiff competition dealers enjoy no profit in installation. Economies of scale in monitoring and the expected decline in monitoring prices will increase the market share of large integrated companies, especially wireless companies and other companies that offer packages of home and business services.

Competition can arise from a wide variety of sources. Utilities and the telecommunications industry, including local, long-distance, cable TV, and environmental services within facilities, can and will be open for competition. Thus, security services as add-ons can be offered by any of the above types of firms. For example, a local electric utility company will be able to offer local telephone services, including alarm services, as a joint product. This may make a local dealer who installs alarms, monitors a small subscriber base, or contracts out the monitoring unable to effectively compete in the marketplace.

The only dealers who can survive in such a competitive environment are niche marketers. Dealers who specialize in wealthy neighborhoods or particular industries will be able to maintain their special niche market share; however, even they will need to adjust to the new business and technological changes. Niche marketers need to consider offering some or all of the following additional services in addition to traditional alarms—access control, CCTV, home automation, and private response. Another possible way to create a market niche is by becoming a comprehensive security provider rather than merely an alarm dealer. This package would include a security check, integrated locksmith service, alarm, CCTV, exterior lights, and target-hardening features.

To conclude, the changing technological, legal, police, and business environments are all expected to affect operations in the alarm industry. Companies that adjust to changes are likely to survive and prosper. Running the business as usual and merely extinguishing fires is risky. Resources should be expended by the industry's associations and by large companies to forecast market conditions, to discover changing consumer motivations, to develop new products, and to modify the way companies are managed. Research efforts to forecast, analyze, and make policy recommendations should be enhanced in order to better prepare for future conditions.

Industry consolidation does not preclude small dealership operations. Small firms, however, will have to establish market niches, change to become overall security providers, concentrate on a particular market segment, provide for specific needs, be consumer-oriented, provide a wide range of business or residential automated services, or offer private response. Small companies that are able to acquire a market niche by adopting some of these practices may be successful in competing against the large players that are expected to become more dominant in the alarm industry.

False Alarms

The wide use of wireless systems and their integration with wired telephone and personal communication devices makes an effective means of reducing false activations. In the case of activation at the alarm premises, the owner can be alerted as a source for first verification. In the case of an unknown cause, the owner can be automatically connected to the central station.

The trend in communities nationwide is to reduce both the number of free responses by police and to increase the fines for repeat false activators. These two facts will encourage many businesses and some wealthy homeowners to contract with private response companies, an area which could become competitive now with more expensive and/or less responsive police response.

Global Marketing

Alarms are perceived as a luxury products regardless of their low installation prices. Our surveys have consistently shown that as income rises, alarm ownership rises at an ever-increasing rate. Actually, only at incomes of at least $150,000 a year does alarm ownership reach the 50 percent threshold. In the next few years personal income is expected to rise somewhat.

Police budgets will remain the same or increase slightly. Thus, in order to maintain the same level of security, businesses and households will need to supplement police protection with private measures like alarms.

Prices of installation will remain at the same level or even decline. Monthly charges will decline due to mounting competition and improved technology.

The burglary rate has been constantly declining since 1973, reaching in 1993 half the level of 1973. Much of the reason for this is attributed to the aging of the American population and the decline in the number of teenagers. However, demographic conditions suggest that the trend may change, and the burglary rate will rise in the next few years.

All the above factors determine the demand for burglar alarms. Increased income, lower levels of effective policing (which is a substitute good), low prices of installation and lower prices for monitoring, an expected increase in burglary rates, and improved service all suggest a greater demand for alarm systems.

Foreign markets for alarms will open. The shift of Eastern European economies to democracy, the rise of high- and medium-income groups, and the rapid increase in burglaries are all indicators for rise in demand for alarms in that part of the world. The flow of unskilled workers from Eastern Europe to Central European nations will result in an increase in the number of burglaries and thus an increased demand for alarm systems. The creation of the European Community is expected to significantly improve the income level of its citizens. Again, since the purchase of alarms is closely related to income and wealth, alarm purchase in Western Europe is expected to rise.

Success in actualizing potential demand for alarm systems depends upon achieving solutions to false alarms. If police do not respond, then demand for alarms will be adversely affected.

Clearly, the problem of false alarm exists only if the police are obligated to respond to activations. If government does not intervene by offering response, then the private sector needs to provide and price it accordingly. The false alarm problem exists only when police retain the service. Thus, the alarm industry should try to significantly reduce false activation calls to the police in order to capitalize on potential alarm purchases.

CONCLUSIONS

This chapter attempts to accomplish the impossible: to predict the future of the various segments of the industry. The determining factors are new technology and the erosion of legal barriers. These two factors place the security industry in the midst of the telecommunications and computer industries, which are both on a rapid growth path.

Integration of alarms with other security systems such as CCTV and access control, and with other telecommunication systems, is inevitable. Wireless systems will spread and will be sold by retail stores. Monitoring will be contracted directly by end users, avoiding the dealers' share of the revenues. Indeed, competition in monitoring and prices will significantly fall. Mass marketing and the change in technology will alter the operations of the traditional alarm dealers; survival will require greater territorial and/or functional specialization to compete with large discount firms.

NOTES

1. Paul Hallam, "Vision of the Future," *Canadian Security* (December 1995). For the University of Pennsylvania case, contact The Protection Bureau, Eagle, Pennsylvania.

Index